F*CK

———— the ————

SCALE

The Naked Truth

in becoming a *Warr;or*

Samantha Sutherland

DEDICATION

To all the brave men and women
who choose LIFE every day.

To all the brave men and women
who choose to speak up about their own
personal struggles when it comes to the debilitating
effects of mental illness.

Let's close the stigma that surrounds
mental illness and EMPOWER others to be brave
enough to speak their #nakedtruth.

THE STORIES IN THIS BOOK

All of the stories and people in this book are real. The writings were taken from the author's journals, which were written during her recovery period with mental illness beginning in 2005. The names with an '*' have been changed to protect the privacy of those whom she's had a privilege to meet in the past and still call a friend today.

THE ADVICE IN THIS BOOK

This book contains opinions and ideas of its author and is not meant in either parts or its entirety to be a substitute for medical advice. It is intended to provide information on the realities of the author's 365 day journey with mental illness and is offered with the understanding that the author and publisher, are not engaged in rendering medical, health or any other kind of personal, professional services. The reader should consult a medical professional before applying or adopting any of the suggestions in this book or drawing any inferences from them. The author and publisher disclaim all responsibility for any liability or risk that is incurred as a consequence, directly or indirectly, from the use or application of any of the contents in this book.

SAVING LIVES ONE NAKED TRUTH AT A TIME

In addition to donating a percentage of the sales from each copy of F*CK THE SCALE to 'It's OK to be Awesome' and 'Capital Region Mental Health & Addictions Association', additional copies of the book have been donated to hospitals, organizations and individuals that are in desperate need of hope.

My mission is to get F*CK THE SCALE in the hands of over 1, 000,000 people so that I can change......

One Million Lives,
One #nakedtruth at a Time!

Much Love and Gratitude for your support,

Sam xo

NAKED TRUTH CONTENTS

WHAT IS A *Warr;or*

A brave fighter who has experienced self-harm, addiction, anxiety, depression and/or suicide; not ready to give up no matter how many demons lie ahead. The ';' (semi-colon) represents a sentence the author could have ended, but chose not to. The author is me, and the sentence is my life.

A warr;or is an individual with incredible strength who is extraordinarily brave. We fight a difficult batter every day, and endure pain of the mind, body and spirit. We are strong. We are brave, but sometimes the battles we fight and the pain we feel causes us to fall but only temporarily. Because we are warr;ors, we get back up and keep fighting.

Mental illness is our battle. We fight every day to get out of bed, take care of our bodies and protect our minds from the torpedo of emotions that are brought on by our mental illness. We fight for control over our lives when our mental illness tries to take that control away from us.

The battle is exhausting, and can leave us feeling weak and tired. Sometimes, the battle seems too grueling, too much for us to handle. It's those times we warr;ors fall slightly and contemplate what it would mean to not have to fight anymore.

Many warr;ors have lost their battle, and many of us sometimes wish we would. Sometimes, we just want to find an end to our suffering. Sometimes, we are too tired to be strong and too broken to be brave. We let our thoughts of giving-up consume our strong and capable minds until those thoughts become a battle themselves. Then we have to fight to stay alive. As we fight for our lives, we look to one little symbol, one small weapon, one glimpse of hope, to help restore our strength.

The semicolon is our symbol of strength and hope. It is our small weapon against suicidal thoughts. We look to the semicolon to remind us we can't end our sentence and to gain hope and inspiration through its meaning. The semicolon means keep going, don't give up, you are worth it and don't stop writing…………

My third tattoo on my forearm (see book cover) was the word '*warr;or*' with an arrow. This powerful tattoo embodies everything we are, and everything we do to fight our battle against mental illness. The power this tattoo holds is incredible. It means so much to those of us who struggle. This tattoo does NOT define me, it reminds me. It encases my strength and bravery and tells me and the rest of the world to keep fighting our battle with mental illness.

It is just one word with one tiny symbol replacing a letter. But it is inked deep into my skin to send a message to myself and everyone who struggles with mental illness. You are a warr;or. You must not give up. It reminds me I am a *warr;or.* I am STRONG.
I am EXTRAORDINARY.
I am BRAVE.
I may fight a battle, but I will win every damn time.

ACKNOWLEDGMENTS
FIRST & FOREMOST

Thank-You certainly doesn't cut it when it comes to all the amazing people in my life, but here goes nothing.

To my daughter Madyson, I know without you that my road to recovery would have been longer. Becoming pregnant with you helped put into perspective what truly mattered and lit a spark inside of me. That spark enabled me to learn more about nutrition and to love myself and my body no matter the shape or size. Your huge heart makes me smile every day and I'm so grateful that God chose you for me. Beautiful. Powerful. Intelligent. ALWAYS remember that!

To my spouse Mike, whose support, guidance, patience and abundant heart have helped push me through times, when I thought writing a book was completely foolish. No matter what time of day or how many hours I'd been writing you knew just how much therapy this book was providing me.

To my step-daughter Kaleigh, thank-you for teaching me patience and love, on a whole other level. Your strong silent side never goes unnoticed. The energy and self-confidence that surrounds you is absolutely beautiful. Never change that powerful voice inside of you.

To my Ma, who has always believed and supported me through each and every endeavor I have ever taken on and no matter how many times they didn't work out (let's not talk numbers here because that lemonade and popcorn stand rocked!). Who has shown me the value of hard work and compassion since the day I was born. You are always proud and ready to come along the next adventure with me.

To my step-Dad Bobby for proof reading my book a thousand and one times. Your constructive criticism and honesty helped me realize during my tough times my words are powerful and can help open the eyes of others who need heeling or just an eye opener.

IT TAKES A VILLAGE

When the cover of "F*CK THE SCALE" was created, I was truly in the depths of despair trying to reclaim my life. I cannot thank the following people enough for helping me feel a little better that day. They are friends, but they show love and compassion like family.

♥My hairstylist, Alexandar Von Alstyne from Avalon Salon Spa Uptown Fredericton, who makes me feel fab every damn time I sit in his chair.

♥My makeup artist, Emily Brawley who not only makes my eyes pop but is the funniest damn women and momprenneur I know.

♥My photographer, Denise Trask from Making Memories with Denise for making me feel so comfortable when I was far from comfortable in my own skin on that day shooting the naked front cover of the book.

♥My hobby photographer & step-daughter Kaleigh Leblanc for making me smile big for my back cover where I'm most comfortable, inside our home.

♥My hobby photographer & esthetician, Jessica Morehouse from BME MediStudio & Esthetics for allowing me to smile big for the inside back cover of the book and creating my dream eyebrows.

♥My graphic artist, Steve Boulter from Cap City Creative for designing my book cover and logo. Steve truly listened to my vision that had been in my head for so long and created the perfect masterpiece all the while keeping my vision in check.

♥My tattoo artist, Dave Cummings from Peep Show Tattoos. This guy is not only an incredibly talented artist, he listened to my warr;or story and truly understood what this 'ink' represented and what it meant to me.

♥And last but not least, thank-you to my 4 cats from CARMA for keeping me company and walking over my computer in the wee hours of the morning and night. This book would have been written in ½ the time, but with ½ the cuddles. #thestruggleisreal #crazycatlady

BUCKET FILLER RECOGNITION

"Someone who says or does something nice for other people."

There is nothing more rewarding than being able to impact another person's life in a meaningful way all the while impacting your own.

The following people are THE reason that 76 '*warr;or* SOCK PACKS' from my Kickstarter campaign are being praised as #bucketfillers.

Each pack included a pair of socks, a granola bar and a Tim Horton's gift card for a coffee which were hand delivered and donated to the Fredericton Homeless Shelters just before the Christmas of 2018.
#christmasmiracle

♥Steve Boulter

♥Victoria Andrews

♥Natasha LeBlanc

♥Jennifer McKay

♥Jessica McKenna

♥Shelley Polchies

♥Crystal Hubscher

♥John Menniger

♥Katherine Toner

♥Laurie Robichaud

♥Amy Donovan

♥Cynthia Ratelle

♥Kerri Robichaud

♥Elizabeth & JC LeBlanc

♥Dallas Fortin

♥Margaret Ann Dinan

♥Cheryl McGuire

♥Sherry Yu

♥Ashley Yerxa

♥Jana Long

♥Tara MacKinnon

♥Jesika Garsch

♥Pierette Gervais

♥Jennifer Grant

♥Krista O'Connor

♥Christina Walsh

♥Eveline LeBlanc

♥Eve Connolly

♥Natalie Ouellet

♥Jessie Dinan

♥Jason Chakravorty

♥Debbie Chezenko

♥Tina Crossman

♥Dana Neuman

♥Shona O'Brien

♥Jennifer Murray

♥Matthew Freeman

♥Dan Hermans

♥Lisa MacKenzie

♥Kathy Dinan

♥Cathy Clowater

♥Lori Spilman

♥Sarah Forward

♥Louis Belliveau

♥Chantal Robichaud

♥Laurie Hansen

♥Erin Klinghammer

♥Lori Shea

♥Jamie & Jason London

♥Anonymous

♥Nicole & Chris Boyd

♥Kait Dutcher

♥Laura Romano

♥Emma & John Gillam

♥Debi Hawkes

♥Sheri Sutherland

♥Megan Hampsey

♥Amanda Hope

♥Kara Campbell

♥Lori Ramsay

♥Michael Barth

♥Chrissy Hollis

♥Sarah Belmore

♥Melissa Morris

♥Charlie Hawkes

♥Lynsey Wilson Norrad

♥Laura Gibson

♥Cathy Belmore

♥Lindsay Betts

♥Lloyd & Murielle Sutherland

♥ Dave & Anne Marie Dixon

♥Claudette Levesque

WHY the NAKED BOOK COVER?

Your first thought when you saw the book was "Why the naked body on the cover Sutherland?" Believe me it was not easy, but it felt so freeing! This book is about bearing it all when it comes to the day to day struggles of mental illness and by making myself vulnerable, I hope you too can see that scary can oftentimes be the best medicine.

Thanks to my photographer Denise for making me feel like a goddess which included lots of laughs and retakes of course. Who needs another Elaine from Seinfeld incident, am I right?

I've spent many years covering up both physically and mentally and it's time to get f*cking naked with the truth. Oftentimes as women we masque ourselves in ways that we truly believe makes us "better women" such as working too much, taking less time for ourselves to help others, saying YES to everything and being so wrapped up in the day to day that you don't realize that life is passing and you are sinking deeper and deeper into an unhealthy hole. You constantly keep telling yourself tomorrow until you stop in your tracks and wonder if tomorrow will even come.

I used to hold back my past for fear of hurting others. In turn, it hurt me more.

I used to hold back my emotions and how I wanted to end my life. In turn, it hurt me more.

I used to think time instead of talking to others would heal all my traumas. In turn, it hurt me more.

I've fought f*cking hard to get where I am today – to this place of FREEDOM. I used to feel defined by the number on the scale, whether or not my tummy was flat! But now thankfully, I know better. That shit was bondage – and I refuse to life my life like that. It doesn't mean that I don't get faced with self-doubt, or sometimes battle that inner critic, but it's a whole lot rarer that it ever used to be and when I do find myself going down that road of self-criticism, I catch myself, redirect and start practicing gratitude for everything my body is, has done and does for my daily – which is A LOT!

You can have abs. You cannot have abs. You can have a thigh gap. You cannot have a thigh gap. You can have big boobs. You can have small boobs. You can be whatever shape you are. You can be whatever size you are. And guess what? It's all YOU, so be-YOU-ti-ful!!!
Stop the madness of comparing. Stop thinking you'll love yourself more if this, if that. LOVE YOURSELF NOW. You can be YOU and practice self-love simultaneously, give yourself permission.

So here I am, being naked and it feels scary but good. It's time to show the world the #nakedtruth when it comes to mental illness and the realities that one faces every damn day. It's time to get loud and take action! Stand tall. Reach out. You are beyond worth it. Share your #nakedtruth and help end the stigma.

GET NAKED and F*CK the SCALE

IMPROVE BODY IMAGE
Ideals of beauty are slowly changing (if only they would change as fast as I eat a bag of popcorn, we'd be all set) but it is still hard to accept body image that differs from your desired one or one that you feel is accepted. Getting naked can improve your self-esteem by increasing comfort with your body parts. And ladies, let's be honest, is there anything better than taking off your bra at the end of the day?!?! Can I get a HELL YEAH! Embrace the naked. Embrace the beauty of it ALL!

COSTS LESS
Clothes and scales can be expensive and need to be replaced. Going naked decreases the need to purchase clothes and trying to figure out the mathematical equation required when weighing yourself with a pair of pants on....subtract the one, add the 2 and multiply by what??? PLUS no need to find a little corner in your bathroom for the scale demon that loves to stare at you every time you sit on your toilet. See, it's a win win!

HELP OVERCOME FEARS
As crazy as it may sound, many adults are afraid to get naked and to step on the scale, I used to be one of them! I was afraid of being judged and letting a number determine my self-worth. We are taught at a young age to stay covered up, bodies are not acceptable to show. This only leads to feeling ashamed on many levels later in life. Now I'm not about to hop on the next train to the Hedonism Resort, but I am all for increasing the look and feel of the human body.

BOOSTS VULNERABILITY

So......you jump on the scale naked, the one thing we all know has ruined more self-esteems, hopes, dreams and days in this world and yet continually we go back for more torture. But yet, strutting down the beach in your swimsuit freaks you out??? Girl, stop running away from the awesome, because each scar, stretch mark, varicose vein, bulge etc. has a story! It's time to get naked, accept yo'self and tell your story because you only have ONE body to live in and that shit kicks some serious ass!

ENHANCE YOUR QOL a.k.a. QUALITY OF LIFE

Embrace your so called "imperfections" and love it for what it is. Let go of the f*cking scale and your insecurities (easier said than done yes) but make a conscious effort. I had a million thoughts a day about my body with and without a six pack so I'm here to tell you size or the number on a scale doesn't matter. Get naked with yo' bad self both mentally and physically and ditch the f*cking scale!

P.S. Sex is better when you're naked too! The scale only makes you groan instead of moan. ♥

LIVING A LIE IN QUIET DESPERATION

Being naked when it comes to my own personal mental illness issues can be very difficult and overwhelming, even after 11 years of my journals being transcribed into this book. Sharing secret information can be both courageous and make one feel super vulnerable, in a world where stigma around mental illness still exists.

Throughout the years, I've realized that healing can only begin once you start to speak your #nakedtruth. Own your feelings. Own your thoughts. Take back control and create the life you want. I get it, seeking help is scary. The second time I faced mental illness head on once again, I held so much back because I thought I knew what to do and how to heal but I didn't. I desperately needed professional help and I had to constantly remind myself that seeking help is not a sign of weakness.

Weakness only remains when help is not sought. You are worth it every damn day of your life you've been given. There are so many others who are suffering in silence as perhaps you are, so let's lock arms and join together to get loud on this #nakedtruth journey. The world deserves to hear your story because you are a somebody. An incredible human who is here to make a difference in your own life and the life of others.

The truth is, as I share this dark side of my experiences with mental illness, I fear that others may perceive me differently. I've always been the 'happy' and 'strong' one, all my life. For people to see this dark shadow that hovered over me for many years, makes me feel hypocritical in telling my story. Today (2017) as I begin to write this book, I have relapsed after my 11-year anniversary and as I'm currently suffering through another depression, anxiety and paranoia episode. Just 12 short months ago, I was an outgoing and successful fitness leader in the city of Fredericton, New Brunswick. I was energetic, happy, confident and full of life. But once again the dark shadows have returned and the wind has been blown out of my sails, forcing me to take a step back to reflect and do some healing and the best way I know how, is to write. Although my depression is completely different than 11 years ago, it has made me realize that NOBODY is immune to mental illness, even those in the health and wellness industry.

When someone has a physical illness, you can see it, you can touch it, you can somewhat feel their pain; you have empathy. On the other hand, when someone has a mental illness, 99 percent of the time it cannot be seen, it's only sometimes mistaken for being over emotional, tired and working too much. It cannot be touched, yet fingers continuously get pointed in their direction. You cannot feel their pain and therefore your empathy and patience, diminish to the point where friends vanish and lose compassion for you and your illness. You end up feeling like you have the most contagious virus, which then evolves into a zombie apocalypse. Now let's be honest, there is no competing with Carol from television series 'The Walking Dead'.

The best part of mental illness is that it is something you can hear, if you listen carefully. Listen to the sounds of distance, which was once a close relationship. Listen to the sounds of silence, that was once was laughter. Listen to the sounds of lashing out, which was once patience. Listen to the sounds of tears, which was once joy. Just LISTEN, as the sounds of mental illness surround each and every one of us every day. Truth be told, the realities of mental illness and let's be blunt here, fu*king suck! They suck the life out of you each and every day. The simplest of tasks become struggles, even for those with a Type "A" personality like me. It crushes your dreams and realities of what you once thought would come true and makes you question each and every decision you make. Not only does your heart race like you're running frantically away from a June bug, (yes, I have a fear of June bugs and if you live in the Eastern part of Canada, I would be very surprised if you didn't have a freakish fear too) but your mind never stops. Each breath you take comes with a new crazy thought of how you perceive the world to be, knowing it can't possibly be reality......but yet in knowing it can't be reality, you continue with the same crazy thoughts that surround your every move, it just NEVER stops!

I still have days that getting out of bed is tough. I still have days where my body doesn't look like I want it to. I still have days where eating out of box is fun. I still have days where I have to DRRRRAAAGGG my ass to the gym. I still have days where I want to escape from everyone and everything.
It's time to get over the physical being of someone and believing you can determine who he or she is......that bullshit is over. We all have a story, you just need to open up your ears and LISTEN to the power it represents. Become naked in your thoughts and opinions to what you think mental illness may look like. Be proud of your story. You are a warr;or and you WILL inspire others.

If you would have asked me just 11 short years ago, I would have been all about the physical of EVERYTHING and EVERYONE...nothing else mattered. I was obsessed, and by obsessed, I can't even express what that would look like to some of you but it got me nowhere! It f*cking got me nowhere!

The best days become when you truly believe that the scale doesn't determine your worth or your day – good or bad. It's incredible once you become more than your physical self – once you allow the physical self to be your strength and do the things you want to do, the mental self becomes so badass! So I don't think most women have a problem with their physical self, it is the mental self that is impeding them to be the most badass empowered women they could possibly be!

STOP RIGHT THERE, I know what you are thinking..... "She is not as bad as me. I've gone through shit too. I've got my own story!" You're right, I don't know you and your story however I know it would be an honor if I did and your bravery would certainly not go unnoticed. My goal is to tell my story in hopes that others will feel empowered enough to do the same.

Look, I was hospitalized for almost two years, tried to commit suicide, cut myself, puked multiples times a day and thought my life was worthless. What I felt at the time, was hell on earth! My life felt worthless......do you get that? I HAD HIT ROCK BOTTOM!

Do you have to hit rock bottom to become AWESOME? NOPE not at all! There are so many mentors/coaches that I have, that are freaking AWESOME and I mean out of this world awesome, BUT……for me, it was what needed to happen for change to finally occur. It doesn't make me better or worse, I just think that I can relate a lot to most people, when it comes to mental illness and having hope for a future and ending the stigma that surrounds it.

Sooooo, did I just turn to exercise and eating healthy overnight? HELL NO, I went to the other extreme….from not eating enough to stuffing my f*cking face with food when I got pregnant! I used the excuse of 'I'm pregnant'. Yeah I had cravings and my hormones were nuts, but come on, 65lbs in nine months must be a new world record! Oh gosh, as I write this I giggle because at the time I didn't really care….UNTIL……I went to the OB at 38 weeks and tipped the 200's …….200 pounds. Now keep in mind that this is after me not giving a shit about my weight, however, seeing that number made me gulp and then probably go and eat another slice of pizza and a bagel with strawberry cream cheese! I wish I would have purchased Tim Horton's stocks, as I swear, that had become a new food group during my 40 weeks of pregnancy. Just to note, I have not had a bagel with strawberry cream cheese since….ok maybe just an 'everything' bagel with herb and garlic cream cheese. Yummo!

So where am I going with all of this? I really don't know….writing is my sanity, my real, my get it down and who gives a shit how many 'likes', 'comments' or books you sell, it is me just being me. If I happen to resonate with you, offer you guidance and hope, then my mission is complete.

My ultimate mission on earth is to **EMPOWER** women to believe in themselves; to believe that there is **HOPE;** to **BELIEVE** that there is life past an illness, no matter what that might be.

In the beginning drugs are necessary, I can 100 percent attest to that. There comes a time where you have to also try to incorporate some of the other methods out there. They do require effort, they do take commitment and you do need to put your heart and soul into each of them! But guess what…they are SO much more worth ANY Ativan I ever had! Nourishing my body is a gift. Moving my body is a blessing. Stretching my body is my euphoric Zen. Meditation is my Ativan, even on the craziest of days.

Eating all my favorites such as nachos, plain chips with Philadelphia whipped chive cream cheese, Oreos, Whoppers, wine, brownies and the list goes on and on; but enjoying EACH AND EVERY morsel and mouthful is possible, without ever feeling guilt. How? Because I don't overindulge – I eat mindfully and listen to my body. Call it hocus pocus or read above again to remember where I came from…….this is real, this is me. I try to live each day to the fullest, for not only me, but my family and especially my girls. EMPOWERED girls, turn into POWERFUL women.

I share my past and my present lifestyle, to offer hope to every women I know young and old because as women, we are WAY too hard on ourselves. If I can touch the life of just one, I have lived life with purpose.

It is with great sadness that I inform you that in the spring of 2012, the Dr. Everett Chalmers Hospital concluded the outpatient day therapy program. I truly believe that had it of not been for this program, I would not be here today telling you my story. I am so grateful that I was able to be part of such an incredible program that believed in my progress and my healing. The nurses and doctors in this program understood the struggles and complications of mental illness and were such an incredible support system throughout my journey.

A portion of the proceeds from the sale of this book, will go to:

Capital Region Mental Health and Addictions Association CRMHAA in Fredericton, NB
Increasing awareness and support for mental health in our region.
www.crmhaa.ca

It's OK to be AWESOME in Fredericton, NB
A mental wellness and empowerment program for youth.
www.itsoktobeawesome.ca

WHERE IT ALL STARTED
When the scale mattered and getting naked was dumb.

These writings were taken from my journals, which were written during my recovery period, 2005-2006.

I'm here to tell you that 27 years ago, time did not matter. Time only prolonged my self-destruction for 17 years because I had no plan or goal set in place. I had no direction and was on the path to self-destruction. I've hit rock bottom with my health, so I know what it is like to find the strength to recover, dig deep and find hope to be living what I once thought was a dream.

Saying F*CK THE SCALE did not come easily for me.

October, 1990 – 13 years old
My first purge. I felt exhilarated! I had done it! I had accomplished something just for me, 'ED' and no one else! It was our little secret, on our time and I know my body thanked me – 'ED' was so proud of me!

January, 1995 – 18 years old
My secret had been found. I was not embarrassed I was MAD! How could anyone have figured me out? I was not going to let this little hiccup get in my way of 'ED' and I being together. He was mine after all and no one else could have a man like mine – he was different than all the rest.

May, 2003 – 25 years old
I was out of control in so many ways. I had no self-respect,

'ED' had taken over. He loved me though and he knew what was best for me and only me. He would comfort me in times of self-doubt by holding my hand and my hair in times of binging and purging. When that was not enough, cocaine seemed to subside the feeling of worthlessness for a bit longer. In turn, 'ED' loved me even more by making me realize I did not have to eat because doing lines would fill my void on countless 48 hours binges.

March, 2005 – 27 years old
A knee surgery set me back for the worst once again. 'ED' came through, however with so much time to think on my hands which I didn't want to do because that would mean facing reality I spiraled downward into a depression which I had been hiding for so long. I had a case of the "Don't worry about me" cause I had 'ED' and he would never leave me and always take care of me.

November, 2005 – 28 years old
I began seeing things, hearing voices and had terrible anxious bodily twitches. Where was 'ED' when I needed him? I was doing what I was told. Not eating and if I did I would purge. Why was he purposefully hurting our relationship?

December, 2005 – 28 years old
'ED' left my side for just a second and the next thing I knew I was being admitted through the emergency room into 2SE at the Dr. Everett Chalmers Hospital, THE PSYCH WARD.

FIRST
QUARTER
OF THE NAKED TRUTH

Warr;or

MUST HAVES

Kleenex.
Cozy Blankie.
Wine.

DAY 1 – Thursday December 15, 2005

I don't think I have gone to sleep from the night before or was it the night before that? What day is it? Was I supposed to get up to go to work?

I sit here on the couch by my lonesome after speaking with my best friend Monika at 3am. I can't stop the voices, my body keeps twitching and I know there is someone outside my window ready to break in. I keep hearing someone outside but I can't see them. Monika wanted to come over and to be honest I feel bad as it's 3 in the morning but I needed someone by my side. Andrew was away for work in Toronto and I didn't want to bother him. She stayed and we talked and to what I thought was normal behavior I mean there had to be someone outside, to Monika it was troubling, I could see it on her face. She left an hour or so later.

I sat on the couch all day contemplating an appointment I have later on with my counsellor Julia at Family Enrichment Services. I hate talking to people about my 'issues'. I mean really, what's the point? I don't know the last time I showered, I have no idea what I'm wearing but I get in the car and realize driving seems so odd yet somehow I arrive for my counselling appointment downtown for 4:00pm.

I have been seeing Julia at Family Enrichment Services for a few months talking about the issues that I'm having and trying to make changes but as time passed, my symptoms become worse. Although the memories surrounding Thursday December 15, 2005 are sporadic, I do remember arriving at her office and after checking in at the reception, I began to pace in the waiting area back and forth. To me, this was normal as I was in a frantic state of panic and pacing is what I needed to do so I wouldn't take off like Forest Gump! To those working in the office, this was far from 'normal' behavior and I can remember the receptionist peeking in the door way a few times looking at me and I was not sure why. I would sit, shake my head, shake my body and get back up to pace once again for 12 paces and continue this same behavior. The bodily twitches were so extreme. Stop this feeling inside of me. Stop the voices. Stop the constant panic that someone is watching me. I know I'm being followed, I can sense it. Sit down, look left, look right as my head moved around like the exorcist I can't stop it, I can't f*cking stop it!

Suddenly Julia my counsellor poked her head out and quietly said "Sam?" All I can remember thinking was yeah it's me why are you so confused? She took me into her office and sitting down was impossible. I can remember looking out the window wondering who knew I was with her. I remember her asking me "What do you see?" I said those people down there, they know I'm in here, close the curtains. My body began to shake, the twitches became more intense, I can't breathe, stop the voices, stop the panic, STOP! She immediately said "I'm taking you to the hospital" to which I replied, "Why?" And within minutes the next thing I knew I was sitting in her car.

I don't remember getting in but I remember driving up Regent Street thinking we are being followed and why can't I stop my neck from spinning around and my body from moving sporadically? Suddenly Monika arrives at the ER, how the hell did she get here? Did I call her? From there they place me in a separate room from everyone else and give me some Ativan, of which I have no idea what that is but it doesn't do much. The pacing begins in the room, the head to toe twitches continue and we wait for the Psych Doctor to arrive which seemed like forever. I just want to leave, I don't understand why I am here! Thankfully Monika calms me down and later the Doctor arrives. I don't remember too many details but I do remember being interrogated and questioned "Why are you twitching like that and pacing", to which I replied "I can't stop!" The doctor becomes frustrated and says "You need to stop that now, you are doing that on purpose!" Purpose? I don't get it. This has been going on for weeks now and it's frustrating as hell but I just assume its normal stress. I do remember Monika getting angry with him and saying "You need to admit her, she needs help and this is my best friend whom I know very well and she is not faking! This is not her normal behavior from the past!"

DAY 2 – Friday December 16, 2005

Andrew arrives home from Toronto and is very worried about me. The Psych Doctor arrives and I am being admitted to the Psych Ward?!? Ok, hold on I'm really ok. You guys are going overboard. I just work too much and need to talk to someone, I'll be ok in a week or two. Of course this was not what any of my family or friends, nor the Psych Doctor thought, so up through the back elevator and within seconds I am at 2SE, the Psych Ward. Just the thought of it all frightens me. I mean I am not like the others, what I do when it comes to binging, purging, twitching, hearing voices is all normal, right?

I am somewhat patted down to make sure I don't have anything that may harm myself or others and all of my toiletries that Andrew brought are taken away from me other than plastic bottles. I'm then escorted to a room that has another bed and a roommate. I quickly run to my bed and begin to cry. This all must be a nightmare, I'm begging you it's time to wake up!

DAY 3 – Saturday December 17, 2005

I am highly medicated and I don't move from my bed for fear that I will see someone, anyone. I just want to crawl into a hole and NO I don't need food. Seriously stop coming into my room to let me know that my tray is ready cause there can't possibly be anything that this hospital can provide that will not make me gain more weight or make me want to puke. Your constant watch is driving me nuts!

When can I go home, it's been 3 days, that surely is enough right?

DAY 4 – Sunday December 18, 2005

Went to bed last night around 11:00pm. The nurse gave me an Ativan and that really seemed to help me calm down and have a better sleep. I'm having a really hard time remembering all the nurses' names around here, I think last night was Michelle or something. After Andrew left, I was very upset. It's so hard to see him go every night knowing that I won't be going with him or lying in bed beside him. You would think that each day would get easier when he leaves, but it seems to be getting harder. He has been so supportive and there for me every step of the way. Without him I don't know where I would be right now – he is my rock and knight in shining armor.

So last night I only woke up about 3 times, however I quickly feel back asleep. I finally woke up around 7:00am and did crosswords for about an hour. They help keep my brain stimulated which sometimes can be hard to focus in here. I got up, had a shower and threw in a load of laundry. Having showers here freaks me out! There is no lock on the door, just a simple sign that says "In Use" and no curtain to the shower just an open area near the washer and dryer.

I made the attempt to eat breakfast, however failed. Andrew always tells me to look at things in a positive way so the positive is that I walked into the common room, pulled out my tray and looked at the oatmeal and chose the prune juice. So breakfast today is prune juice which is better than having nothing the past 2 weeks. Had a new patient arrive last night, not sure of her name, however she is 90 years old and believes that everyone is trying to poison her. Also had a code blue last night that was supposed to be arriving by ambulance in 7 minutes but then this morning I heard the nurses whispering that they are not sure why they announced a code blue over loud speaker since they were dead upon arrival.

Today I'm feeling a little down. I miss doing all the things I'm used to doing at home. The time here is 'somewhat' relaxing, however I have found it so hard. The eating, the anxiousness, the depression etc. I guess arriving here was bound to happen, 28 years of self-destruction had finally taken its toll.

I want a better life for myself, my family and of course my husband. I know I have all the great qualities of a giving person to everyone else but now it's time to earn to give back to myself and gain respect and self-esteem too. I can't really remember there being a day in my life where I thought I was absolutely beautiful without a doubt, and that is something I like to strive for. Realizing beauty both on the inside and outside. Andrew tells me every day just how beautiful I am and I am one day going to believe him and in myself. I have to stop blaming my past for the way I feel today. I guess I have just never dealt with my past and once I can put that behind me I can move on to my brighter future.

So I just woke up from an hour and a half nap and I did not wake up to anything good. I now have a roommate. I have no idea what her name is, however she is the girl that was put in the padded room for 72 hours the other day with and has a 4 year old. At first she says "Don't worry I won't wake you. I like it when other people are quiet" then she doesn't shut up! She is going to drive me nuts! I am not here to make friends or talk to anyone. I am here to get better and get home to my family as quickly as possible! I can already tell that she is untidy. Totally left her bra sitting on the bathroom counter! Uh, disgusting! So I moved it cautiously with paper towel. I can see there is going to be some conflict! Maybe this is a good thing, in that it will make me more motivated to want to get the f*ck out of here!

Woohoo, they just called dinner, F*CK MY LIFE! I will go check once everyone leaves to see what is on the tray of shit. If there is broth, for Andrew I will eat it. I looked at myself in the mirror today when I went to have a shower and only a few more pounds to go until I'm happy. It sounds so weird because I have never once liked my body, however a few more pounds and I think I might be there. If I can just get out of here and begin working out and eating what I want to eat I know that will help too. I would just love to be able to maintain my weight, one that I look great in, to me. When I say I'm fat, it just means that I am not at the weight where I think I'm beautiful.

Well lunch today was ½ cup tossed salad with light Thousand Island dressing, minestrone soup, crackers, banana and tea. I improvised and ate ¼ cup of salad with salt and pepper, tea and brought my banana back to my room. I feel like I have achieved a small goal today, however I am feeling so guilty for eating. I want to puke it up as bad as I know how great it would feel! I promised Andrew however that I wouldn't which is definitely hard if he wants me to eat. I hope he gets here soon as I really miss him. Unfortunately he has to leave at 5:00pm for volleyball but will be back afterwards but only for an hour since visiting hours end at 9:00pm.

I am scared and looking forward to this week. My therapy begins and it is going to be hard doing so with all the others around. I am so self-conscious of myself right now that I find it hard to be around others.

I want to be happy for being alive and not worry about having to look in the mirror. I want to be able to go out in public and not worry that people are staring or talking about me behind my back. If they are staring and talking I want it to be in a positive way and learn to accept, appreciate and love the body and attitude that I am displaying. I want all these things because I hope someday to be able to teach them to my children so they don't' have to go through the same things that I have both emotionally and physically. I know I should appreciate the body I have now because in 50 years I'll wonder where it went.

Andrew has come and gone and it's so hard to see him leave. He just seems to make everything that is bad go away for a moment in time. I hate having a roommate! I feel as though I cannot show my emotions or feelings.

This week I believe is going to be tougher than I thought. I just want to be home now. I feel so lost here. Relaxed in some ways but empty in others. I really need to work hard this week to get strong so I can go home and enjoy Christmas with my family. I'm so sad right now as the tears fall my down face uncontrollably. I want all this to be over.

FOOD JOURNAL for Today
BREAKFAST – ½ prune juice
LUNCH – ¼ cup tossed salad with S&P, tea & water
SNACK – Strawberry Ensure, 2 celery sticks & ¼ tomato

SUPPER – ½ Booster Juice, 1 Banana & water
SNACK – Orange

DAY 5 – Monday December 19, 2005

Had an absolutely terrible restless sleep last night. Having a roommate didn't help matters. I did my relaxation breathing exercises after I woke up but didn't bother going to breakfast. Have I mentioned that my roommate is driving me berserk! Her side of the room is a pigsty! Her bed is not made, pillow on the floor, her toiletries everywhere – uh it's f*cking filthy! I decided I would go to morning meeting and get out my room. So I get up and head to the common room where most of the 'crazies' are gone and of course a nurse quickly comes in, to make sure I'm going to eat my breakfast – pulls out my tray for me.

They watch me here worse than if I were in Shawshank! I had 2 prunes, a yogurt and water so I feel proud of myself! I then played a couple of games of solitaire waiting for morning meeting to start at 9:00am, however it didn't start until 9:10am how f*cking frustrating that is not starting on time! I was ready to reach across the table and throttle *Paula* my roommate, as she wouldn't shut up! Always has something to say! Morning meeting was definitely boring, however it was nice to hear what is going on around the world and in the news. I decided that going to morning meeting was good enough for me and venturing outside for the 10 minute walk, was going to be too much. Parading around the building as the "crazy group" while being chaperoned was never going to happen for as long as I had to stay here.

I decide to call Andrew on the pay phone and he said he spoke to Bobby last night for an hour and a half. Bobby really is such a great guy. He is the only great father figure that I've truly ever had. He's funny, caring, giving, smart and most times easy to talk to. I guess I just have a hard time talking to him sometimes for fear of opening up too much of the past and Ma getting pissed off at me. Not quite sure why she is like that, however Andrew tells me it's because she so protective of me all my life and is still trying to do the same, however it is still quite irritating.

It's 9:52am and I have my psychology appointment today at 10:30am with Dr. David. I find him quite odd at times – like he's nervous or shy just awkward. We had our meeting and had a good chat and we are beginning to work on self-esteem issues. He said we would talk more tomorrow at 10:30am. My biggest esteem issues are feeling ugly/fat and feeling a sense of people talking badly about me or behind my back. I am on kitchen duty today with crazy *Corinne*, so it'll just be me on kitchen duty as she'll never do anything between all her smoke breaks. Before lunch, I tidy up the kitchen and *Paula* my annoying roommate, would not leave me alone as much as I tried to ignore her Cathy (my night nurse) told me this might be a good time to practice my assertiveness, as this is another issue we are working on as well. So I think my next response to her when she is annoying the f*ck out of me will be "Sorry if this comes across the wrong way, however I just really need my space right now."

Just finished eating lunch, had a ½ cup tossed salad with salt and pepper and water. I thought I was having vegetable soup today so I took it but it ended up being turkey noodle so I threw it out as it looked like it had too much fat.

I have Skills Therapy Group and TAG this afternoon for the first time – Therapeutic Activities Group. Should be one of the many things that I find stressful and annoying – maybe I'll learn something.

Ma and Bobby sent me a package this morning. Tons of things of course. Art pencils, markers, drawing paper, cards, crib board, chocolates, nice magnet that made me think a lot, card, journal, note pad and a few others things. You can always count on Ma for those things for sure. I definitely know where I get my warm, giving and caring heart from. If only the emotions came with her love of giving. I still have not talked or seen them since I have been admitted. Not sure if I am ready for that or not. Not sure I am ready to see anyone other than Andrew, Monika and Jamie. I guess I just really want to focus on myself and have my time when I want it. Having the visitors that I have now is enough.

I rest my eyes for 15 minutes then it was skills therapy group. It was the hardest f*cking thing I've done today! We sat around in a circle and had to talk. I felt so anxious the whole time, it was awful! I got a lot of great information from the session. A lot of quotes really touched home. Now if I can just implement them I will be so far ahead. It really made me think about issues that I'm going through and making the right choices for me first and foremost.

After I left skills class I was feeling so anxious, so I found a nurse and got an Ativan. After the Ativan kicked in, I decided to go to TAG and I'm so glad I did! It really helped to relax me and calm me down. I chose to make a trivet with tiles and it will be a reminder of my time here.

I come back to my room and my flowers from Andrew had been moved! I am not impressed so I quickly ask *Paula* how come my flowers were moved and she said the janitor had been in here…..funny everything else was in place but not that. Then she said she moved some of my gift bags around, I'm GONNA LOSE IT!

Andrew came by to visit for supper. I had poached fish, green beans and beef consommé. We then came back to the room and I started painting. Andrew just enjoyed watching me paint while I enjoyed his company and the relaxation. Once again when it was time for him to leave it was a hard goodbye. He tucked me into bed and told me he loved me and that he is proud of me and that everyone is thinking about me and loves me very much. Things are progressing but I still have so much fear!

The best part of today, they moved *Paula* from my room at suppertime! She asked the nurse why and was told "Well there's an empty room, so were giving it to you!" Thank f*ck, back to normal and home sweet home her at 2SE.

As I'm sitting here in bed trying to relax I'm feeling very lonely and sad. I miss everyone so much and I'm tired of being in here.

I feel so isolated from the outside world. I have been here for a while, that I'm almost fearful to go out into the real world again. My time in here stresses me out to think of all the things that are piling up at work, around the house, banking, bill payments etc. I know I can't think of all those things as I am here to focus on the important issues, however sometimes that make me feel selfish for doing so. I just want to get back to my routine.

FOOD JOURNAL for today
BREAKFAST – 2 prunes, fat free yogurt & water
LUNCH – ½ cup tossed salad with salt & pepper, 3 tablespoons couscous, water
SUPPER – poached white fish, green beans, beef consommé & water
SNACK – ½ Orange with water

DAY 6 – Tuesday December 20, 2005

Slept from 11:00pm – 5:00am this morning! I think not having a roommate helped a lot. I got up and had a shower and FINALLY was allowed to shave with a razor or should I say sign out a razor at the nurse's station. I had 20 minutes to use it before they would ambush me before signing it back in. For breakfast I had 2 hardboiled egg whites and a fat free yogurt with bran, tea and water. I'm feeling really good this morning and ready to face what comes at me, we will see what the afternoon brings.

I just got done my meeting with Dr. David the Psychologist

and the session went well, however I felt it was too long. I have realized that my attention span is less than an hour. Any more than that and I begin to have bodily twitches and get agitated. We discussed lots of issues but mainly the reason why I can't sit still and the feeling of failure if something is not accomplished or completed in its entirety. Dr. David also asked me "What is something that keeps coming up in your day to day life that occurred in the past?" My answer was "My alcoholic step Father coming home drunk all the time, me doing cocaine without any of my friends and family knowing and the loss of an ex-boyfriend whom I used to do cocaine with. He then asked me if I felt responsible for his loss, to which my answer was a very quick YES, with tears streaming down my face. I explained to Dr. David that I felt this way because when I first found out that *Mitch* was doing coke I tried to get him help on many occasions, which failed. Then I became an addict for a short period of time and stopped suddenly, when I realized what I would lose if I continued. I feel that I left *Mitch* out there to fend for himself, when he probably didn't have the same support system as I did. I feel that I am somewhat to blame for his death. I know I couldn't have stopped him from going out to Penniac that night but I feel as though maybe with a better support system, he would have made a much better decision.

We also talked about our family session coming up on Thursday with myself, psychologist, psychiatrist, Ma, Bobby, Andrew and my day nurse Cathy. I am feeling nervous, anxious for that as that will be the first time that I have seen Ma and Bobby in a very long time and this will also be the first time that Ma will hear and find out about how I have truly been feeling all these years, in trying to hide my pain and anxiety.

I was going to eat my lunch after my session, however everyone piled into the common room and since they won't allow me to eat in my room I'll come back. 20 minutes later I come back and it's a shitty salad plate, so I picked off 2 cucumbers, 2 tomatoes and ate a hardboiled egg white the other full of fat crap can stay, like potato salad, coleslaw and cheese. The soup was not edible either too salty. Cathy came in and gave me my Ativan before Emotional Therapy group. I made out a lot better today and even said a couple of words and my heart didn't start racing. After group I came back to my room only to find a new roommate even worse than *Paula*, *Kathy* PARTY GIRL, and holy f*ck! If I thought *Paula* was a handful, she is tame compared to *Kathy*! All she keeps saying in the common room is "I'm sorry for what I did to my husband and I don't wanna do the marijuana anymore." This should make things interesting. I give her some crayons and paper and hope she is able to calm down. After relaxation session I'm feeling really good. For every inhale I say to myself I AM BEAUTIFUL and for every exhale I say to myself I DON'T HAVE TO BE AFRAID. As I'm sitting in bed Monika walks in for a visit, it is so great to see her. I haven't seen her since Monday. We talked for a bit then I was forced to go to supper with everyone, UH! It was so gross so I just took the steamed broccoli and mixed it with my beef consommé. I warmed up some couscous for Monika that Andrew had made and she ate my muffin.

Andrew arrived and we signed the house papers to finalize

our purchase, as we move in in February, 2006. I began to feel down for some reason and I just couldn't seem to shake it. We decided just to cuddle in bed and talk and that's when I lost it, I began bawling. Part of my fear is going back out into the real world and the other part is going back to my old habits and taking on too much.

Lastly and certainly not least, is the fact that one day I just want to look in the mirror and think I'm beautiful both on the outside and inside and not worry about other people's judgment or what they are thinking about me. The nurse quickly came in as I was crying and asked if I was alright and told me that I don't have to worry, as I won't have to take everything on and nor will I be expected to take everything on. She asked if I wanted an Ativan but I said no at first, however before Andrew left I went back out and told her I would like one before bed. So Andrew tucked me in and of course I cried even more and poor *Kathy* asked "Why are you crying?" and Andrew said "She does this every time I leave, as it makes her sad." So I'm going to bed tonight feeling fearful of what the next few days are going to bring.

FOOD JOURNAL for Today
BREAKFAST – 2 boiled egg whites, fat free yogurt & water
SNACK – banana
LUNCH – 2 cucumbers slices, 2 tomato slices, 1 hardboiled egg white & water
SNACK – orange & muffin
SUPPER – steamed broccoli & beef consommé

DAY 7 – Wednesday December 21, 2005

I had a pretty restless and terrible sleep last night having
Kathy in the room probably didn't help either. I woke up at
6:30am but fell back asleep until 9am. I got out of bed and
went and had breakfast since they would be taking the trays
away soon. I had 2 hardboiled egg whites and prune juice. I
saved the yogurt for later as I was full. I came back to my
room as I decided to make Thank-You cards for all the people
who had sent me cards, gifts or visited, as I will be leaving
soon. I cannot forget to make one for the staff of 2SE, as I will
never forget them. This is definitely one special floor, with
people who are very unique and unbelievably caring in what
they do.

I had lunch and decided to weigh myself, because all the other
days they would not let me. I was so happy, 132.5lbs and at
5'10", just a bit more to go but for the first time I'm seeing
some results. When I arrived I was 148lbs, so I am happy I
have lost 15lbs. The weight I would like to maintain is 130lbs
and I feel like I would be great, more confident when I walk
around. I wouldn't have to worry that everyone is looking at
my giggly fat ass!

I was thinking that I would like to get *Kathy*, a little
something for Christmas. I thought maybe some sugar free
candies, some toiletries, socks and I was thinking maybe a
teddy bear or something. She says she feels lonely and I think
this may give her some comfort at night especially this
weekend as she is already not looking forward to it, as she
fear nobody will be around other than the staff. I reassured

her that there would probably be a few people around that are not allowed to go home.

The nurse came in and we discussed how I was feeling about tomorrow's family meeting and leaving 2SE on Friday. She really focused on forgiving and accepting some of the past issues that I've had to deal with, it was a really great talk.

The afternoon went by really fast and the next thing I knew Andrew arrived. We talked about what was going to go on for Christmas and we also talked about tomorrow's family meeting and how I was feeling which was very anxious. He reassured me not to worry and that there was no pressure on me. I then decided that I wanted to get a 1 hour leave pass to go with him to Walmart, the first time I've been out of the hospital in 8 days. We asked *Kathy* if she wanted anything and she only requested a Diet Coke. Andrew and I got talking to *Kathy* beforehand and found out she is 36 years old, has 4 kids (1 son and 3 daughters) along with a grandson. Her son and 1 daughter live in Fredericton. *Kathy* comes from Woodstock and has turrets. Not sure about her husband/boyfriend, however I believe that is a pretty touchy subject based upon the picture she drew the other day. She says she used to be a party girl who did a lot of marijuana. She loves to sing and dance and to Charlie Pride.

So off we headed to Walmart, got freaked out a couple of times, but ending up picking up a few things for *Kathy* including a CD player and Charlie Pride CD. Well the look on her face when we told her Xmas had come early, was simply PRICELESS! We got back around 7:00pm and I don't think she stopped listening and singing to Charlie until 9:00pm, when it was lights out. She ate chocolates like it was her first time, was drooling everywhere and downed a can of diet coke like nobody's business with big burps during and after. The nurses even came into the common room, to tell us they ran to my room because they thought they heard someone crying from room 2075, but it was just *Kathy* singing her little heart out. Andrew and I just laughed. The nurse couldn't believe that we had done that out of our own money. It made me feel great to give something to someone whom I know would appreciate the gifts, use them and find joy in every moment. When we came back to the room we danced, sang, laughed and talked with *Kathy* then it was time for Andrew to go. He tucked me in and I asked him to promise me to hold my hand during tomorrow's meeting the whole time. *Kathy* kept singing her little heart out, while the nurse came in to talk to me about how I was feeling about tomorrow. I decided to take an Ativan to try and get a good night's sleep since so many thoughts are running through my head and I can't stop them. I also asked for an Ativan before tomorrow's meeting and she said it wouldn't be a problem.

FOOD JOURNAL for today
BREAKFAST – 2 hardboiled egg whites, prune juice & water
SNACK – fat free yogurt
LUNCH – 1cup mixed veggies (carrots, celery, cucumber, tomatoes, broccoli & cauliflower), ½ cup beef & barley soup, tea & water
SNACK – banana, 2 kiwis & muffin
SUPPER – beef consommé with 2 Tablespoons couscous salad & ½ baked potato with cranberry sauce

SNACK – 1 apple & 1 tablespoon peanut butter

DAY 8 – Thursday December 22, 2005

Had a terrible night's sleep and finally woke up at 5am to
Kathy's snoring, deep breathing, tossing and turning. Then
at 6am she decides to get up and get dressed by slamming the
dresser drawers then tops it all off with downing 2 cans of diet
coke with tons of f*cking belching in between. I got up
needless to say, had breakfast and by 9am I decided to have a
nap before my meeting. *Kathy* one the other hand decided
to have a dance party with Charlie Pride cranked on the CD
player! We both had a laugh. It honestly has been great
having *Kathy* as a roommate the only negative thing is that I
am having a hard time sleeping. Hopefully that will get
worked out on its own.

Just got done my family meeting and it went ok. I gave Ma a
huge hug when I saw her and told her that I loved her and
began to cry. Dr. Shahid (psychiatrist) went over why I was
there and granted me a weekend pass, needless to say I was
surprised. I thought I was getting out tomorrow for good. He
said it would be another 1-2 weeks of treatment here at 2SE.
Its mind draining being here, however I know this will only
make me stronger in the end.

Lunch has come and gone and I decide it's time to clean
Kathy's side of the room. So we rounded up all of her
clothes that needed to be cleaned, tidied up her desk and
removed all her bedding and remade her bed. I can handle
this room now, whereas before it was revolting to see.

F*ck, this is one hell of an emotional and exhausting day. Family Meeting at 10:30am, Emotions Group at 1:00pm, Psychology appointment at 2:00pm, Relaxation Group at 3:00pm, Ma, Bobby and Andrew coming at 4:00pm. Needless to say I fell asleep, to only have Dr. David waking me up for my appointment. We discussed the meeting this morning and maybe setting up another meeting with both my Ma and myself. We also discussed some of the issues I may have with respect to the weekend food wise. I think it is going to be difficult and just the whole aura of the house this Christmas will be different. So I'm not exactly sure how the weekend will go exactly. We also talked about forgiveness and how to go about doing it or accepting things. Something which is very different for me. I have a very hard time forgiving people and learning to let things go. Dr. David game me some reading for the weekend, a chapter from the book "Building Self-Confidence and Self-Esteem". I am very interested to read it. Ma, Bobby and Andrew are coming at 4:00pm and I'm very nervous and anxious for that, since this will be the first time they are coming or I should say that I am allowing them to come and visit with me in my room.

I think going home for the weekend although it is scary to me will be good for me to get away from it all and not have to think on the level I'm thinking now. One thing and one day at a time. I will get through this for me, my husband and the rest of our family and of course the family we hope to have in the future.

FOOD JOURNAL for today
BREAKFAST – 2 poached egg whites, prune juice & water

SNACK – banana
LUNCH – ½ cup tossed salad with salt & pepper, chicken broth with 2 tablespoons of couscous, & water
SNACK – orange, muffin & 5 grapes
SUPPER – beef broth, green beans & 2 slices turkey
SNACK – snack size booster juice

DAY 9 – Friday December 23, 2005

So I'm headed home on a weekend pass today – excited, anxious, nervous and probably over worrying what the weekend will bring. Once again I had a terrible sleep. I woke up at 3am to *Kathy* in the bathroom talking to herself, then I had a nightmare that she was looking over me and I woke up in a panic! She is a great person but I finally had to tell my day nurse Michelle this morning that *Kathy* has got to shower, because it was absolutely awful going into the bathroom this morning. I couldn't even stand going in there even a half hour later, it smelt like dying f*cking fish on a hot day, UH! So about 2 minutes later *Kathy* comes into the room saying she is going to take a shower, thanks goodness! The only thing that bothered me was that the nurse said "Well you won't have to worry about it this weekend." That's not the point dumbass! The point is that it's unsanitary and she needs to be told, as she doesn't know or realize just like doing her laundry yesterday. I went and had breakfast, came back and packed my bags for the weekend. I decided to just get cleaned up in the bathroom and save the shower for home, I can't wait!

I decided to go to TAG before Andrew arrives to pick me up and it was so much fun! I got to try the pottery wheel for the first time in my life and loved the feeling on my hands! I had the 'perfect bowl' about 4-5 times, however one little move and it was gone in an instant. So in the end I did not come out with a finished product, but I will try again next week when I come back.

Andrew arrived and we headed home, it felt so strange.

FOOD JOURNAL for today
BREAKFAST – 4 prunes, 2 boiled egg whites & water
LUNCH – ½ cup tossed salad with salt/pepper & ½ cup chicken broth
SNACK – apple & 1 tablespoon peanut butter
SUPPER – beef stroganoff & water

DAY 10 – Saturday December 24, 2005
home on weekend pass

Got up, had some breakfast and then headed to the mall with Andrew to finish up the last of the Christmas list, which went ok. Went home and wrapped the last of the gifts then it was time to head to Andrew's Mom's for Christmas Eve Supper, in which I OVERSTUFFED myself! The great thing about Andrew's family is that they have fun when they see each other, which is perfect timing for me to slip away and throw up every bit of supper. GOD that never gets old and feels so good! It's been so long since I'm monitored every f*cking second at the hospital! After supper we left and went to Ma and Bobby's to open only one of our gifts, PJ's my favorite thing on Christmas Eve!

FOOD JOURNAL for today
BREAKFAST – yogurt, banana, pecans & water
LUNCH – beef stroganoff, orange & water
SUPPER – turkey, potatoes, squash, corn, beets, 2 turtles, cranberry juice & glass of red wine.

DAY 11 – Sunday December 25, 2005
home on weekend pass

So we wake up and it's Christmas day! I am actually feeling really good, my spirits are up and the 3 things that I am grateful for are:

1. I had a warm bed to sleep in last night.
2. I have a friends and family to visit today.
3. My tummy won't go hungry today.

We get ready and drive to Andrew's mom's house for our gift exchange, then quickly to my Ma's for breakfast and gifts. I had 2 boiled egg whites, 2 slices black forest ham and fruit salad while the rest of them had eggs benedict, hash browns and OJ with champagne. After, we came home to relax before heading off to Andrew's Dad's for supper.

We arrive at Andrew's Dad's house and are the 5th/6th person to arrive, however 30 minutes later there was 21 of us, including 7 children!!!! So before dinner I was feeling a little overwhelmed and anxious. I went over to Andrew and my hands were shaking. He asked if everything was ok and I said "No". I quickly went upstairs and I lost it, crying, pacing back and forth and the anxiety building like I had never felt before.

Unfortunately we forgot the Ativan and nobody at the house had any, so Andrew and I quickly drove home and it took a good 45 minutes until I settled. I then laid on the couch, stuffed my face with beef stroganoff, antipasto, crackers, turtles, Lindt chocolates and with Andrew as my overly protective "eagle eye" I was f*cked and not able to puke, worst guilt ever! We watched a movie, fell asleep around 9:30 and didn't wake up until 9:30am the next morning.

FOOD JOURNAL for today
BREAKFAST – 2 boiled eggs whites, 2 slices black forest ham, fruit salad & OJ
SNACK – clementine
LUNCH - yogurt, banana, pecans, chocolate covered cashews & water
SUPPER – beef stroganoff, antipasto, crackers, turtles & Lindt chocolate

DAY 12 – Monday December 26, 2005
home on weekend pass until 8:30pm

I woke up this morning feeling a little down for so many reasons – Christmas is over so I'm going back to the psych ward today. There are so many things still left to work on; not being with Andrew as much as I would like, feeling guilty for all that I have eaten this weekend etc. etc. etc. We were invited over to Monika and Jamie's for supper, however when it came time to leave I started having a panic attack, so Andrew got me an Ativan and called to let them know we wouldn't be coming, I went to bed and cried myself to sleep. I feel like I'm always letting people down. The Ativan knocked me out for 2 hours and then it was time to leave to head back to the hospital, as it was 8:15pm and I had to arrive by 8:30pm. When we arrived *Kathy* was happy to see me. Andrew tucked me and I cried myself to sleep once again.

FOOD JOURNAL for today
BREAKFAST – ¼ omelet
LUNCH – turkey, squash, stuffing, potatoes, carrots, beets, 10 slowpokes & 4 Ferrero Rocher
SUPPER – yogurt, 2 kiwis, flax seed, pecans, English muffin, 1 slice cheese & water

DAY 13 – Tuesday December 27, 2005 131.4lbs

Well it is day 13 but day 1 for my diet again! I have not weighed myself yet, however I will before the morning is done. I know that I have gained a couple of pounds. WAY too many temptations in the outside world that I have a hard time saying "NO!" to. I couldn't believe *Kathy* last night, I honestly think she has gotten worse. She did not stop going on about death and burning in hell and finally fell asleep from 9:00pm – 11:30pm. And this morning it started early once again, 5:45am. I like *Kathy* as a roommate, however I need some sleep to help me feel better. Breakfast was a little later than usual today. I had 1 hardboiled egg white and ¼ cup orange juice. I will probably have a pear later on, but I really have to watch what I eat, as I feel so disgusting after the weekend. I noticed lots of tossed salads in the common room fridge over the weekend, so I'm sure I can have one of those for lunch as I'm sure the rest of the things I get today will not be diet approved.

There are no treatment sessions today, so I think I'm just going to read the book Andrew got me and do crosswords. So much for that, I've become anxious, agitated and I'm ready to scream at *Kathy*, she won't shut up! So the nurse came in and gave me an Ativan and told *Kathy* to go to the common room as I needed to rest. I had a pear and this is so bad, but I stole 4 Hershey's kisses from *Kathy's* stash, and completely devoured them! Got a glass of water, chugged it and immediately went to the bathroom to puke – f*ck why am I so weak?!? You seriously just ate like a f*cking pig this weekend and now you're eating chocolates?!? F*ck f*ck f*ck!

I'm feeling so down and unmotivated today. Haven't had a shower, taken off my pj's. I just feel like staying in bed and not talking or seeing anyone today. Sometimes I wonder what it would be like to be far away all by myself. Sometimes I regret not doing that in the past. But then I realize it would be worse not to be with Andrew because I can honestly say I may or may not be alive at this time or I would be doing things that are very harmful to my body. I wish I knew my calling, the reason why God put me on this earth. I know it is to help others, give support and hope, but how does that become my 'job'? I guess those are things that will hopefully come to me someday. I just feel so lost with what steps I am to take to make myself feel better. I know that positive thinking is one, but for some reason you can think it and say it, however if you don't believe it doesn't do much good. I just want to love me the outside as I already love most of my inside. There are a few things I need to work on such as jealousy, not questioning people's intentions, underestimating people etc., however I think all these have to do with my own self esteem.

I have a 3 hour pass tonight, so Andrew is taking me out to see the movie "Dick & Jane". I will want to eat nachos or popcorn, however if we can get the movie done around 8:30pm or so that will give Andrew just enough time to get me back to hospital and have to leave so I can puke. Sorry Andrew, however it just has to be done. Just like yesterday I felt so guilty for all I had eaten I purged in the shower knowing you would never find out. I'm sorry I didn't tell you!

FOOD JOURNAL for today
BREAKFAST – hardboiled egg white, ¼ cup orange juice & water
SNACK – banana & water
LUNCH – ½ cup vegetable soup, ¼ cup tossed salad & water
SNACK – apple
SUPPER – ½ cup broth, carrots & ¼ cup tossed salad with salt & pepper
SNACK – popcorn, chocolate bar & sprite

DAY 14 – Wednesday December 28, 2005 131.3lbs

Dr. Shahid came in today and asked how I was doing. He said that I would be in here for another 1-2 weeks and that he would take care of getting the social worker to see me about EI and those types of things. That eases my mind of a little bit of stress as I hate not having answers or a plan.

I told *Kathy* that she has to do her laundry, not sure how that went. I know she brought her laundry somewhere....and I also told her that she needed to have a shower, NOT just wash her hair but have a shower well that didn't work so well. She came back 5 minutes later with a towel on her head then said "You blow dry it Richard". You see *Kathy* has this thing with calling me Richard, I have no idea where she got it from, and sadly I should not laugh but the way she says it over and over makes me giggle sometimes. I told her that I wasn't going to dry her hair until she called me by my right name, so she did.

My meeting with Dr. David went well. We talked about how my weekend went and how I felt a little disappointed that my Ma didn't call the night I left Andrew's Dad's house at Christmas supper. We also went over the test that I did and he highlighted the main things that he thought were of concern such as PTSD (post-traumatic stress disorder) from my cocaine use and *Mitch's* death, low self-esteem/confidence were very high off the charts.

I did find out that I have a weekend pass from Friday until Monday this weekend not sure how I feel about that after last weekend.

Before bed I began to cry, just staring at the wall. I cried for a long time just continuing to stare at the wall. I just feel so lost. Not knowing what to do next to make myself feel better. I feel so numb, no emotion like a zombie – not sure maybe it's the drugs or maybe just me. Finally I began to read but *Kathy* was really getting on my nerves – she sees things and voices and of course never stops saying it out loud. I couldn't take it any longer so I went across from my room to the nurse's station and said "Can I please have an Ativan before I lose it on *Kathy*!" The nurses quickly came in and asked *Kathy* if she wanted a room to herself and she said "NO, I don't' want to be alone!" So then they asked me to move to another room, a single where *Kathy* used to be for the night and in the morning, they would get things straightened out. I felt bad as I really like having *Kathy* as a roommate, however I was not getting any sleep and she was getting worse, making me more irritated. So I went to my new room down the hall more isolated from everyone and sat there for what seemed forever and ever……

FOOD JOURNAL for today
BREAKFAST – 1 hardboiled egg white, fat free yogurt, natural bran, banana & water
LUNCH – ½ cup beef & barley soup, spinach, 2 carrots sticks, 2 celery sticks, 1 slice cucumber, 1 slice tomato & water
SNACK – banana
SUPPER – ½ baked potato, ½ cup beef broth, carrots, applesauce & water
SNACK – snack size sonic soy smoothie at booster juice

DAY 15 – Thursday December 29, 2005 131.9lbs

Stacey my day nurse came to talk to me as *Kathy* has been moved out of my room into a private room #1070. She is not happy and nor is she very friendly to me right now. I feel so bad, however I know that I have to look out for me right now and I wasn't getting my rest. Dr. Shahid came to talk to me as well and asked me how I was doing and I told him that I am feeling really down these past few days and emotionless. He said it could be the Zoloft, however we would wait until Tuesday to make a decision on the medication and on my stay. I'm beginning to think that maybe this place is bringing me down, I really don't know. I feel almost as low as when I came in, but not as much anxiety, bodily twitches and room pacing. I just don't know what to do, I feel so lost and I wish this would all just go away. I'm tired of feeling emotionless and sad when I know deep down inside I am a happy person.

I decided to get *Kathy* to come to TAG with me this afternoon as I think it will be a good stress reliever for her…..so much for that. She pops in an Anne Murray tape into the tape deck, sits down, starts singing and then crying! The nurse ended up having to take her back upstairs, f*ck I feel terrible for dragging her here!

After TAG, I went back to my room and started journaling which immediately made me cry. My day nurse Stacey came in and asked what was wrong. I said "I just want to feel like my old self once again and I don't understand what I'm supposed to be doing in order to get better. I guess I'm really confused as to what's going on now and what is to go on in the future."

When Monika and Jamie came last night, I felt like a zombie, I hardly spoke. I just really want things to start progressing and getting better. I know that I have gotten a little better since I have been in here, because I've eaten, haven't vomited in a few days and my anxiety has greatly diminished, however it seems my depression has gone up! Maybe because my anxiety was first symptom that took over in the beginning.

FOOD JOURNAL for today
BREAKFAST – 2 hardboiled egg whites, prune juice, fat free yogurt, banana & water
LUNCH – ½ cup tossed salad with salt & pepper, chicken broth & water
SNACK – banana, apple, 1 tablespoon peanut butter & water
SUPPER – beef broth, green beans, 1 slice roast beef, ¼ bowl orange Jell-O & water

DAY 16 – Friday December 30, 2005 130.9lbs
home weekend pass

Worst sleep ever. I think I was awake all night then finally at 6:30am I was greeted by a light, a roommate and her friend, what the f*ck is going on?!? Ok calm down, she's not being admitted, however she is having ECT (Electro Convulsive Therapy) today, YIKES!

I'm looking forward to going home for the weekend but I'm so scared of all the temptations that are going to await me especially when I'm alone! When we got home Andrew had all the candles lit and spa music playing. He had made me a little bed on the couch and told me to relax. I couldn't relax, so I turned on the TV as he was going out to visit his friends. Well soon after I got into the Doritos, chocolates and Ritz crackers. Note to self, DRINK WATER before purging a bunch of dry shit! Jesus that is the hardest thing to ever have to puke up! Andrew got home and I was eating rhubarb pie, so while he was in the computer room I quickly went to the bathroom to purge, water makes all the difference in the world!

FOOD JOURNAL for today
BREAKFAST – 2 hardboiled egg whites, 2 prunes, fat free yogurt, banana, bran flakes & water
LUNCH – ½ Wendy's mandarin chicken salad no dressing, 3 sips root beer & 1 glass Ovaltine
SUPPER – salmon & stir fried veggies
SNACK – ½ box Ritz crackers, 13 chocolates, ½ strawberry rhubarb pie & ½ bag dill Doritos

DAY 17 – Saturday December 31, 2005

New Year's Eve so we decided to have a few friends and family members over to play Cranium and Taboo but then it turned into a full-fledged party. The music was blastin' while we were all dancing in the middle of the living room, it was great! I drank so much vodka, which is a huge 'no no', which made me obsessively crave! So, I ate some bad food which means I had to purge, twice! The first time Andrew caught me and I confessed to doing it and he was of course disappointed but with all that yummy yet off limits food, it was so hard to say no to all of it! The party didn't get over until 5am! What a way to ring in the New Year!

FOOD JOURNAL for today
BREAKFAST – 2 hardboiled egg whites, 4 prunes, ½ English muffin with PB&J & orange juice
LUNCH – stir fried vegetables leftover
SUPPER – Almost quart vodka and a shit ton of bad food

DAY 18 – Sunday January 1, 2006

Completely hungover. I have nothing else to say.

FOOD JOURNAL for today
BREAKFAST – McDonalds Egg McMuffin
SNACK – crackers & Swiss cheese
SUPPER – chicken chow mein, 2 chicken balls, 4 honey garlic spareribs & 1 glass diet Pepsi

DAY 19 – Monday January 2, 2006 133.3lbs

Woke up this morning having had some very vivid and terrible dreams. I did absolutely nothing at all this morning, not even eat breakfast. I felt nauseous for some reason. Around 1:00pm I made Kraft Dinner and ate 1/3 of that. The dishes and the house were still a disaster from New Year's, what the f*ck! So I pride myself off the couch tidied up the kitchen, living room and did 2 loads of laundry. I also packed my bags for the hospital and ate the rest of the KD.

I started to feel really anxious and when I spoke to Andrew on the phone I told him that I wanted to go back to the hospital early, as soon as he got home. The anxiety kept getting worse and when Andrew arrived I was pacing the house and the bodily twitches came on strong. I needed an Ativan desperately, I can't settle down and all I wanted to do, was pace the house which obviously bothers Andrew. He dropped me off at the hospital doors and that made me feel really bad that he didn't want to come up and tuck me in. He didn't call either….I do know *Laura* his ex was in town and she called so that is probably where he was all day, f*ck!

FOOD JOURNAL for today
BREAKFAST – nothing
LUNCH – 2/3 box KD & 1 glass of lemonade
SUPPER – 1/3 box KD, 3 Ritz Crackers & 1 bite vegetarian chili

DAY 20 – Tuesday January 3, 2006 133.3lbs

Had a great sleep last night, slept from 11:00pm-8:45am. The staff changed my room on me over the weekend, I'm now in 1072A the room right beside my old room. I can't believe that I gained 2lbs over the weekend, f*ck I feel so fat!!!

I'm feeling odd today, not quite sure of my mood. Definitely feeling fat and very uncomfortable around people.

I had an appointment with Dr. David at 10:30am and he immediately sensed that I was not doing well. I began rocking in the chair uncontrollably and my legs would not stop moving. We talked about my negative body image, how I look at food and what I like and dislike about myself. He asked what I liked and as soon as I said "My back", it quickly turned into a quick negative of I hate the way the flab shows when I have a t-shirt and bra on etc. etc. etc. I guess I like that my thighs don't rub together since I've lost weight….even though I've put on 2lbs. The things I totally hate about myself are my flabby stomach, arms, legs, back, the flabby fat that hangs over my jeans, fatty sides, my fat by my armpits that sags, my back fat, my flabby cellulite ass, my stretch marked hips, the lump on my left upper thigh from the car accident and I hate the way I look especially without makeup on.

I told Dr. David once again that I feel lost. I feel fed up feeling this way and I'm not quite sure what I am supposed to be doing to help myself. He also talked to me about a Day Therapy program that is offered for 'crazies' like me I guess. It is a minimum of 3 months and it is for patients that do not need to be in the hospital, however you would come to the hospital for the program 2-4 days/week for 2-3 hours per day.

I would then be allowed to eat and sleep at home – this is the option that Andrew wants, however my concern is the food. I know at some point I will have to face it, but right now I am not strong enough to do so.

Back to my room after my appointment and I have a

roommate. She was formerly in one of the padded rooms in the locked area behind the nurse's station, as I recognize her name from the board. Her name is *Shelley* and she is very quiet, won't eat anything.

I'm really tired today and feeling pressure from Andrew to come home, to eat, to relax and to talk. Maybe it's just my sensitivity, however I feel like not telling him what I say to the doctors for fear of what he'll have to say about it all. Sometimes I feel like he gets mad at me for not knowing the answers to some of his questions. He thinks that my feeling depressed or anxious is a result of me being at the hospital. I tried to tell him that I am going to have my good and bad days but it didn't work. I just feel so hopeless and I want to quit. I knew that is the easy way out but I'm tired of feeling sad and angry with myself all the time.

My day nurse came in to talk to me and I began to cry. She asked me how my anxiety was and I said a 7 and my depression an 8. I feel so hopeless and angry with my body and I feel no end in my journey. She asked me "Do you have any suicidal thoughts?" I said "Yes". She asked "Have you thought of how?" I said "Not really." She said "Have you thought of committing suicide or just being dead?" I said "I'm tired of living my life this way. I feel like there is no end to this depression or feeling the way that I am feeling."

Andrew called and apologize for the way he reacted today. He just wants to know from the Doctors what is going on. I know with him being on the outside it must be difficult and to be honest I don't think there are any answers at this point. Of course with all this talk, I start feeling sick to my stomach, anxious and I begin rocking back and forth while fidgeting with my ring, my hands, my legs, my jeans. It's like ants are crawling all over my body and I'm just trying to shew them away! The pacing starts and the deep gasps for air begin.....panic attack take 1000! Imagine being trapped in a glass bubble, the oxygen is depleting around you. Your breathing becomes quicker and quicker by the second as your heart races faster and fast. Your eyes start bulging out of your head because you truly feel you are drowning. Your arms stretch out for help but nothing can save you. You begin prying at the glass that surrounds you trying to break free. The simplicity of one breath is all you want yet you can't have it.

Andrew got me a new book tonight called "A Million Little Pieces" part of the Oprah Book Club, it's is about a guy in rehab. He decides to take me to the movies and as we get in line to get popcorn Andrew sees two of our friends *Dick* and *Jane* that I have not seen since I was admitted to the hospital. He says to me "Go to theatre number 6, I'll meet you there." I quickly dart out and go to number 6. I felt very uneasy walking in there by myself and the anxiety started coming on. The thoughts of being alone in the theatre made me think of people thinking what a loser sitting by yourself, she's so ugly, no makeup on etc. etc. etc. Being surrounded by people I felt like I had no escape, what an awful feeling.

On a daily basis I hate myself, feel stupid, feel inadequate, feel ugly, scrutinized for my body, want to die and kill myself. So the best thing to do to feel in control, purge up all the movie shit I ate, AH RELIEF!!! Oh ED, you never disappoint me.

FOOD JOURNAL for today
BREAKFAST – 1 hardboiled egg white, fat free yogurt & water
SNACK – 3 prunes
LUNCH – 2 bites chicken & tea
SNACK – tangerine
SUPPER – ½ cup chicken broth & ¼ cup carrots
SNACK – kids pack popcorn, chocolate bar & diet coke

DAY 21 – Wednesday January 4, 2006
Morning: 130.9lbs Night: 130.8lbs

Weighed myself this morning and I'm almost back down to the weight I want to be. Must have been the shit I had yesterday, who knows it fluctuates so much. I'm going to start weighing myself in the morning and then again in the evening hopefully they won't catch on but I should be able to fool them with a day nurse and night nurse at the station. I'm so happy that we have bought a scale for the house. I think this will really help me stay motivated to maintain my weight and hopefully stop this yo-yo thing that I have been doing all my life. I'm feeling pretty good today, probably has a lot to do with what I saw on the scales, but oh well……

My meeting with Dr. David was ok. We talked about the cognitive therapy we are working on and working on self-esteem when it comes to my body image and the scrutinizing that I do. He asked, "How often do you look at your body?" I said "First thing in the morning every day for 2-5 minutes depending upon what type of fat day I'm having and ultimately this determines part of the way that I will feel for the day based on how I see myself in the mirror. I look at the acne on my face, the blackheads, if my nose looks big or small, if my boobs look ok – are they perky or are my nipples inverted. Is my stomach fat and bulging out? Is my ass saggy with lots of cellulite, do my hips look big and how many stretch marks do I see today? How does my left hip/thigh look and how big is the bulge in which I'll never be able to get rid of due to the car accident? When I sit down on the toilet how many rolls on my stomach, do my thighs squish over the sides?" Seriously Dr. David, do you want me to go on?!? He decided that my therapy for this would be 'Time and Frequency'. Reducing the amount of time that I scrutinize my body along with the frequency that I look in the mirror. Our next family meeting will be Friday January 6, at 9:30am – this will be to find out whether or not I'm getting discharged. This scares me because of all the food temptations, feeling vulnerable to seeing people I know in the outside world. When Dr. David and I are walking back from our session back to the psych ward, of all the people that could be in the Day Therapy room waiting was *Tina* F*CKING *Pope*! I NEARLY DIE!!! That's all I need to worry about her blabbing her big mouth.

Thankfully Dr. Shahid came in to calm me down after Dr. David left but I also found out bad news that if I am discharged and placed into the day therapy program and Dr. David will no longer be my Psychologist. I feel these past couple of days Dr. David and I have made progress in that he has given me specific things to work on. Dr. Shahid does not want me to leave until I am ready as he has seen so many patients leave and end up back in 2SE in worse condition then when they arrived the first time.

Ma came to visit and of course came bearing gifts, her way of communicating I love you, I miss you and I hope you are alright…whatever works right? I guess my focus is my relationship with myself not with her right now. We played crib for a couple hours then I walked her to the prison doors. If you get too close, the alarm goes off! Kidding, but it seems that way! it's like Shawshank in here!

Cathy my night nurse came in as she was sensing my anxiety towards my discharge. I asked her "Did you feel this fearful when you were going through your thing" She said "What thing was that?" I said "When you were going through your disorder." She said "I told you about that?" "I said "Yeah when I had been here for only 4 or 5 days and you became my nurse. Funny how things work out because from the beginning Cathy has been my favorite nurse and I couldn't exactly pinpoint why, but now it all comes together. Cathy said to me "Yes I was fearful and to keep each and every accomplishment held high no matter how small they may seem." She then recited this prayer which really resonated with me.

> *"God, grant me the serenity to accept the things I cannot change, Courage to change the things I can, and wisdom to know the difference."*

FOOD JOURNAL for today
BREAKFAST – fat free yogurt, banana, bran flakes & water
LUNCH – 2 celery sticks, 2 cucumber slices, tomato wedge, ½ cup beef & barley soup & tea
SNACK – banana & orange

SUPPER – ½ cup beef broth, 2 slices turkey, ¼ cup carrots &
peas & water
SNACK – apple

DAY 22 – Thursday January 5, 2006
Morning: 131.6lbs Night: Unknown they would not let me
on the scale, F*CK seriously!

Not feeling good today, feeling very shaky, weak and tired.
Cathy told me to use 'HALT' when I feel anxiety coming on.
H – am I HUNGRY
A – am I ANGRY
L – am I LONELY
T – am I TIRED

I guess I'm tired as I was having really weird dreams last
night.

Dr. David comes to get me for my appointment, yup one must
be escorted of course – I guess the crazies are not allowed to
roam…I'm sure there's a code for that. As soon as I sit down
in his office, begin to rock viciously. I need to release some of
this energy. My hands begin to fidget, neck start twitching
from side to side and my heart rate begins to quicken!
STOP!!!!! I always wonder what Dr. David must think when
this starts to happen as I'm sure it looks like an enactment
from the exorcist!

There have been some weird people that freak me right out
that have been admitted in the past 2 days. These 2 guys are
very odd. I believe one has anger issues, the other, well he

honestly looks like he is ready to kill you with his eyes. I thought anger management guy was going to lose it today at lunch because he had to have plastic cutlery when the rest of us had regular.

I called Andrew and the questions start. The one that really got me really f*cking pissed off was "When we go into the family meeting tomorrow, I want to talk to your psychologist and psychiatrist by myself." I said "Why, you want to talk about me behind my back?" He says "I don't want to talk about you, but about me." He then tells me that instead of relaxing at home last night, which is the reason why he said he couldn't come visit, he went to *Greg's* and they went out and played pool and that he would be late tonight, as he's playing squash with *Aaron*. Well, I am angry, frustrated, sad, disappointed etc. at this point so I let him go and storm away from the phone. I need a place to be alone! I can't go back to my room because:

1. My roommate might be there.
2. Michelle or someone may come to my room
3. The day nurse would come running if she heard me crying.

My only available option is the secluded bathroom/shower in the creepy section of the ward. I get the key, open the door, quickly shut it and completely lose it! I begin bawling my eyes out wanting my world to end! I get into a deep depressive low and think the worst, I want to die! I imagine all the ways in the bathroom it could be done.

Suffocation with the shower curtain (wait there is none), hitting my head over and over again on the tiled wall, take the drain cap off and cut myself and bleed to death and that is all I can come up with. They don't give you many options in the psych ward, f*ck them, and f*ck it all! I'm in a bathroom that has NO LOCKS. A door that does not go up all the way to the ceiling, no toilet paper holder, and no push handle flush and therefore no privacy. I sat there in a shower without water turned on for about 45 minutes and sobbed.

FOOD JOURNAL for today
BREAKFAST – 1 hardboiled egg white, fat free yogurt, banana, bran flakes & water
SNACK – tangerine
LUNCH – ½ baked potato, ½ cup beef broth, ½ cup peas & carrots
SUPPER – ½ cup beef broth, 2 slices turkey, ½ cup beans & water
SNACK – 2 tangerines, 1 banana, 2 plain rice cakes & 1 tablespoon light peanut butter

DAY 23 – Friday January 6, 2006
Morning: 131.3lbs Night: 132lbs

I wake up and realize today is family meeting day, my stomach instantly goes into knots! I don't like confrontation and I am scared of what everyone will have to say. I go and weigh myself and I'm still not down in weight! I'll have to watch myself this weekend. My day nurse Gloria comes in and by her tone and words, they are going to be sending me home. I am so scared and fearful. Fearful that I will gain weight, fearful of seeing people I don't want to see and have to talk to them. Gloria takes me into the meeting room, Andrew, Dr. Shadid, Dr. David and my other day nurse Melanie are sitting down. Andrew gets up and gives me a kiss and we sit down and he holds my hand, it feels good. Of course my body starts to shake and it doesn't stop the entire hour I'm in the meeting. The verdict is they are keeping me in the hospital for another week and then I will be put into the day therapy program for 3-6 months.

We arrive home for the weekend and in less than 12 hours I have eaten more than I do in 3 days! What the f*ck is wrong with me?!?!? This is not good! At least we do have a scale at home and I can monitor my weight that way and not have to ask a nurse every time and get the evil eye and hesitation before saying yes or no. I'm over 135lbs it will have to come off no matter what I have to do so I chug a litre of water and head to the bathroom to purge up every last f*cking bit I can until bile is the only thing to come up! F*ck, that feeling never gets old, I feel so exhilarated and damn proud every time!

FOOD JOURNAL for today
BREAKFAST – 2 hardboiled egg whites & water
SNACK – tangerine
LUNCH – ½ cup tomato rice soup, ½ fat free yogurt, ½ peach & water
SNACK – tangerine, 4 plain rice cakes, ½ jar natural peanut butter, ½ block cheddar cheese, 1 can veggie chili and water
SUPPER – 1 box potato & cheese pierogis, ½ container fat free sour cream & water
SNACK – apple, tangerine, Mexican cocoa & water

DAY 24 – Saturday January 7, 2006
Morning: 132lbs Night: 133.4lbs

Decided to drive my car for the first time in over a month today and run a couple of errands. The anxiety is killing me just driving, I feel like I'm driving for the first time ever. Went to the bank ATM and felt that people were too close to me, but I stuck to what I had to do. Decided that I would head to the grocery store to pass some time since Andrew was away in Shediac for a volleyball tournament, BAD IDEA!

I only had to get a few things, veggies, fruit, buttermilk, rice cakes so I figured it wouldn't take long and I would be ok. My chest started feeling tight, my breathing began to get really fast, people are way too close to me, and it was awful! I felt like throwing my basket down but I figured that would bring more attention to myself. So, I gathered up my things and quickly got out of there literally running to my car. Threw the groceries in the trunk and got into the driver's seat and literally collapsed! I close my eyes, throw my head back, and begin to breathe even more heavily as tears streamed down my face. I turned on the car and see the gas light, f*ck I'll never make it home! I stop at the closest place get gas and make a mad dash for Ma and Bobby's house, I'll never make it home without having a panic attack, I need safety right away! I run into their house, beeline for the kitchen, sit down and Ma has no idea what is going on! I quickly poured a glass of water, popped an Ativan and try to breathe. I know that relief is on its way.

FOOD JOURNAL for today
BREAKFAST – banana, fat free yogurt & bran flakes
LUNCH – nothing
SNACK – apple, ½ cup peanuts, 1 macadamia nuts cluster & 2 chocolate covered pretzels
SUPPPER – 1cup vegetable & shrimp stir fry, 3 glasses red wine & 1 macadamia nut cluster

DAY 25 – Sunday January 8, 2006
I'm so disappointed in my weight I can't even write it down

Back to the hospital today. Andrew didn't come up with me and I wonder if it's because he has to pay for parking. So I get dropped off, head upstairs and put away my things. It feels good to be home in my safe place even though those around me are completely unsafe to themselves and sometimes others. Andrew asked me "do you get scared in here?" I think it scares him to see the patients that are in here, but for me it feels like there is no judgment, just people being who they know who to be.

FOOD JOURNAL for today
BREAKFAST – omelet with 1 egg & 2 egg whites & 2 glasses of orange juice
LUNCH – 1 cup shrimp stir fry & 1/3 homemade muffin
SUPPER – ¾ homemade chicken cordon bleu, 1 cup spinach salad with black beans, pears & pecans
SNACK – 1 macadamia nut cluster & clementine

DAY 26 – Monday January 9, 2006
Morning: 129.3lbs Night: 129.2lbs OMG I fell below
130lbs, this is going to be the best day ever!!!

I woke up in the middle of the night to the night nurses playing crib and couldn't get back to sleep. I should have gotten up and played with them.

Dr. Shahid came early in the morning and told me he is going to get in touch with the Dietician. Not long after, Catherine McCain the Dietician came in to talk to me. We talked about the foods I normally eat during the run of a day, what makes me want to purge, my idea weight, how I see myself etc. She said she would try and take me on as a patient and set up a couple of appointments for this week.

Went to skills group today and it was really helpful. We talked about "Initial responses to people with a problem". It helps you focus on things that would be positive feedback vs. negative and how the best thing you can do is "REPEAT and PAUSE" before answering someone's difficult questions. Therefore validate and think before opening your mouth, as once it's said you can't take it back. I'm trying so hard to become a better person for myself one day and of course see myself the way others see me.

Andrew picked me up after supper and we went to another movie and of course I had the kids pack. The theatre was pretty empty so I felt more at ease. When he dropped me off, I quickly went up to my room and purged the poison. I just wanted to get up during the movie and go to the washroom to purge so bad, but Andrew would have caught on too quickly.

Had he of not been there I would have, but then again I would not have been at the movies by myself either. God it's such an incredible relief to release that crap out of my stomach!

FOOD JOURNAL for today
BREAKFAST – fat free yogurt & banana
LUNCH – ½ cup chicken broth & ½ cup tossed salad with salt & pepper
SNACK – tangerine, banana & apple
SUPPER – piece poached sole, ½ cup beef broth, ½ cup beans & carrots, 2 rice cakes & 1 tablespoon peanut butter
SNACK – popcorn, chocolate bar & diet coke

DAY 27 – Tuesday January 10, 2006
Morning: 129.8lbs Night: 129.6lbs

I woke up early this morning to *Kathy* saying she couldn't sleep so she left the room went and got a sandwich and watched TV. I overheard one of the nurses saying to her "as long as you're quiet *Kathy* because you are not allowed to watch TV before 7am." Poor *Kathy* she seems so much worse now than when I first met her. I almost feel it is the needle they gave her with some crazy shit inside. She seems to have gotten so much crazier since then, her dreams are f*cked up. Probably doesn't help that she has no support here, I feel so bad for her.

I got up, had a shower and a shit too! I don't know what makes me more excited, purging or having a shit. Either one I know, gets out the evil. As I was walking to the common room to have breakfast, there were all these girls that I didn't recognize, so I felt like the center of attention as they were all looking at me. I didn't want to walk through the crowd so I said "What are all these extra people doing here!" Went to the other door instead and as I walked in the common room, they were all looking at me. F*CK just let me crawl in a hole and die. As I was eating, Margaret the Dietician came in. We talked about weight fluctuation and dieting and she gave me a couple articles to read before our meeting tomorrow.

While I was in the shower room, I overheard *Mark* talking to his roommate as to why he ended up in here again. He had taken his whole months' worth of Ativan and his anti-depressants, crushed them and then snorted them. I was like WOW, *Mark* and I have a lot in common. I snorted coke before and since being hospitalized thought about what it would be like to snort Ativan and my anti-depressants, when I feel super low. The only difference, he actually did it! He must have been totally f*cked up! Probably the reason he was in CNC (Critical Nursing Care) aka the 'padded room' for so damn long!

I walk into my room and *Kathy* is now sitting on my bed singing, she must have gotten lost along the way. One of the student nurses is trying to talk with her, good luck with that! Just dance and sing with her, you'll get more accomplished. I must have a student nurse as well, f*ck I do not feel like telling my problem to someone my own age, let alone some skinny little f*cking UNB nursing student.

After lunch it is managing emotions class. But speaking of

lunch, the unit must be full because every seat is taken. Holy shit, I think CNC is full too, sad really. But I'm really beginning to enjoy the therapy sessions, as I find them challenging at times, however very useful. I begin to talk in to the room and there is a super skinny, beautiful and tall blonde young UNB f*cking social worker student there. I immediately feel like f*cking shit! My anxiety level increases and I either want to start crying or run out of the room! Instead, I literally turn inside myself and drop my head and don't speak the entire session. After the hour long grueling session, *Shelley* one of my day nurses comes into my room to chat about the session. I tell her "I feel like a lab rat with all the student nurses around!"

Thankfully, relaxation group is next and 6 of us head down supervised of course and all lay down on the floor. Poor Judy fell asleep and began snoring. We all had a chuckle afterwards. We get escorted back to 2SE and we were in for a crazy awakening after our relaxation session. We walk in to *Madelaine* f*cking losing her shit! She was hollering "You're f*cking hurting me, stop it you f*cking asshole!" Along with some very loud screams! What the hell is going on....that we'll probably never find out and perhaps it was nothing. It shook us all up pretty good and we lost the whole feeling of relaxation.

Andrew arrived for supper and as we left my room and walked out to the hall, there were 6 nursing students talking and Andrew said "Excuse me ladies" and I was behind him and said "Oh my GOD!" Why, because I felt low from all of today's craziness, feeling fat, inadequate and also felt that they were judging me. I began to cry terribly, so Andrew took me to the end of the hall and calmed me down. It is hard for him to understand the way that I am feeling, but having skinny bitches with their hair all done and makeup on invading a 'safe place', is the worst feeling ever and I'm sure I'm not the only one that feels that way!

Andrew came for supper and after he left I went back to my room and my night nurse Cheryl came in and said "Your day was ok?" and began to walk out. I said "No it was not" and told her what happened and why I felt this way. She has got to be the worst nurse ever. She is NOT sympathetic and I feel she hates her job, hates talking as she has already told me she is not good at communicating. Why in the f*ck are you on this floor then??!? I find her quite odd actually. She is the only nurse that I know around here that does not go around talking to her patients. She may come in to your room and ask, but she is walking out before you answer as I know she doesn't want to hear it.

"God, grant me the serenity to accept the things I cannot change, Courage to change the things I can, and wisdom to know the difference."

FOOD JOURNAL for today
BREAKFAST – 2 hardboiled egg whites, fat free yogurt, banana & water
SNACK – orange, 3 prunes, 2 rice cakes & 1 tablespoon of peanut butter
LUNCH – ½ cup chicken broth, 2 slices turkey, ¼ cup carrots & ½ cup tossed salad with salt & pepper

SUPPER – ½ cup beef broth, 2 slices roasted pork, ½ cup broccoli & carrots, tea & water
SNACK - 1 banana, ½ banana chocolate chip flax bran muffin, ½ bag Dorito's & fat free yogurt

DAY 28 – Wednesday January 11, 2006
Morning: 130.7lbs Night: 130.4lbs

Finally got to sleep at 1am and woke up a few times after that. *Shelley* my roommate and I were woken up 6 times by "Breakfast is here ladies!" 3 times by nurses and 3 times by this annoying little f*cking UNB student! Ok, enough with breakfast we get the f*cking point! *Shelley* and I were both laughing afterwards. I call *Shelley's* student nurse her 'girlfriend' and she calls her a 'stalker'! Finally we got up and went to breakfast and it is always comic relief to listen and watch *Mary*. I don't know why I'm so captivated by her. Not sure if captivating is the right word, but I think it's because she's so obsessed with food as well. She sits there and plays with her food, complains about everything that is on her plate, hates the fact that they won't give her metal cutlery and decides that is the reason why she can't eat, because plastic cutlery is not acceptable and too hard to cut stuff.

I'm feeling a little anxious as my time here at 2SE is coming to an end. I do however want to look at it in a positive way so I should say my time here is coming to an end, however my new life will just begin. I do feel a little more relief knowing that I will be coming back for day therapy. I want to make myself better. I am tired and my body is tired of living the way I have been. I know I have done so many positive things in my life, however my heart and energy into those positive things I don't believe were 100%. I have focused everything that I do around food and me. By 'me', I don't mean in a self-centered sort of way, but always worrying about negative or any attention for that matter. I am only here on this earth once and God has given me some pretty amazing opportunities to be here. There were times in my life when I look back now that I think he didn't have to be by my side, but he was and I am still here today. Why he chooses some people over others I'm not quite sure why, but I do know that I have been chosen and I should feel pretty special about that. I would like to see myself the way that my true friends and family view me. I want to respect by body. I want to react to situations or events in my life in a controlled manner. I want to believe I can do things. I want to think on days I feel low that I am worth it. I want to think to put myself before other's sometimes. I want to believe that family and friends are here to support and love me. I want to believe that everyone does not judge me. I want to believe that I am wonderful person. I want to believe that I am beautiful on the inside and out. I want to believe that I am strong, powerful and successful women. I want to believe that what I am on the outside that day will not make or break my day. I want to believe all of these things about me one day. I WANT TO BELIEVE IN ME!

WOW, these sessions have really helped me look at myself and figure out how I am feeling. Not just to assume or try to hide my feelings, but to explain to someone how I am feeling. Expressing the way you feel is not a bad thing like I had been taught for so many years, 'stop crying', 'don't tell anyone', 'we don't talk about that' etc. It does help to relieve some of the stress that I may be feeling. My 28 days here have been an eye opener. I have learned so much and realize I have so much more to learn; However instead of being scared all the time, I realize that scary sometimes means overcoming fear. Overcoming fear leads to accomplishments.

Accomplishments mean feeling good about myself. I owe so much to Julia my therapist at FECSF (Family Enrichment and Counseling Services Fredericton) for bringing me up here. I had to let my mask and makeup come off to reveal how I was truly feeling on the inside. This feels good, I look good.

I went to my session with Dr. David and found out the best possible news, he is going to keep treating me during day therapy! This is not normal practice as once you are no longer an 'in-patient', you lose those services. However, I'm so happy I don't have to switch and feel like I'm starting over again.

When I came back from my appointment with Dr. David, *Mary* was just sitting and waiting for her lunch to arrive, so I brought us both of our trays. I found out the reason that she is so concerned with food is because of the steroids and the pesticides. She is afraid of getting cancer and therefore does not use conventional deodorant as well. Makes sense I guess, since we need to all consider this epidemic of cancer and why it is being brought on.

The afternoon brought on Managing Emotions session with today's topic being Sleep and Caffeine. We begin going around the circle confessing our caffeine habits. When we first open the session and everyone was saying their name and caffeine addiction we get to Frank and he says "Hi, I'm Frank and I'm and addict." We all giggle not because it's true, but it was so unexpected. As everyone confesses their caffeine addiction we then get to *Mark* and he says "*Mark*, prior addict as well." It makes me begin to think…..maybe this is the perfect time to open up about my cocaine addiction about 2 years ago. Maybe this would be the beginning of the mourning process that I should have done a long time ago when *Mitch* passed away. My turn comes and I say "Well since we are all confessing our sins… I'm a former cocaine addict and I gave up coffee for lent. A few months after stopping drugs, I had some coffee and it freaked me out so much I felt like I was on cocaine as the high completely caught me off guard! Coming off of the coffee high, was the worst thing in the world. It felt like losing the coke high and wanting more. I was willing to do anything to get it!" I guess that got the ball rolling as before I knew it, *Frank*, *Mark* and *Kylie* of all people were all spilling the beans on their addictions and the other patients were asking questions because of friends and family members they knew that were addicts.

FOOD JOURNAL for today
BREAKFAST – 2 hardboiled egg whites, banana, fat free yogurt, natural bran & prune juice
SNACK – 1 rice cake
LUNCH – ½ cup beef broth, 2 celery sticks, 2 carrot sticks, 1 slice cucumber & 1 tomato wedge
SNACK – apple

SUPPER – ½ cup peas & carrots, 2 slices turkey, ½ cup beef broth, ½ baked potato & 1 tablespoon applesauce
SNACK – 2 rice cakes with 1 tablespoon peanut butter, apple, 2 rice cakes & 2 tablespoons of Cheez Whiz

DAY 29 – Thursday January 12, 2006
Morning: 130lbs Night: 129.1lbs

Had a meeting with Dr. David today, we discussed how I was feeling about my discharge – scared, excited, happy, anxious, nervous. All of these for different reasons of course.
SCARED – wondering what it's going to be like in the real world again, all the time with no escape.
EXCITED – to overcome challenges and meet my goals
HAPPY – that I have made progress since Day 1
ANXIOUS - to do some of the 'normal' daily activities such as going to the store, driving etc.
NERVOUS – for the tasks/challenges that I have ahead of me.

After lunch it was managing emotions class and today's topic is 'SELF-ESTEEM' – perfect for me! I began to cry when we discussed checking out. I said to them "The hardest thing for me and dealing with myself esteem is admitting to myself that I have a problem and that I am never going to be perfect. That is the hardest thing in the world."

After supper I made progress I went out to the common room by myself and watched some TV with *Shelley*, *Christine*, *Kathy* and *Mark*. There was a huge commotion going on in CNC. I heard terrible banging on the door. I found out that it was *Dianna*, she got put back in their today. I overheard one of the nurses saying "That girl likes to hurt herself." Poor *Dianna* she has been in and out of there so many times. They ended up having to sedate her and security had to come up.

FOOD JOURNAL for today
BREAKFAST – 1 ½ boiled egg whites, fat free yogurt, banana, natural bran & water
LUNCH – ½ cup chicken & rice soup, ½ cup tossed salad with salt & pepper & water
SNACK – 2 rice cakes with 1 tablespoon of PB, banana & water
SUPPER – ½ cup beef broth, 2 slices roast beef, ½ cup green beans, 2 crackers, 1 apple & 1 tablespoon PB
SNACK – ½ cup seaweed & 5 small sushi

DAY 30 – Friday January 13, 2006
Morning: 130.2lbs

The day has finally come, I'm leaving the 'crazy' psych ward for good…..well as an in-patient that is! We were quickly awoken to Mary's screaming as her shampoo bottle had been opened mysteriously and the 'fumes' of algaecide came seeping out and now she has a heavy chest, her lungs are burnt and she has a headache. Holy shit, get me the f*ck out of here! After I got ready the most amazing nurse I've had my entire stay came in, Cathy. I gave her a book that I bought last night "Chicken Soup for the Nurse's Soul" and I almost started to cry when I gave her the gift. She said she really appreciated the gift and I went above and beyond. I said that she actually did the same thing for me. Most nights she would stay with me and talk for an hour or so and she opened up about some of her past which really helped me to feel I wasn't alone. It was Cathy who used to recite the serenity prayer to me every night.

"God, grant me the serenity to accept the things I cannot change, Courage to change the things I can, and wisdom to know the difference."

As I'm walking towards the doors in 2SE I begin to cry, tears of joy and fear. I had held it in all morning in front of Cathy, *Shelley* and *Kathy*. I gave *Kathy* a hug before I left and told her I would be in to visit and that I would bring her a Diet Coke. I really feel that *Kathy* and I became roommates for a reason. As we head out to the car I am feeling excited for the future of my treatment but at the same time fear of the unknown world and fear of gaining weight especially.

FOOD JOURNAL for today
BREAKFAST – 2 boiled egg whites, fat free yogurt, banana & 1 prune
LUNCH – 6" ww roasted chicken sub from Subway
SNACK – ½ homemade muffin & ½ banana
SUPPER – bite vegetarian spring roll, ½ cup yellow curry with chicken and sweet potato, 2 ½ glasses wine & 2 sips of Spanish coffee

DAY 31 – Saturday January 14, 2006
Morning: Unknown Night: 134lbs

We had a birthday party to go to that evening, so I made nacho dip, got ready and we headed out. I tried not to eat but it was so hard! I had 6 pieces of rye bread with spinach dip, peanuts, 2 mini pita pockets, 4 glasses of red wine and 2 glasses of white. I felt so guilty when we got home for eating all that shit! I immediately went to the scale to weigh myself. At first it said 135.5lbs, I put my head down, what the f*ck have I done, I began to cry. I feel awful seeing those numbers so I hop on again and it reads 134lbs no better.

I need to start working out again. I told myself I would never let myself get past 135lbs. I cannot let myself get fatter than I am! I feel disgusting now with all that terrible poisonous food I ate! I have to get rid of all that stuff now, if I flush the toilet and purge he will never hear me. Tomorrow I get rid of all the tempting foods in the house, it's my only way. I have no willpower I am weak!

FOOD JOURNAL for today
BREAKFAST – ½ cup all bran cereal with skim milk, 2 cubes cantaloupe, 2 cubes honeydew melon, 2 cubes watermelon & tea
LUNCH – ½ cup minestrone soup, 4 pieces sushi & water
SNACK – 2 servings' sour cream & cheddar baked chips, 1 banana, 1 piece turkey jerky & 1 mini box raisins
SUPPER – 1 slice lasagna, 2 boxes raisins & green tea
SNACK – 6 pieces rye bread with spinach dip, 2 mini pita pockets, handful peanuts, 4 glasses red wine & 2 glasses white wine

DAY 32 – Sunday January 15, 2006
Morning: 1335.lbs Night: I was too scared to look!

My eating this weekend has been awful for me! My intake was way too much and I feel even more stressed, as I know Andrew is watching me like a hawk and therefore I am unable to purge when I feel the strong urge to do so. I feel so fat, I look terrible so this week I have got to get into a routine! I feel so guilty for eating and the lack of activity I have done. A new week and I have to do better! NO more fat can be added to this body....IT JUST CAN'T!!!

FOOD JOURNAL for today
BREAKFAST – ¼ cup oatmeal, ½ banana, pecans and water
SNACK – 1 small box raisins
LUNCH – 1 flax and whole wheat tortilla & 1 slice light cheese
SNACK – 2 Breton crackers & water
SUPPER – French onion soup, chicken, spinach, mushrooms, 10 Glosette raisins, 1 glass red wine, 1 macadamia nut cluster & 1 chocolate leaf
SNACK – 1 rice cake, ½ banana, 1 tablespoon PB & 1 cup homemade cocoa

DAY 33 – Monday January 16, 2006
Morning: I just can't! Night: 133.5lbs

My first day as a DT (Day Therapy) patient. I head up to the hospital to meet Marion my DT nurse to have my evaluation. The interview was 2 f*cking hours long! I got so anxious and tired of answering questions she could sense my stress.

Finally at 12 noon I was done. Now a new dilemma, what was I going to do for lunch? I only have 1 hour until I meet Dr. David and the roads are awful so going home is not an option, eating in the cafeteria is f*cking nuts especially by myself so off to McDonalds I go like a failure. I get a chicken McGrill on a whole wheat bun, fruit and yogurt parfait and a bottle of water. I drive back to the hospital and park the car and begin to gorge my sandwich crazily like it's the first thing I've had to eat in years. The bread tasted so good. I skimmed off the mayonnaise and I knew there was a ton of salt in the chicken but I couldn't stop myself. I knew I was out of control eating but it was so yummy! Before I knew it, I was eating my last bite.

As I realized what I had just done, a feeling of guilt, sickness came over me. OH MY GOD you fat f*cking pig you just ate the whole sandwich in less than 3 minutes!!! Ok PUKE now! Puke now in the bag! So, I do it in the bag, in the car and I don't give a shit if anyone is watching, this is more important thing right now! It gets messy but I don't care. I clean up a bit and run into the hospital to release the rest of the evil. I check in to the reception desk and head straight to the washroom and release the evil. How could I let myself eat that shit! I purge and it feels incredible once again. I purge even more and F*CK it is better than 3 orgasms in a row! I pop a piece of gum in my mouth and I am as good as new!

Dr. David comes to get me and we talk about how my dreams have now increased regarding food and purging. My anxiety level around food has increased and I can honestly not get it out of my mind! It consumes me and I think about the negative impacts of food all the time! What am I going to eat? When am I going to eat? How much will I eat? Will I be able to purge if I eat? How much weight have I gained since I left the hospital? I am letting myself go by eating this much. I have no willpower. I am weak! I am worthless! I am fat! I'm a useless f*cking piece of shit!

Trying out yoga with Andrew, Tracy and Chris for the first time tonight. I'm not looking forward to going as yoga is for skinny people and I am not one of them.

FOOD JOURNAL for today
BREAKFAST – ½ cup oatmeal, 1 banana, 1 tablespoon flax seeds, 1 tablespoon pecans & water
LUNCH – McDonalds McGrill Sandwich on w/w bread & water
SNACK – McDonald's fruit & yogurt parfait, orange & 2 small boxes raisins
SUPPER – 1 cup red curry shrimp, 4 caramel rice cakes & water
SNACK – fat free yogurt, 1 banana & water

DAY 34 – Tuesday January 17, 2006
Morning: 136.6 HOLY F*CK! Night: unknown, shame sets in at full force.

Today was horrible there are no words.

DAY 35 – Wednesday January 18, 2006
Morning: FAT Night: FAT

Another awful f*cking day.

DAY 36 – Thursday January 19, 2006

My life f*cking sucks. My body is shameful. I have no willpower, I am weak. What the hell is wrong with me?

DAY 37 – Friday January 20, 2006

I'm feeling very unmotivated, very low and worthless. I feel like I have nobody. It may be good to go to Ma's today to visit Cosmo (my cat). He will sleep and cuddle with me. He makes me feel like my worries are gone when I'm around him. I really need an animal in my life. I miss not having a pet. I know we can't have a cat since Andrew is allergic, but a dog would be amazing!

My appointment with Dr. David was awful! I cried the whole time. I feel so unmotivated and worthless. Not being able to concentrate and forgetting everything. I am also stressing with Andrew being away. I felt almost no emotion when he left because I feel as if something bad is going to happen like him cheating on me or utilizing his flirting skills a little too much. I left Dr. David's and since Monika was working, we had lunch at the cafeteria. I went to the washroom afterwards and purged before TAG. This being out of the hospital is much better than I thought, more opportunities to puke the poison without anyone finding out.

FOOD JOURNAL for today
BREAKFAST – 1/3 cup oatmeal, 1 tablespoon pecans, 1 tablespoon raisins & water
LUNCH – ½ cup tomato rice soup, whole wheat roll, banana, fat free blueberry yogurt & water
SNACK – pear, 2 celery stalks & 2 tablespoons light Cheez Whiz
SUPPER – slice pork tenderloin, ¼ cup chutney, 4 pieces broccoli, 3 sweet potato fries & 1 glass white wine
SNACK – 4 carrot sticks, 4 cherry tomatoes & water

DAY 38 – Saturday January 21, 2006
Morning: unable at Ma's Night: unable at Ma's

Woke up to Cosmo by my side. He makes me instantly smile. As soon as you begin to pet him, he begins to purr, too cute! Ma and I run errands then later they were off to the STU Gala. I stayed home and Andrew called. I told him I was a little worried all day as he didn't call and I thought he was avoiding me. He felt bad. I just wish I could trust and believe him all the time. He is my husband and I should be able to do this. I love him so much and my biggest fear is obviously being hurt or not knowing that I'm being hurt. I really must focus on healing this aspect of my life.

FOOD JOURNAL for today
BREAKFAST – 2 boiled egg whites, yogurt, 3 strawberries, 1 tablespoon, 1 tablespoon bran flakes & water
SNACK – homemade bran & blueberry muffin & water
LUNCH – wonton soup & water

SNACK – homemade bran & blueberry muffin & ½ apple & water
SUPPER – 1 cup beef & broccoli & water
SNACK – ½ cup yogurt, ½ banana, 3 strawberries, 1 tablespoon almonds, ½ banana & 2 servings baked lays chips

DAY 39 – Sunday January 22, 2006
Morning: Unknown at Ma's Night: Unknown at Ma's

Decided that I would go to church today with Ma and Bobby, the sermon was titled 'When will you ever be Happy?' which was fitting. Went to volleyball later on that night and it felt good to get out. We won 3-2.

Today was a good day. I was however feeling anxious when I went to church and sat down, but I did some deep breathing. I need to start working out my body is so flabby. Tomorrow I'm going to do a workout tape. My eating was good today, however still ate too much. I have to start working out to burn off all those extra calories. I will get back on the scale tomorrow, I'm scared to see what it says.

FOOD JOURNAL for today
BREAKFAST – 1 cup cereal, 3 strawberries, 1 tablespoon almonds, 1 cup soy milk, 1 hardboiled egg white & water
LUNCH – 1 homemade bran blueberry muffin, yogurt, pear & water
SNACK – 1 carrot
SUPPER – 1 cup veggie chili, 10 baked tortilla chips & 1 tablespoon light marble cheese

SNACK – yogurt, 3 strawberries, 1 banana, 1 tablespoon almonds, and 10 baked lays chips with fat free herb spice dip & water

DAY 40 – Monday January 23, 2006
Morning: unknown at Ma's Night: unknown at Ma's

Once again last night, weird dreams. I was in this house and this guy that was there looked like *Mitch* and I knew he was either on ecstasy or cocaine. So I took him aside and asked him, he said ecstasy then asked "Why, what's so bad about cocaine?" I said "It's the most addictive drug I've ever had and it can ruin your life or take it away." What a weird f*cking dream.

Had my appointment with Dr. David and we spoke about the weekend and how he believes some of my anxiousness may be from playing crib, as I play so much every day to keep my thoughts at bay. However, it brings me back to when I was an addict. During those times, *Mitch* and I would play for 12 hours at a time. The PTSD is creating flashbacks and is related to the excessive crib playing when I was using. I talked to him about my eating and how I try to have snacks available to me especially if I know that I'm going to be out for an extended period of time, so I have less urge to binge and purge.

Went to supper with Monika at Blue Door and ordered the roasted chipotle lime and honey ½ roasted chicken with black beans, corn and red peppers. Then after supper, the waiter brought us over dessert menus, however we were all too stuffed, to order. The waiter looked at me and said "No crème brulé tonight?" I said "No, I'm so stuffed, however that is my favorite!" About 10 minutes later he comes out with brownies on the moon with a candle in the middle for Monika's birthday and 3-mini crème brulé for me. So after woofing down the dessert, I had to purge! I may have been ok with just the supper, however with the desserts....definitely not! So I went to the bathroom and purged at the restaurant. When I came back, I knew Monika knew….. but I didn't care.

Today was an ok eating day until supper....oh well at least I was able to purge up the evil!

FOOD JOURNAL for today
BREAKFAST – 1 cup organic soy cereal, 4 tablespoons blueberries & 1 cup soy milk
SNACK – banana & water
LUNCH – homemade flatbread sandwich with chicken, spinach, avocado & chutney
SUPPER – 1 cup tossed salad with 1 tablespoon balsamic vinaigrette, ½ chicken breast, ½ cup black beans with red pepper & corn, 2 glasses white wine & 3 mini crème brulé
SNACK – 1 yogurt, 4 strawberries & 1 tablespoon almonds

DAY 41 – Tuesday January 24, 2006
Weight: Beyond frustrated with myself

I think I will begin going back to work after we move in in February. The problem is that I don't know what my day therapy schedule will be yet.

I need to go get my scales from the house. I so need to know how much weight I have gained. I know it's at least 5-7 pounds. I have been eating too much at supper, along with too many carbs!

FOOD JOURNAL for today
BREAKFAST – 1 c soy crunch cereal, 4 tablespoons blueberries & 1 cup soy milk
SNACK – banana
LUNCH – flat bread, 4 strips chicken breast, 2 tablespoons chutney & ½ cup spinach
SNACK – homemade muffin
SUPPER – 2 cups spinach salad with apple & peppers
SNACK – yogurt, ½ cup pineapple, 6 strawberries, 1 serving all natural chips, kiwi, 2 rice cakes, 1 tablespoon PB & banana

DAY 42 – Wednesday January 25, 2006
Weight: Beyond frustrated with myself

Went to the communication session at the hospital, it was on friends. What is a friend, what are the qualities we look for in a friend, when do friends not become friends etc.? It was a good session with some good handout material to read.

Sometimes I forget that Andrew is my best friend and I oftentimes don't treat him that way. Sometimes the way that I talk to him, is not the way I should or the way I would talk to any of my other friends. It really put some perspective on what I want our relationship to be like. I have to put what happened in the past and move on, as it does not make our relationship any better by me hanging onto it. Unfortunately, that is easier said than done. I have a hard time allowing someone to regain my trust. I'm having baby fever lately. I really can't wait to have kids. Another chapter in our lives that's for sure.

The time came that I had to call Mike (my boss), I talked to Mica (admin support) first and she said "Oh Sammy it's so good to your voice!" That was nice to hear. She asked "How are you doing?" I said "Just needed a break, one day at a time." I then spoke with Mike and he said it would be fine to get sick time and work part-time, so I could attend day therapy. I said that I would be back to work in 2-3 weeks. He said "Sam you take all the time you need, I know you will be back up 100% when you are ready, I'm your biggest fan!" That was very reassuring and I could not ask for a better boss! He is incredible and so understanding and supportive. He said he was doing better after his Mom passed, however one day at a time. He said his family was very fortunate that she had her finances in order. I made the joke and said "Oh your Mother left her money in the curtains eh?" He laughed and I think that is just what he needed.

For supper I had way too much! I totally never even thought about portion control when I dished that shit on my plate. God I hate myself when I eat that much! I had a piece of salmon, green and yellow beans, asparagus. Then even though I was fat and stuffed, I had blueberry crisp. Seriously Sam you're such a f*cking looser! So of course I headed to the bathroom to purge, Ahhhh RELIEF!! Amazing how good that can feel!

Andrew called and I got upset at him because he was not paying attention to our conversation but more his cell phone and someone else that was in his room. I said "Well you know what I'm tired of that f*cking cell phone! I'm talking to you right now and I haven't since last night so you should be interested in what I have to say, not that other line beeping! You need to be a little more considerate. Anyways you're going to supper and you have to get ready, so I will talk to you tomorrow." I then hung up the phone and cried. I was so upset because I felt totally neglected and ignored, not what I deserved at all. Then of course to stuff my feelings I ate a muffin! What the hell! F*ck I'm such a looser and have no willpower. Here's to a better day tomorrow as I'm off to purge up the muffin man.

FOOD JOURNAL for today
BREAKFAST – ¾ cup soy cereal, 4 Tablespoons blueberries & 1 cup soy milk
LUNCH – flatbread, 6 pieces chicken breast, ½ cup spinach & 2 tablespoons chutney
SNACK – yogurt & orange
SUPPER – 1 piece salmon, green & yellow beans, asparagus & blueberry crisp
SNACK – ½ serving no preservative chips & fat free dip, 1 muffin, 1 slice cheese & water

DAY 43 – Thursday January 26, 2006
Weight: Beyond frustrated with myself

I weighed myself on Ma's scale, 130lbs. However I HIGHLY

doubt that, more like 140lbs probably! I guess I will find out this weekend when we get our scales back.

I'm a little down today for some reason. I'm sure it didn't help that I had a fight with Andrew last night and probably overreacted, however I definitely had every right to be upset.

Well I guess I should get my fat ass up and go get ready. Wow, it's even hard for me to do that right now. I just feel like staying in bed all day. I would if I didn't have a lunch date with Bobby. I'm so tired these past couple of days. Probably a cold I'm coming down with. I'm almost positive I have a sinus infection.

FOOD JOURNAL for today
BREAKFAST – yogurt, ½ cup pineapple, 1 tablespoon cranberries, 1 tablespoon almonds & 2 tablespoons natural bran
LUNCH – ¾ cup cereal, 1 banana & 1 tablespoon almonds
SUPPER – ½ piece haddock, 1 cup stir fried veggies & soya sauce
SNACK – 5 Twizzlers, ½ cup homemade cocoa, and 5 no preservative chips & water

DAY 44 – Friday January 27, 2006

My appointment with Dr. David went well today. We did a lot of exercises and he gave me the results from my evaluation from Monday. Most of the things I was in the same range as the eating disorder people – low body imagine, however my self-esteem was off the charts low. Not that this was surprising to me. I came to the realization that I have not accepted myself for fear of being put down and caught off guard. Sometimes I may look in the mirror and think that I look pretty, however that through quickly passes as I fear that I am thinking something that is not true.

It was lunch so I decided to go to the hospital parking lot and eat in my car. In the car I feel at peace and in my own world.

Tomorrow I leave Ma and Bobby's place and I'm not looking forward to it. I've developed a routine here and I'm not looking forward to going back to chaos at home.

I'm excited for tomorrow's volleyball tournament. I hope I play well. I have been getting so down and frustrated with myself when I make mistakes lately to the point that I want to cry and run off the court. I also feel that Andrew and I have been distant. I know I shouldn't worry as I'm sure its temporary and all, with what I'm going through.

FOOD JOURNAL for today
BREAKFAST – ¾ cup soy cereal, ½ cup berries & 1 cup soy milk
LUNCH – 1 homemade muffin, 1 cup spinach, 3 pieces chicken & 1 tablespoon Japanese vinaigrette
SUPPER – ½ BBQ chicken pizza on whole wheat pita & 1 cup stir fried veggies
SNACK – 1 cup blueberry crisp, all natural cinnamon apple cookie, 5 Twizzlers, 8 Breton cracker, 4 slices light marble cheese & tons of water

DAY 45 – Saturday January 28, 2006

Woke up feeling great on Saturday ready to play volleyball and see Andrew! I really like the new digs I got, my legs and hips are still big but my butt looks ok. Ended up in the finals and we won.

FOOD JOURNAL for today
BREAKFAST - 1/3 cup oatmeal, 1 cup soy milk, 1 tablespoon almonds & 1 banana
SNACK – 1 rice cake with 1 tablespoon PB
LUNCH – 1 cup tossed salad with chicken, 1 tablespoon light ranch, 1 vodka & OJ
SNACK – 6 dried apricots, 3 Twizzlers, 1 vodka & OJ, 8 Jujube's
SUPPER – ½ pita pit pita falafel & tzatziki

DAY 46 – Sunday January 29, 2006

Woke up at 8:45am as we had to play volleyball once again at 10:00am and 12:00pm for league. So exhausted from playing 13 games yesterday and then 12 hours later playing another 10 games. We then had to go to Ma and Bobby's after our games, as I forgot my crazy pills there and there was no way I can go more than a few hours without them.

FOOD JOURNAL for today
BREAKFAST – 1/3 oatmeal, 1 tablespoon almonds & 8 apricots
SNACK – 2 tablespoons soy nuts, 1 all natural bran & apple cookie & 6 apricots

LUNCH – 1 cup veggie chili, 15 baked tortilla chips & 2 tablespoons light marble cheese
SNACK – 1 yogurt, ½ homemade muffin & ½ large box raisins
SUPPER – ½ cup rice noodles, 1 cup yellow & green beans & carrots & ½ cup tomato sauce
SNACK – ½ homemade muffin, ½ cup muesli & ½ cup soy milk

DAY 47 – Monday January 30, 2006

I felt a little down, as I feel Andrew is acting so differently than he normally does when he comes home. I know that his days were long, however I'm beginning to feel that his nights were even longer.

Feeling weird today. Just got done my appointment with Dr. David. He gave me a cognitive mirror desensitization worksheet to work on. The exercise begins with my shoulders and I rated them a 5 out of 10 then as I get more comfortable I work to my lower torso, which I rated as a 1. You do deep breathing in between the 15, 30 and 60 second intervals of looking at those specific body parts, while thinking positively and negatively.

Well it's final, the house is now ours! We signed all the papers and its official, how exciting!

I'm so black and white. I can't communicate properly and I'm a basket case. Andrew and I seem to fight all the time.

Andrew tries to reassure me that in my past relationships I

never communicated and therefore anytime we discuss, I think of it as a fight. I instantly feel low and worthless. I just wanted to lay on the couch and die. The last thing I wanted to do was go to yoga. Finally after much begging from Andrew I went but not happily.

FOOD JOURNAL for today
BREAKFAST – 1/3 cup oatmeal, 1 tablespoon almonds, 6 dried apricots and ¾ cup soy milk
SNACK – 6 Twizzlers
LUNCH – Wendy's grilled chicken burger, small garden salad & water
SNACK – ½ homemade muffin & 2 tablespoons soy nuts
SUPPER – ½ cup rice noodles, 1 cup green & yellow beans & carrots, shrimp & ½ cup tomato sauce
SNACK – 3 clementine's, 2 serving's ketchup mini rice cakes & water

DAY 48 – Tuesday January 31, 2006
Weight: 132lbs

Went over to the house and I began to paint. I helped Papa lift up the baseboards. Holy crap, what a job that was! I also lifted all the carpet in the living room.

FOOD JOURNAL for today
BREAKFAST – ¾ cup cereal, 1 banana, 1 tablespoon almonds & ½ cup soy milk
SNACK – 2 tangerines

LUNCH – Subway roasted chicken wrap with mustard, ½ bag baked plain lays chips & ¼ bottle sprite
SNACK – ¼ small bag sun chips
SUPPER – ¾ cup cereal, 1 banana & ½ cup soy milk
SNACK – 3 strips pork tenderloin & 1 tablespoon soy nuts

DAY 49 – Wednesday February 1, 2006

I finished painting the kitchen then it was time to pick up Ma. When we came back I made supper, then afterwards Ma helped me with the hallway. We got it all painted, it was great help! When Ma left I got another coat on the kitchen. Another long ass day, it's 11:45pm and it's time for me to head home and sleep.

FOOD JOURNAL for today
BREAKFAST – 1/3 cup oatmeal, 2 tablespoons raisin, 1 tablespoon walnuts & ¼ cup soy milk

LUNCH – 1 tuna sandwich on ciabatta bread & water
SNACK – ¼ small bag baked lays & yogurt
SUPPER – 2 slices veggie pizza & glass diet Pepsi
SNACK – 1 slice veggie pizza, ½ cup muesli & ¼ cup soy milk

DAY 50-54 – Thursday February 2, 2006 – Monday February 6, 2006

Too tired physically and exhausted mentally to journal.

DAY 55 – Friday February 3, 2006

Still feeling exhausted from the weekend. I feel as guilty, as I haven't had a chance to write in my journal for a while. Things have been crazy around here with the renovations and moving into the new house. I really have to refocus myself on me. I have been neglecting the things that help me get better such as my journal, deep breathing, and food journaling. I have to remember to set aside time each day for these things just as I would time to eat and sleep. So tomorrow is a new day to begin all these things, once again. I can't be too hard on myself, I have been trying to get the house in order so that way I can stay sane. I hate having the house in disorder.

FOOD JOURNAL for today
BREAKFAST – ½ cup cereal, 1 banana & ½ cup soy milk
SNACK – clementine
LUNCH – low carb wrap with chicken mushrooms & BBQ sauce, 2 tablespoons cheese & ¼ cup spinach
SNACK – 2 servings dill pickle chips, 1 whole wheat pita, 2 tablespoons PB & banana
SUPPER – ¾ cup cereal & ½ cup soy milk
SNACK – yogurt, 1 banana, 1 tablespoon walnuts & water

DAY 56 – Wednesday February 8, 2006

So I am ready for breakfast, however I'm feeling guilty for what I ate yesterday. The couple handfuls of chips were terrible. I have to throw those in the garbage today, so I am not tempted. I'm even feeling guilty for having any snacks lately. I try to wait for my lunch but I'm starved, I have no self-control.

Went to the Dollarstore to pick up a few things for the house but unfortunately I couldn't pass up a chocolate bar. I was so hungry and it was sooooo calling my name! There were people staring at me in the isle and I felt like they were looking at me thinking oh my God she is so fat and she's buying a chocolate bar, no wonder her ass is fat! She is actually going to eat that! I felt embarrassed for picking it up, but f*ck them! I quickly paid for my things, ran to my car and had the chocolate bar gone before I even got out of the parking lot. I was craving it so bad, I needed it now! I feel so guilty and sick to my stomach I can't wait to get home to throw it the f*ck up! I had to stop at the Co-op first, so thought what the hell might as well get a few more chocolate bars gonna purge when I get home anyways! I feel so sick to my stomach walking in the Co-op but that won't f*cking stop me from stuffing my face with more on the drive home. As soon as I got home, I threw the groceries down to the floor and ran to the bathroom. Aaahhhh relief! I immediately felt better. It's like poison in my body when I eat those things yet I just can't stop once I start! Why can't I stop eating? God I could seriously just stuff my face until I exploded! Food is all that is on my mind all the damn time! What am I going to eat? When am I going to eat? How much am I going to eat? Will I be able to purge? Will someone question what I am eating? Well now I feel like a super fat, crazy f*cking food maniac. When will these food issues ever end? When will I be able to eat something and not feel guilty or obsess over it?!?!!

FOOD JOURNAL for today
BREAKFAST – 1/3 cup oatmeal, 1 banana & ¾ cup soy milk
SNACK – 1 plain rice cake & 3 slices mozzarella cheese
LUNCH – 1 low carb flour tortilla, ½ chicken breast, 2
tablespoons BBQ sauce, 2 tablespoons marble cheese, yogurt
& clementine
SNACK – 4 chocolate bars (Crispy Crunch, Reese PB cups, Kit
Kat & Coffee Crisp)
SUPPER – 1 cup spinach, ¼ pear, 2 strawberries, 1 tablespoon
almonds, 1 tablespoon red onion, 1 tablespoon raspberry
vinaigrette, ½ w/w pita, 3 tablespoons cheese & 2 organic
brownies
SNACK – 6 organic brownies

DAY 57 – Thursday February 9, 2006

Ate breakfast and I feel full, too full and I want to puke, but
hopefully with everything I have to do this morning I will
burn it off quickly.
I called Leo Burke, Psychologist from day therapy and I will
begin my Mind over Mood course on Tuesday and Thursdays
from 10:30am – 12:00pm. I already missed 2 classes and
normally mind over mood is the last class you take, however
they are offering it to me, because they really feel I will benefit
from it.

Ate way too much again today, no f*cking willpower what is
wrong with me? After supper I kept drinking wine and
sitting alone by myself. I suddenly had this urge to start
hurting and cutting myself. This is a new feeling. Not so much

the hurting myself but the cutting. I tried to cut my wrists with the knife that I was using to cut the bread but it was too dull. Many times I thought about taking a bottle of Tylenol or anti-depressants, however the effects wouldn't be immediate and I would be afraid of what would happen. Then I thought of calling people such as my Ma or Monika and asking them to come over. Tonight I was ready to put myself back into the Psych ward.

Andrew came home from volleyball and I am just blah. Blah because I feel worthless and have no willpower to go through what I was going to do. F*ck I'm too damn lazy to get up off the couch and get a sharper knife. I am so f*cked up, why am I still alive? Why am I here? I am so worthless. I am worth nothing to nobody. I am a piece of shit, I don't belong here or anywhere.

When Andrew arrived home we began talking about the shit that's going on with me. Of course we began arguing/discussing and I of course got super upset and began bawling profusely and I couldn't stop. I felt so stupid, ugly and I wanted to die. I told him that I tried to cut myself with the knife that I was cutting thread with, but it was too dull. Of course he flipped and said I was selfish, so I got pissed off and went into the bathroom and took 8 extra strength Tylenol and went to bed. He came in and asked what I had taken and I told him and of course he flipped out again, worrying about me. I honestly did not see what the big deal was, it's not like that was going to kill me. I started seeing double and then I passed out. At least it put me out of my crying misery for a while.

FOOD JOURNAL for today
BREAKFAST – ¾ cup cereal, 1 banana & ¾ cup soy milk
LUNCH – w/w pita pizza with chicken, 1 clementine, & water
SNACK – yogurt, 1 tablespoon almonds & 1 banana
SUPPER – 1 bottle red wine, ½ w/w pita pizza, 1 cup spinach,
3 strawberries, ½ apple, 1 tablespoon almonds & 2
tablespoons raspberry vinaigrette

DAY 58 – Friday February 10, 2006
Weight: 131lbs

Woke up this morning feeling no emotion. I knew I had a
body but couldn't feel it. I do not feel like eating, I am
emotionless and even the motion of the spoon going to my
mouth is weird. I quickly got ready and went to the hospital
for my appointment with Dr. David. When I met with him, I
felt like I was in another world, like my mouth was moving
and words were coming out of it, however I had no idea why.
I told Dr. David what happened Saturday night and he was
very surprised and suggested I not drink anymore as my
thoughts/feelings are inhibited by the alcohol are causing me
not to think straight, especially when I'm already in a
depressive state.

Went to wellness therapy class and didn't learn much. My
problems are a lot deeper than anyone else in here and I
wasn't about to spill my problems when I was asked
questions. I'm sure the shock value would have been good for
a laugh though. Marion my day therapy nurse met me
outside the room and asked if I wanted to start the Grieving

Therapy session on Mondays & Fridays from 10:30-12:00, so I guess I will be going to that as well.

I went out to my car to eat lunch by myself. It was so cold out, I couldn't even eat. Lately every time I do eat I feel like a fat f*cking pig. No normal person would ever eat this much! STOP f*cking eating! You are only eating because it is around and you're so weak, you have no willpower! You fat f*ck!

FOOD JOURNAL for today
BREAKFAST – ¼ cup oatmeal, 1 tablespoon almonds, ½ banana & ½ cup soy milk
SNACK – 3 slices low fat Mozzarella cheese, 1 clementine & 8 almonds
LUNCH – ¼ BBQ chicken pita pizza, 1 ½ cups spinach, 2 tablespoons raspberry vinaigrette, 1 clementine, 1 all natural cookie & 1 yogurt
SNACK – 1 yogurt, banana, ½ cup organic granola, low carb tortilla, 3 slices honey ham & 3 slices cheese
SUPPER – 1 potato, 2 tablespoons sour cream & 2 glasses sprite

DAY 59 – Saturday February 11, 2006
Weight: 132.5lbs

Once again feeling emotionless. Had breakfast with Monika and Jamie at the Big Stop, what a shit show. I hate being around others and I hate trying to pick over the menu asking for "no this, or not" that and the entire time I'm eating, I feel disgusting and guilty. I should have just eaten the f*cking newspaper and a cup of coffee. Later we had a party to go to for Sheri, which I did not want to go. I'm not allowed to drink, I don't want to be around anyone, I'm going to be tempted by the demons of poisonous food and I just want to stay the f*ck home.

MY CRAZY DAY THERAPY SCHEDULE
MONDAY
9:30-11am – Grieving Class
11-12pm – Psychology with Dr. David
TUESDAY
10:30-12:00pm – Mind Over Mood Class
WEDNESDAY
11-12pm – Wellness Class
1-2pm – TAG
THURSDAY
10:30-12:00pm – Mind Over Mood Class
FRIDAY
9:30-11am – Grieving Class
11-12pm – Wellness Class
1-2pm – TAG

FOOD JOURNAL for today
BREAKFAST – 1 slice w/w toast, 2 tablespoons jam, ½ tablespoon PB, ¼ veggie omelet no cheese, ½ cup hot chocolate & water
LUNCH – 1 low card flour tortilla, 3 slices ham, 1 slice low fat cheese, & water
SNACK – yogurt & all natural oatmeal chocolate chip cookie, ¾ cup cereal, 1 banana & ¾ cup soy milk

SUPPER – 5 pieces flax w/w baguette, 8 pieces cheese, 4 carrots, 4 celery sticks, 4 red & green pepper slices, 1 tablespoon light ranch dip, 4 shrimp with seafood sauce, 10 olives & 1 piece vanilla pound cake

DAY 60 – Sunday February 12, 2006
Weight: 131.5lbs

Andrew had to run a few errands, so I decided to watch a movie and stuff my face! I'm craving great binge and purge! A big ass plate of nachos is exactly what I need! These are going to taste sooooo f*cking good, yummy, yummy, get in my fat tummy! Those went down so fast, I don't even think I tasted one. I feel so full but want more. Time to purge the poison out of my body. I feel so fat now. No control whatsoever and I wonder why I'm gaining weight!

FOOD JOURNAL for today
BREAKFAST – omelet with 1 egg, 2 egg whites, 2 tablespoons low fat cheese, red pepper, mushrooms, onions & spinach, ½ grapefruit & water
LUNCH – a BIG ASS cookie sheet full of nachos with sour cream & salsa
SNACK – clementine, ½ w/w pita with garlic butter, 2 spoonful's veggie soup, 1 Rice Krispy square, 2 cups coffee with soy milk & 2tsp sugar

DAY 61 – Monday February 13, 2006
Weight: 133.5lbs

Andrew and I had a great discussion regarding my therapy and progress. He felt left out and that was my fault. I told him things that I have accomplished like being able to go get groceries, and not have a panic attack, being able to drive and not losing it, going to social events and not puking every time I eat. He didn't realize that those things had been so difficult for me.

I have so much homework to do for my classes, it's making me dizzy! It is helping to get my thoughts on paper, but I do find my days so hectic, this is certainly not an easy breezy sick leave by any means. I'm sure people at work think differently. People just don't understand the severity of mental illnesses, they can be so judgmental which makes being sick even harder. Jennifer and Sandra from the Human Resources at my work are coming over to the house on Friday to discuss my options regarding my time off, not looking forward to that at all!

I've come to the conclusion that I may have to go elsewhere to do my homework and journal writing during the day, as being home makes me want to eat! I must get rid of all the temptations – cheese, baking goods as those are my 2 biggest sins right now! I made brownies for friends of ours and as soon as Andrew left, I downed a couple then the next thing I knew there were only 4 left! I feel so disgusting, I know I have put on weight! I can feel it therefore, I must get rid of the poison as I keep lifting my shirt to check out my fat and flabby stomach!

FOOD JOURNAL for today

LUNCH – 1 cup homemade vegetable soup with beans, 1 baked potato with 2 tablespoons fat free sour cream & 2 tablespoons mild salsa

SNACK – homemade banana blueberry bran muffin, 2 plain rice cakes & 1 slice low fat marble cheese & ¾ of a pan of homemade brownies

SUPPER – 1 yogurt, ½ apple, ½ banana, ½ clementine, 3 strawberries & 2 tablespoons almonds

DAY 62 – Tuesday February 14, 2006
Weight Morning 128.5lbs Noon: 131.5lbs Night: 133.5lbs

Happy Valentine's Day! I am feeling tired today but not as numb as on the weekend or as hopeless. Mind over mood therapy was good. IT really helped me once again just like the exercise I did to put feelings, thoughts, moods and situations a little more into perspective. I think I may have been the only one that took the homework seriously. I don't get it, people aren't taking this seriously and I know it's not easy, but I feel lucky to be in this program because only a select few are chosen, not everyone that ends up in the psych ward gets to attend day therapy.

Sandra and Jennifer are meeting Andrew and I at the house, to discuss my option for work at 1:30pm. I am so nervous, anxious – my stomach feel terrible, I just used the bathroom and my chest is so heavy it feels like it's going to explode! Just so nervous to see those as they will be the second and third person that I have seen from work in 3 months. The first person was Mike at his Mom's funeral. I'm worried about what they will go back to work and tell people.

Andrew and I cooked Valentine's supper, salmon, sweet potatoes, asparagus, chai tea and chocolate covered strawberries. I felt so disgusting afterwards! I wanted to puke and I let Andrew know this! I had to do it, I needed to do it, and it would instantly make me feel better! Andrew suggested we go for a walk. I said if I don't feel better when I get back he has to let me puke. We went for a 30 minute walk and I did feel better when we came back and I also had to use the washroom, so I felt great!

FOOD JOURNAL for today
BREAKFAST – ¾ cup cereal & ¾ cup soy milk
SNACK – yogurt, ½ clementine, ½ apple, homemade banana blueberry muffin & 1 clementine
LUNCH – Subway grilled chicken wrap with mustard, baked lays & iced tea
SNACK – all-natural oatmeal chocolate chip cookie & brownie
SUPPER – salmon, asparagus, sweet potatoes, 2 glasses red wine, chai tea & chocolate covered strawberries

DAY 63 – Wednesday February 15, 2006
Morning: 131lbs Afternoon: 132.5lbs Night: 133.5lbs

Had my appointment with Dr. David today and we talked about how I'm feeling food wise in regards to the retreat I'm going on this weekend. I feel like I won't have any control over what is served and people will question my choices.

FOOD JOURNAL for today

BREAKFAST – yogurt, homemade banana blueberry muffin &
2 hardboiled egg whites

LUNCH – 1 ½ cups spinach, 3 strawberries, 2 tablespoons
raspberry vinaigrette, 1 homemade muffin & yogurt

SNACK – banana & clementine

SUPPER – 4 bites lasagna, baked potato, 2 tablespoons fat free
sour cream & salsa

SNACK – yogurt, apple, clementine, 3 strawberries & 1
tablespoon almonds

DAY 64 – Thursday February 16, 2006
Morning: 133lbs Afternoon: 132lbs Night: 134lbs

Mind over mood class today was good, however I was not
into talking. I felt shy today. I know that I was feeling
stressed because I was rushed leaving home since I slept in,
but I've just been so exhausted lately. I also felt shy because I
didn't feel like dishing out some of the things I had written in
my book. So when it came to my turn to share, I was very
frightened.

After class, I fled to my car for a snack then home for lunch.
Decided to make an egg salad sandwich, I haven't had sliced
bread in over 3 months! I feel so guilty for the bread and I
added too much mayo, the binge comes at me like a freight
train. I reach for the apple cinnamon Cheerios, poison cereal
with all artificial ingredients! Almost a whole box later I'm in
the bathroom releasing the poison! F*CK, I know better than
to let myself get hungry but I forgot my snacks in the car
during my mind over mood class. Failed yet again today.

Talked to Ma today, she is really excited and happy for me to go on this retreat. She has called me like 4 times in the past 2 days about it. I packed my clothes and bedding and I'll pack my food tomorrow. I'm both nervous and excited to go.

Nervous – food, meeting new people, different religion, being by myself, not knowing enough about religion and being with Ma all weekend.
Excited – being relaxed, taking care of me, learning new things, have time with Ma, be alone on my time and seeing what others have to say.

FOOD JOURNAL for today
BREAKFAST – 1/3 cup oatmeal, ¾ cup soy milk, 1 banana, 1 tablespoon almonds & cinnamon
SNACK – 2 clementine's
LUNCH – 1 ½ cups vegetable bean soup, 1 egg, 2 slices organic bread, 1 tablespoon mayo, 3 gherkins, celery & onion
SNACK – almost whole box apple cinnamon Cheerios & soy milk
SUPPER – 1 cup veggie stir fry, pork tenderloin, 2 tablespoons applesauce & 1 red wine
SNACK – fat free chocolate pudding

DAY 65 – Friday February 17, 2006
Morning: 134lbs

Another sleepy morning. I have been getting back into my routine, however it will take some time. I really think therapy has been wearing me out mentally.

Grieving session today was very difficult. We all had to go around and say what we were grieving about. My eyes welled up when some people spoke.

1. Because I could relate to what they were saying and
2. I could feel their pain and I just wanted to say thank you for sharing and give them a hug.

I cried the entire time I was telling mine, however what I am most proud of is that I did speak. When they first started going around the table, I was ready to say 'pass' as I was feeling I would look stupid for what I had to say or that I would be judged for my actions. After class, *Roxy* one of the patients came over and gave me a gig hug and said "Anytime you need one of those, you know where to come." Then Jane (nurse) said "If you were my daughter I would tell you how proud I am of you, not for speaking up, but for getting out of the situation and becoming a better person. Then I would probably yell at you for not coming to me sooner." I just smiled and giggled.

After class I went to Sobeys to pick up some snacks for the weekend, then went home. Andrew had still not left for work and he began nagging at me about my EI claim which irritated me as I've done as much as I can but I'm waiting for information on others before I can submit it. My work called 3 times today but he didn't feel like answering it and that was the information I was waiting for. So after I spoke with them, I was able to complete my EI application and then packed the rest of my things for the retreat and get the f*ck out of there.

There was definitely no sentimental goodbye. Frankly I was quite happy to be leaving at that point and honestly if I never returned the better. I went and picked Ma and we stopped at the Irving for coffee – I know I'm not supposed to drink it, but I'm exhausted and I have 2 hours of driving ahead of me.

Finally after 2 hours of driving Ma's 'scenic route' aka got lost, we arrive at Camp Beulah. We check-in and the rooms are like a motel but no linens, radio or TV. Ma and Bobby bought me a little gift for the weekend, 'The Purpose Driven Life' book and journal. I started laughing and Ma couldn't figure out why until I pulled the same book out of my suitcase! I guess great minds think alike.

FOOD JOURNAL for today
BREAKFAST – 1/3 oatmeal, ½ cup blueberries, ¾ soy milk & 2 tablespoons pecans
SNACK - 1 clementine & yogurt
LUNCH – 1 ½ cups spinach, pork tenderloin, 4 strawberries, 2 slices organic bread & 2 spoons natural PB
SNACK – 7 organic chocolate mint cookies, 1 w/w pita, 1 tablespoon PB & ½ banana
SUPPER – ½ cup mixed veggies, piece salmon & w/w roll
SNACK – clementine

DAY 66 – Saturday February 18, 2006

Our first morning of the retreat. We both had a terrible sleep so we both stayed up and read. Our first session after breakfast was with Mary Pratt. She is so inspirational and interesting. I honestly could listen to her talk for hours. She is such a happy and warm spirited women. It really made me think about my life or I should say our life, Andrew and I together and how I hate the tension and difficulties we have been suffering through lately. It does not make me the person whom I want to be. Life has become so complicated these days that oftentimes I feel like we think we have to complicate it more to keep up with the 'Jones'. I really want Andrew and me to be able to settle our differences in a more respectful manner. For me, I need to look at our 'discussions' as discussions and not arguments every damn time.

At lunch I had a HUGE accomplishment! Although I felt guilty for eating ½ of a sandwich, I felt calm and relaxed eating my cookie….epically MIND BLOWING! It is so weird, because I was slowly eating the cookie and not trying to hide it from anyone while enjoying my tea, I enjoyed my cookie with no guilt!!! I've never f*cking felt that before!!!

After supper there was a 'play time' session but I didn't want to go so Ma went and I hung out in the bedroom by myself. Of course alone time usually means eating, which means binging! Why did I bring all this food with me? Binged on a bag of cookies, a bag of chips, an apple and 2 glasses of red wine. So I had no other choice but to purge before Ma came back. It truly was the biggest and best purge I've had in a long time! Oh the exhilaration, it never gets old!

FOOD JOURNAL for today
BREAKFAST – 1 cup scrambled eggs, 12 grapes, ½ apple & homemade muffin

SNACK – 1/3 banana, 1 orange slice, ¼ apple, 10 almonds, 4 all-natural chips, ½ organic chocolate cookie, 1 clementine & 4 Triscuit crackers
LUNCH – 1 ½ cups corn chowder, ¼ w/w ham sandwich with mustard, ¼ w/w tuna sandwich, oatmeal raisin cookie & tea
SUPPER – turkey, scoop mashed potatoes, squash, apple crisp & water

DAY 67 – Sunday February 19, 2006
Morning: 134.5lbs Night: 133lbs

I'm anxious, self-conscious and have little concentration this morning. The church service was really good. Not your typical service but it had all the elements. During the final prayer, one of the volunteers asked "Would anyone would like to pray for someone. Please do so and speak up." Surprisingly I spoke up and said "I pray for my niece Jessica at the Moncton Hospital". I then felt tears streaming down my face. Then Ma spoke up and said "I pray for my daughter Samantha as she begins her new journey." Well the tears kept coming. I had no tissue, my nose was running so when we were all done, I discretely stepped out and went to the washroom. It definitely was a very touching moment.

After the service, we headed home quickly as I had forgotten my meds. I have not had them since Friday and I'm beginning to feel the withdrawal effects of Zoloft, feeling anxious and very dizzy.

Once we arrived home I got ready for volleyball, however my

anxiety was increasing, my self-esteem became worse, I was dizzy and I couldn't see clearly. We won 4-1 but lost the last game and I thought I was going to lose it right there and as soon as I stepped off the court and began to cry. Instead of getting completely upset I quickly got dressed and got out of the building. Once I got in the car, I drove of the parking lot and broke down bawling. All kinds of different thoughts begin to run through my head; killing myself, I'm stupid, I'm no god, I'm fat, I hate my body, I suck at volleyball, I lost the game. I was REALLY upset!

FOOD JOURNAL for today
BREAKFAST – ½ cup oatmeal, 1 banana, 5 grapes, ½ apple & ¼ cup milk
LUNCH – 1 w/w pita with sliced turkey & mayo, homemade muffin, 1 piece cheese, 6 organic cocoa cookies & 1 coffee
SUPPER – ½ beef fajita & 1 cup tossed salad
SNACK – ½ cup cereal & ½ cup milk

DAY 68 – Monday February 20, 2006
Morning: 132lbs Night: 133lbs

I really need to begin writing down my dreams, they seem to be getting worse and more frequent, to the point where I begin recollecting during the day and wonder if it was a dream or reality.

After my therapy sessions I came home and made a batch of muffins and cookies, that was a bad f*cking idea! Had 2 cookies, they were delicious and I felt ok, not guilty. But then

I lost all willpower and went completely crazy on the cookies. I ate the whole f*cking batch! Sam you know better! I know it happened because this morning I missed my snack so I came home starving which is NEVER a good thing mentally and/or physically!

FOOD JOURNAL for today
BREAKFAST – 1/3 cup oatmeal, 1 banana, 2 tablespoons almonds & ¾ cup milk
SNACK – 1 w/w pita, 2 tablespoons PB, 1 clementine & water
LUNCH – 2 slices organic bread, ½ can tuna, 1 tablespoon light mayo & 1/3 can maple baked beans
SNACK – bowl apple cinnamon Cheerios & milk, 12 oatmeal chocolate chip cookies & water
SUPPER – ½ chicken fajita, 2 tablespoons fat free sour cream, 1 cup mixed greens, ¼ avocado, ¼ tomato & 1 tablespoon Japanese vinaigrette

DAY 69 – Tuesday February 21, 2006

What a blah day. Andrew left for Miramichi. I went to my mind over mood therapy class. Watched 2 movies. Stuffed my face. Purged 3 times. Went to bed. My parents must be so proud.

DAY 70 – Wednesday February 22, 2006
Morning: 132lbs Night: 132lbs

Another depressing day. Lazed around all day. Did not go to my therapy sessions. Wrote a letter to Ma. Watched a movie.

Talked to Andrew about 10 times, I think he is worried about me. Ate way too much. Purged 2 times. Making progress……I don't know anymore.

DAY 71 – Thursday February 23, 2006
Morning: 138.5lbs

I have not begun my mirror desensitization worksheet that Dr. David gave me. I find that I can never remember to do it, so I've decided to put the sheet along with a small journal in the bathroom so it will force me to remember. I started with clothes on for just 15 seconds focusing on my shoulders. That is the easiest for me as I love my shoulders. Now if I were to stare long enough I'm sure I would find faults but that is not the purpose of this exercise.

My appointment with Dr. David went well. We talked about how depressed I've been feeling these past couple of days and I've overeaten so much. We talked mainly about my body image and me not trusting the scales.
I'm excited for our volleyball tournament Saturday, a little fun in my life after a depressing week is just what I need.

FOOD JOURNAL for today
BREAKFAST – 1/3 cup oatmeal, 1 cup soy milk, 1 tablespoon almonds, 1 tablespoon natural bran & 1/3 cup blueberries
SNACK – 1 orange & homemade muffin
LUNCH – ½ homemade chicken fajita pizza
SUPPER – chicken breast, 4 strips zucchini, 6 cubes roasted sweet potato, homemade snack ½ with w/w cookies & soy ice cream & ½ bottle red wine

SNACK – homemade chai latte with skim milk & homemade oatmeal raisin cookie

DAY 72 – Friday February 24, 2006
Morning: 130lbs Afternoon: 132lbs Night: 129lbs

Did not journal today, this is not a good habit to be getting into. I've got to get my shit together. Can one really fail at journaling too?

DAY 73 – Saturday February 25, 2006

Made it to the finals, but lost. Had a poker night at the new house and found out some stupid f*cking news that an ex-girlfriend of Andrew's is coming home soon, great just another added stress.

FOOD JOURNAL for today
BREAKFAST – 1/3 cup oatmeal, 1/3 cup blueberries, ¾ cup soy milk, 2 tablespoons almonds & water
SNACK – homemade muffin & orange
LUNCH – charbroiled chicken wrap from Hilltop & double vodka & OJ
SNACK – homemade muffin & banana
SUPPER – ¾ cup cereal, 2 tablespoons almonds & ¾ cup skim milk
SNACK – 5 meatballs, 5 nacho chips with dip, ½ cup peanuts, 1 bruschetta, ½ cup baked Crunchits & 10oz raspberry vodka with club soda

DAY 74 – Sunday February 26, 2006

I'm exhausted, the tournament has taken everything out of me. I don't think that people realize just how exhausting having depression/anxiety is or any mental illness for that matter. It sucks the life out of you plus and I can't sleep restfully. Sometimes I lie awake for 2-4 hours waiting for my eyes to finally shut. It's a sick disease in that the more tired I get, the worse I feel about myself. When will this end, when will I feel 'normal'. Not only is the disease exhausting, so is the questioning of oneself every second of every f*cking day.

DAY 75 – Monday February 27, 2006

I feel like I have so many issues that I have opened up about and have been working on that I got frustrated today when trying to do my homework for grief class. I felt like my head was so full of thoughts and it made me more confused that I couldn't pin point or figure out what we were to do. I began to talk about my trust issues in my marriage and Jane the social worker spoke up when I was done and said she would volunteer herself for couple's therapy if I were interested. After class I told her I was interested, so she is going to get a referral from Dr. Shahid.

FOOD JOURNAL for today
BREAKFAST – 1/3 cup oatmeal, 1/3 cup blueberries, 1 cup soy milk & 2 tablespoons almonds
SNACK – orange

LUNCH – w/w pita with 2 tablespoons pizza sauce, ½ avocado, ½ cup spinach, 4 strips chicken & ½ cup skim mozzarella
SNACK – 2 homemade cookies, 2 cookies & lactose free ice-cream
SUPPER – 1 cup homemade chicken rice curry soup & 1 piece baguette
SNACK – 2 homemade cookies, 1 cup honey nut cheerios & 1 cup milk

DAY 76 – Tuesday February 28, 2006

Phone rang and it was my boss Mike from work. He was calling to see how I was doing and said he didn't want to pry, however he wanted to let me know that everyone is thinking about me and that you don't often get a chance to say that to someone and everyone at work loves you and misses you. It was a nice conversation and it definitely made me feel appreciated and loved.

Tried to do my Mood homework, I'm finding it really hard lately to put my thoughts on paper. I feel my mind is constantly racing and I can't seem to slow it down to focus. Information overload that's for sure! My anxiety today is very high and I'm not exactly sure why nonetheless I did not enjoy our talk during mood therapy class. As I'm sitting there, I feel myself doing deep breathing, my chest is heavy, my foot won`t stop tapping, my mind is racing and I cannot sit still! I also feel guilty that I have not done my homework to my full potential.

As the day progresses I believe my mind and body are sensing what is to come tonight, complete chaos on the home front. As I'm lying on the couch by myself I begin to think, why was I put here on this earth? To see how much pain and suffering a person can go through and still live to talk about it? To prove it can be done? I feel like I just start making progress and begin breaking down my wall and then all of a sudden chaos happens to build it back up again!

I have made the steps to talk to Jane regarding couples counseling. I have not told Andrew yet, not that I think he will object, but it just keeps slipping my mind. What do I have to live for? If I don't have my husband's trust and honesty, what do I have? It feels like I have nothing. Why do I remain here on this earth? What is my purpose? I really don't know if I can go on, I'm sick of feeling this way. I guess Andrew is probably right in thinking that I am paranoid. Why bother staying like this? What would be the easiest way to fall asleep and never wake up? I have nothing if I can't trust him. I really want to crawl into a hole and not see anyone or do anything that way I can't be yelled at or called names. I can't be made to feel guilty for something I didn't do. I don't know how much longer I can handle this. Maybe this was my purpose to give up.

Why me? God, please help me! I'm lost and I don't know what to do! So now what? What do I do? Who do I turn to? Where do I go? I feel so alone in this world, something I have felt all my life. This is the longest period of time that I have ever thought about suicide all my life. Weighing out the pros and cons.

Evidence for and Against – I'm obviously stressing my husband, as I am not pleasing him and therefore he is turning to other things. I frustrate him and he would be happier with someone else, why would he want crazy me – no education, fat, ugly, can't communicate, introverted, yell too much, I'm crazy, I overreact, I, I, I, just don't know anymore!

Who needs me? Who needs my irrational thinking? In my mind it is normal, or is it? I don't know what to f*cking think anymore! How many pills would it take? I wonder how many *Shelley* took. Will I ever be truly happy? Will I ever love myself? What is love? What does it mean? Can you have fake love? If you don't know what it is can you have it? Can you give it? Maybe if I did it in a hotel room, that would be better as nobody would know. Who can I turn to? Is there anyone left in my life?

FOOD JOURNAL for today
BREAKFAST – 1 cup cereal, 6 strawberries, 1 cup soy milk & 2 tablespoons almonds
SNACK – Apple & homemade muffin

DAY 77 – Wednesday March 1, 2006
Morning: 132lbs

Went to Shoppers Drug Mart on the Northside and bought sleeping pills. I've decided this is enough pain for one person to go through. Decided I would go talk to Tracy and give it one more try, she always has a way of calming me and seeing a sliver of light and the end of a very dark tunnel.

DAY 78 – Thursday March 2, 2006

My anxiety is at about 95%, I'm having a hard time breathing let alone journaling.

DAY 79 – Friday March 3, 2006

My anxiety is still really high but our friends from Miramichi are coming down today which excites me. And let's be honest, it's been very hard for me to get excited about anything in a very long time. Ben and Kara mean the world to me, they are truly a match and friendship made in heaven. As much as I love having them around I feel panic because oftentimes others don't realize just what goes on in my head on a second by second basis. I fear that if I have a panic attack it will be around them and I don't know what their reaction will be.

Fast forward to 11:00pm and the night is going well with drinks flowing and stories from years gone past and the next thing I know I get triggered out of the blue and the anxiety sets in like a raging forest fire. I begin to feel dizzy, I'm losing control over my breathing, my breath begins to shorten and I begin to shake and hyperventilate. NO, not now and definitely not here with everyone! I quickly run to the bedroom where I begin to gasp for air like it's my last breathe. I claw at the walls like I'm reaching for my last breathe.

Andrew comes rushing in and he has seen me in this state before and runs to get a cold facecloth, opens up the window and I push my head against the screen into the cold winter air gasping for more air that seems impossible to reach. Finally after what seems like an eternity, my breath finally comes back to normal and I drop on the bed from exhaustion. Because I'd run out of Ativan, Andrew called Jimmy to get a lorazepam and within seconds of taking it my body feels numb and I finally feel at ease. The only downside is that I've never had lorazepam before and the next morning when I wake up, I can't walk! My body is so relaxed that my legs don't function like they should. I hate that this happens around friends, I can't stop it!

DAY 80 – Saturday March 4, 2006

No journaling today, I'm mentally and physically exhausted from yesterday.

DAY 81 – Sunday March 5, 2006
Morning: 132lbs

And yet again, nothing. Get your shit together Sam! Journaling is not rocket science.

DAY 82 – Monday March 6, 2006

I feel like I owe it to myself to write in my journal today. I feel so bad for not doing it the past 3 days. I guess my focus has been on my anxiety, depression and frustration. My anxiety lately has been unbelievably high. Feeling guilty about everything I eat. I feel my willpower is diminishing. I'm going to gain weight if I keep going on. This is terrible and I'm embarrassed to say it, but even my willpower to purge is gone. I'm even too lazy to purge after I had 12 Pringles chips!

I've been neglecting my homework for day therapy, I'm just not motivated. I really need to get back into that and remind myself that even though I have not done homework for the past week that I have not failed and that I have to get back on track to make myself better as it definitely cannot make me worse.

FOOD JOURNAL for today
BREAKFAST – 1cup cereal, 1/3 cup blueberries, 2 tablespoons almonds & 1 cup soy milk
LUNCH – 1 ½ cups homemade clam chowder, 5 Breton crackers & 1 tablespoon margarine
SNACK – banana & 2 homemade chocolate chip cookies & 12 Pringle chips
SUPPER – ½ piece salmon, 6 baby roasted potatoes, ½ cup beets & carrots, 1 cup low fat berry crumble & ¾ bottle wine

DAY 83 – Tuesday March 7, 2006
Morning: 132lbs Night: 131.5lbs

My anger and anxiety seem to be increasing once again. This is not healthy for me as I'm not doing any of my homework. I don't feel like doing anything as my focus is on a letter than Andrew promised he would write me, however still has not. I really don't want to be at therapy today mainly because my homework is not done. My chest has been so heavy sine last

Tuesday. I'm so frustrated at this point and feel like I am hitting my head against a wall, making no progress and unfortunately I feel like I have done all that I can do.

FOOD JOURNAL for today
BREAKFAST – 1 cup cereal, 1 cup soy milk & banana
LUNCH – ½ w/w pita with 1 tablespoon mustard, ½ slice ham, 20 grapes & homemade muffin
SNACK – 1 piece chocolate
SUPPER – 6 roasted potatoes, 1 cup mushrooms, ¾ cup cereal, 2 tablespoons cranberries, 2 tablespoons almonds, 1 cup soy milk, 2 homemade oatmeal raisin cookies & 10 Pringles

DAY 84 – Wednesday March 8, 2006
Morning: 131lbs Night: 129lbs

I'm feeling very self-conscious today about the way I look. Not quite sure why….well other than the obvious. I feel alone lately. I don't want to be around anyone and I feel that I would have less to worry about and be less likely to get hurt if I were alone. I really don't even know why Andrew and I are living in the same house, we are just so distant. I feel his avoidance of the situation and I definitely feel my anger and anxiety towards the situation building as well. We are definitely growing apart in my mind at least. I know it is not easy being with me and I feel so guilty about that.

FOOD JOURNAL for today
BREAKFAST – nothing
LUNCH – seven grain tortilla, 4 slices ham, 1 tablespoon

mustard, 4 thin slices light old cheddar, yogurt & homemade muffin

SNACK – 12 Pringles & orange

SUPPER – 1 cup spinach, 3 strawberries, 1 tablespoon almonds, 2 tablespoon cranberries, 1 tablespoon raspberry vinaigrette, glass red wine, small square piece focaccia bread with grilled veggies, 3 slices light old cheese & 1 tablespoon mayonnaise

SNACK – apple, ½ cup optimum power cereal, banana & ½ cup soy milk

DAY 85 – Thursday March 9, 2006
Morning: 130lbs Night: 132.5lbs

At mood therapy class today it was my turn to speak as I hadn't done so in the past and I know Leo was pretty disappointed last time. So I began to let people know why I haven't spoken out this past week and the reasoning behind my anxiety. I began to cry of course, so Leo asked Nancy the Occupational Therapist to read it instead. It was definitely a bit easier. We went over my thoughts along with evidence and I feel like I did really well, as Leo didn't add much or feel that I had forgotten anything. I definitely feel better afterwards as I had let the class know and it helped to put my thoughts on paper.

After the session I went to Ma's to drop off the letter that I wrote her, which to be honest was more of a book than a letter as she means a lot to me.

FOOD JOURNAL for today
BREAKFAST – 2 boiled egg whites, 4 slices ham, 1slice rye
bread, ½ pink grapefruit, ½ cup yogurt, 1 tablespoon natural
bran & 1 tablespoon cranberries
SUPPER – 1 cup tabbouleh with chickpeas, tomato, parsley &
banana
SNACK – 3 bowls homemade apple crumble & 8 whole wheat
& honey pretzels

DAY 86 – Friday March 10, 2006
Today I have my first day therapy newsletter session and I'm
looking forward to it. We are just brainstorming today,
however it will be every Friday for the month of March and
April. It ended up going really well, but *Shelley* and I were
the only ones that showed up as *Sara* couldn't make it in.
We came up with a lot of great ideas – new ones too that had
not been in other newsletters.

My session with Dr. David went well and we discussed what
my action plan was for tonight. We also spoke a little about
my sex drive being so low and that he would look into the
side effects of Zoloft.

Went to TAG and began to cut out my squares for my quilt.
This will be my first time making a quilt, TAG is the best
therapy ever.

When I got home, I began to do research for the newsletter
and found lots of great information.

Ma called and said she had left a few messages, unfortunately

I never got them. I made a point of checking when I got home. She told me that she knew what had been going on in the past with respect to my drug addiction and had assumed that I had involved myself in something that was not any good. She was actually going to stop lending and giving me money as she knew it was enabling me with whatever I was into.

Andrew called and said he had finished the letter to me, it was 4 pages long. We talked for a bit, it was nice. He said how much he appreciated me pushing him to do this and not letting him off with it. So now I am ready to sit down and read the letter. Andrew really opened up. He says a very harsh statement about himself, that he is not a good communicator. I have to disagree with that. I think he's wonderful at communicating when the situation isn't necessarily focused on him. After all, if the situation is about him, his communication skills lack in the sense that he is not always open and honest with what he is saying as he feels it will be easier this way. He has agreed to talk to someone, Jane the social worker. This makes me very happy. I know that our relationship has turned for many reason, but I think the hardest step can be identifying and accepting the impacts and finding ways to improve on them or at least having some coping mechanisms. I must learn to embrace his accomplishments and forgive his mistakes, I have vowed to do so.

Andrew took me out for supper and we began to discuss in a very calm manner the letter and our feelings towards it. It went well and everything stayed calm. We understood each other. He came into the bedroom when we got home as I was headed to bed, exhausted and I needed to get up early the next morning to meet Ma at Cora's but we began to discuss sex and intimacy which made me cry because I felt like I was the one causing the lack thereof and he was upset. He assured me that was not the case, but of course I still felt bad. Intimacy is honestly the furthest thing from my mind right now.

FOOD JOURNAL for today
BREAKFAST – 2 slices all natural bread, 4 slices ham, 1 whole egg + 1 egg white & 1 tablespoon light Cheez Whiz
SNACK – orange
LUNCH – 1 cup couscous with chickpeas, 2 homemade cookies & banana
SNACK – 2 cup homemade berry crumble
SUPPER – Supper at Oscar's restaurant – seafood soup, Portobello mushroom, salmon, rice, Asian coleslaw & red wine

DAY 87 – Saturday March 11, 2006
Morning 131lbs Afternoon 133lbs Night 135lbs

Feeling overwhelmed.

DAY 88 – Sunday March 12, 2006
Morning 132lbs Night 134lbs

I can't think clearly, I'm confused. What's right? What's wrong? I don't know any more, it all seems the same!

DAY 89 – Monday March 13, 2006
Morning 132lbs

My head is spinning I can't stop the thoughts. What should I do? Where should I go? How to think? How to act? Who am I?

DAY 90 – Tuesday March 14, 2006
Morning 133lbs Night 135lbs

WOW, it's been so long since I have written in my journal. I'm feeling quite overwhelmed with all the work that I have to do for my day therapy classes, psychology appointments and then all the other daily things I do. I probably have not been focusing on myself to the best of my abilities lately. I have however had one huge thing on my mind, my weight increase! I can't believe that the scale reads 135lbs, 3 nights in a row!!! What the f*ck is going on with me, where is my willpower, get your shit together! I am very concerned over this.

I am going to start running/walking as I know this will take the weight off quick. I also have to get rid of some of the BAD FOODS in the house. I am eating way too many carbs! F*ck that, just way too much food even if I am purging!

FOOD JOURNAL for today
BREAKFAST – 1/3 cup oatmeal, 1/3 cup blueberries & ¾ cup soy milk
SNACK – 25 grapes & water
SNACK – 2 oatmeal date cookies (homemade)

LUNCH – 1 ½ cups homemade corn chowder

SNACK – tea biscuit & homemade oatmeal chocolate chip cookie

SUPPER – 1 ½ cups beef stir fry, 1 w/w flour tortilla & 1 tablespoon natural PB & Jam

SNACK – 1 w/w flour tortilla with Cheez Whiz, strawberry yogurt, ½ cup fresh pineapple, ¼ cup muesli, 1 ½ tablespoons natural bran & 8 Breton crackers

SECOND QUARTER
OF THE NAKED TRUTH

Warr;or

MUST HAVES

Hot Bath.
Foot Massage.
Chocolate Chip Cookies.

DAY 91 – Wednesday March 15, 2006
Morning 132.5lbs Night 135lbs

Went to self-esteem class today, it was good even though I found myself getting annoyed as I find people talk way too much and the things that we should be working on and discussing we don't have enough time for, so frustrating!

TAG was really interesting, as I got to learn how to use the quilt cutter to make my squares for my quilt. Nancy brought it in for me and showed me how to use it, it was really neat. I got all my red corduroy material cut and on Friday I will do the brown velvet. I'm wondering if I should keep the quilt or give it away. I hope it turns out ok, there's definitely lots of work ahead of me.

I watched the movie 'Pay It Forward' when I got home, what an inspirational movie. Everyone truly needs to watch it!

FOOD JOURNAL for today
BREAKFAST – 2 boiled egg whites, 2 slices all natural rye toast with 2 tablespoons low sugar jam & yogurt
LUNCH – 1 whole egg, 1 egg white, 1 tablespoon light mayo, blueberry yogurt & 12 almonds
SUPPER – 3 slices pork & 10 spears asparagus
SNACK – 1 cup chocolate soy milk, 15 baked tortilla chips with medium salsa & yogurt

DAY 92 – Thursday March 16, 2006
Morning 1315lbs

Very tired when the alarm went off this morning! Kept hitting snooze for ½ hour. I got up and had a shower. That has got to make me feel better right?

The only purpose of getting up early is to finish my homework. I finally after many attempts got my action plan done! I'm not sure if it is correct, however it definitely was a valid attempt. While I was working on the newsletter the phone rang and it was Sharon calling to tell me that Mind over Mood was cancelled. Someone must have heard my prayers last night!

Got done my meeting with Jane and it went really well. She is so sweet and very understanding. Some of the things she said with respect to trust gave me some relief as I realized I was not the only one who had felt this way and I wasn't going crazy! Our homework is to write down individually and not discuss with each other prior, the type of relationship we would like to have. My list was quite long and extensive:

1. We love each other.
2. We communicate openly.
3. We are honest with each other.
4. We never go to bed angry.
5. We have sex at least 3 times/week.
6. We have a date night at least 3 times/month.
7. We have healthy children.
8. We say 'I love you' at least 2 times/day.
9. We respect each other.
10. We don't name call.
11. We take time for ourselves.

12. We trust each other.
13. We don't discuss issues when drinking.
14. We don't fight/argue/raise our voices in front of our kids.
15. We clean up after ourselves.
16. We don't take each other for granted.
17. We help each other out around the house.
18. We play volleyball together.
19. We lift each other up when one is down.
20. We support each other's careers.
21. We camp together in the Summer.
22. We vacation frequently.
23. We realize everyday how lucky we are to have found each other.
24. We challenge ourselves/each other with new activities.
25. We have a big breakfast on the weekends.
26. We don't have a TV in the bedroom.
27. We eat supper at the table.
28. We go to church.
29. We keep in touch with our friends.
30. We stay in shape together.
31. We make healthy food choices.
32. We volunteer some of our time.
33. We go to bed with each other at least 4 times/week.
34. We wake up at the same time at least 2 times/week.
35. We make supper together sometimes.
36. We surprise each other with cards, flowers, candy etc.
37. We never go a day without speaking to each other.
38. We raise/discipline our children together.
39. We laugh as frequently as we can.
40. We don't feel stupid/self-conscious around each other.
41. We support each other's decisions.
42. We don't lie no matter how difficult it may be.
43. We have a cottage to escape/relax.
44. We educate each other.
45. We complement each other frequently.

46. We encourage each other.
47. We accept/work around each other's differences.
48. We allow time-outs during arguments.
49. We work on our relationship every day.
50. We will support each other's families.

Found out today that I now have another day therapy class that I will be starting on Tuesday and Friday's from 10:30am – 12:00pm 'Relationship Group' from April 4-May16, 2006. My weeks just got every crazier!

MY NEW CRAZY DAY THERAPY SCHEDULE
MONDAY
9:30-11am – Grieving Class
11-12pm – Psychology with Dr. David
TUESDAY
10:30-12:00pm – Relationship Group Class
WEDNESDAY
11-12pm – Wellness Class
1-2pm – TAG
THURSDAY
10:30-12:00pm – Mind Over Mood Class
FRIDAY
9:30-11am – Relationship Group Class
11-12pm – Wellness Class
1-2pm – TAG

FOOD JOURNAL for today
BREAKFAST – 1/3 cup oatmeal, 1 cup soy milk, 1/3 cup blueberries & 2 tablespoons pecans
SNACK – 3 bites omelet with onion, spinach, ham, fresh parsley, cheese & ½ grapefruit

LUNCH – 3 slices pork & ½ cup chutney
SNACK – 1 cup optimum power cereal, 2 tablespoons dried
cranberries, 2 tablespoons almonds & 1 cup soy milk

DAY 93 – Friday March 17, 2006

It's St. Patrick's Day and although I shouldn't be drinking it's
the only thing that numbs the pain. I went from binging
purging, to cocaine, back to binging and purging and now
finding my peace with alcohol. It makes me forget. It makes
me not worry about the smallest of things. It makes me block
out the world around me. I know that there is a history of
alcoholism in my family but right now that is the furthest
thing from my mind.

I remember when I had to leave university because my
binging/purging got so bad. I would load up on ice-cream
after a huge plate of shitty food because ice-cream makes the
purging coming up easier and sweeter. Someone had taken a
picture one night when we were drinking and I looked like a
ghost. Now I didn't realize I looked different from anyone
else until I saw a picture and thought finally I look different!
Does that mean I'm skinny now? After having to leave
university, I had lost what I thought was the 'in' thing to do so
I began experimenting with drugs and drank excessively. I've
lost control like this many times before. Even though I know
that Ativan and alcohol do not mix well, for me it is my one
control with a drink in hand.

DAY 94 – Saturday March 18, 2006

Went to Moncton to watch Andrew play volleyball and I went and visited Mémère and Pépère for a couple of hours. I had lunch with them and of course took home some molasses cookies. They were very surprised and happy to see me. I love them so much, they are like my parents. I honestly don't know what I would do without them. I spent so much of my childhood living there and have created so many great memories of playing, baking and just being a carefree kid.

Andrew kept telling me how happy he was that I came own to see him play, which made me feel good. I made Rice Krispy squares for the boys (Andrew's team) and they ate them all. Had lots of fun and enjoyed watching him play.

DAY 95 – Sunday March 19, 2006

I'm so tired and tomorrow is going to be one long ass day.

DAY 96 – Monday March 20, 2006

I want to write a book someday about my journey these past few months someday. So today I've written down a few ideas and concepts for 'My Journey. My Healing. My Life.'

DAY 97 – Tuesday March 21, 2006

Woke up at 8:00am this morning and I feel so fat! I have

gained so much weight! This is disgusting, I can't believe I have that little willpower now! I couldn't believe my eyes when I saw 136lbs on the scale! I told myself that 135lbs would be my limit.

Today I am going to start my run/walk program! I have to do this for me and my fat body! Yoga was really good last night. I have a volleyball tournament this weekend. I must get my ass a little firmer. I know that running will help me lose weight, but I want it NOW! If I could just limit my food intake, I am such a pig! So now I'm automatically feeling like I should be doing a thought record with all these negative emotions, all the same I do have a fair amount of evidence 'for'

DAY 98 – Wednesday March 22, 2006

I am depressed, feeling so low.

DAY 99 – Thursday March 23, 2006

Life is not worth living.

DAY 100 – Friday March 24, 2006

Why do I feel so blue? I feel so blue because I feel stupid. When you get into an argument and someone makes you feel like shit you realize that maybe you don't belong. You want to kill yourself and make the pain go away. I am tired of being ok one day and absolutely f*cked the next. Going from laughing, joking and carrying on to putting sleeping pills in my purse and planning to take a drive by myself with the intention of ending my life. Why is that? What is wrong with me? Am I really so different from everyone else? I ask myself these questions every time I feel this extreme pathetic way. When I am in the heat of an argument or the lows of depression, I honestly don't think there is anything that can stop me or change my mind on what I want to do to myself. Is this wrong? How am I supposed to cope without people thinking that I am too extreme or ridiculous? I feel that I have no coping mechanism when I get into a depressive state and it's nearly impossible to change the way I am thinking about suicide or hurting myself. It is like hurting myself will give me a purpose. What that is, I'm not sure.

I feel numb inside. I feel like I'm walking around and no one notices me, I feel like I don't know myself, I feel inept. Who am I? Why was I put on this earth? What is my purpose? Is my purpose to constantly try to please people, try to make them like me when I hate myself more than anyone else possibly could? Is my purpose to hide behind a mask and pretend that everything is fine, wonderful, and great and couldn't be better? Is my purpose to stand behind everyone and let him or her take advantage of me and tell me what I should be doing? Or is my purpose to live unhappily and kill myself with passion? Perhaps for the first time I will feel again. How am I to know?

I feel so small compared to everyone else most of the time. I don't know what is fact or fiction anymore. I don't know what is true or false. My eyes deceive me every day when I look into the mirror, however what I am looking at seems true, but I have been told it is not, it is something they call body distortion. If this distortion thing is true, how am I to know if anything else is real? How can I believe anything? They say that you can believe things that make you feel 'right' in your stomach. I have to disagree, because maybe my stomach will not accept anything for fear of being lied to.

My trust in most and almost all things now is like a ferris wheel, spinning out of control. I am oftentimes out of control and when it happens I turn into a different person. This person is not the one that has been in day therapy for the past 3 months, this person is the one that has been living unhappy for the past 28 years. She has control over me and she wins the battle 99.9% of the time. I have fought so long to keep her hidden away that I no longer can do it anymore. My mask has to come off to reveal her and my true identity. I feel that my only way to make her stop is to kill her, to kill me. My mind, my image, my life. Why is it that we let someone that has no physical being, control us? The saying that was always said in school is so far from the truth, "Sticks and stones may break my bones but names will never hurt me." Wow, I only wish I could physically hurt myself or let others hurt me because this mental beating is far worse. I may end up with some visible physical scars, however over time they would probably go away. The mental scars today seem impossible to get rid of. How do you get rid of 15 years of body distortion?

I can honestly say I don't know what is real anymore. Not only do my eyes deceive me every day, my ears don't hear the words coming out of people's mouths the way they intend them to sound. What am I to believe? What do I trust? What am I to understand? In the same respect, who am I to believe? Who am I to trust? Who am I to understand? I feel like I don't belong anywhere, I don't fit in; I am too sensitive for all those around me. What is normal? What is perfection? What am I? Who am I?

Right now I feel like an emotional failure. I feel so secluded from the real world. I sit here in the office typing while laughter goes on around me outside the door. That is how I feel most days, like the world goes on around me and I don't know how I go about asking to participate. I don't feel part of anything right now, will I ever? I feel like an outcast like I have most of my life, but why? My mood changes so quickly how do I control it without going to the extreme either way? Maybe I have been hiding it these past few weeks because I feel that I should be able to carry the weight of the world on my shoulders. I quickly realize that doing so only makes things worse, but how do I stop without feeling guilty and like a failure? How do I stop without ending my life suddenly? How do I stop feeling so blue?

DAY 101 – Saturday March 25, 2006

I want the madness in my head to stop!

DAY 102 – Sunday March 26, 2006

I'm so f*cking confused. What am I supposed to be doing?

DAY 103 – Monday March 27, 2006

I'm so fat! I know people can see it they just don't want to tell me the truth.

DAY 104 – Tuesday March 28, 2006

My head is spinning. What is right, what is wrong? I feel numb. I stare blankly all day long.

DAY 105 – Wednesday March 29, 2006

I feel like such a failure.

DAY 106 – Thursday March 30, 2006
Will things every get better?

DAY 107 – Friday March 31, 2006

Lazy. Depressed. Failure. Not interested in anything. Taking on too much. Just don't want to do anything.

DAY 108 – Saturday April 1, 2006 – DAY 130 – Sunday April 23, 2006

What the f*ck am I even writing for? Do I honestly think

anyone will care to read my thoughts or what depression, anxiety and having an eating disorder is truly like? Nobody will ever be able to relate. I'm sure I'm the only one that feels this way. I know when I was in day therapy and others were sharing their story, that I did nod my head a few times because 'those' people I could relate with. But those outside of the Psych ward, how could they possibly relate to me and my issues?

DAY 131 – Monday April 24, 2006

I've got nothing. I am nothing.

ANOTHER F*CKING FOOD JOURNAL for today
BREAKFAST – 1/3 cup oatmeal, 6 dried apricots, 1 cup soy milk & 6 almonds
SNACK – 8 organic 7 grain crackers & apple
LUNCH – 2 slices 12 grain bread, 2 boiled eggs, 4 tablespoons fat free mayo, 2 tablespoons onions, 3 gherkins, 2 thin slices light marble cheese & 1 cup chocolate soy milk
SNACK – ¾ cup fat free yogurt ice-cream, 3 tablespoons chocolate sauce, 2 tablespoons peanuts & banana
SUPPER – 1 cup chicken curry soup, ½ cup Chinese veggies, 2 organic homemade biscuits & 2 tablespoons molasses
SNACK – 1 decaf chai tea, 3 tablespoons skim milk & 1 tablespoon honey

DAY 132 – Tuesday April 25, 2006
Morning 133.5lbs Night 135.5lbs

The only thing I can write about is food? What the hell is wrong with me?

FOOD JOURNAL for today
BREAKFAST – 1/3 cup oatmeal, 8 almonds, banana & ¾ cup soy milk
SNACK – ½ grapefruit & 8 organic 7-grain crackers
LUNCH – 1 cup homemade chicken curry soup, ½ cup Chinese veggies & 1 homemade organic biscuit
SNACK – fat free yogurt, 3 rye crackers with 3 pieces Gouda & 3 raspberry coolers
SUPPER – 7 homemade roasted potato wedges, salmon & 1 cup homemade black bean & corn salad
SNACK – 5 plain lay's potato chips

DAY 133 – Wednesday April 26, 2006
Morning 133.5lbs Night 133.5lbs

Just another boring food journal and how I have no willpower.

FOOD JOURNAL for today
BREAKFAST – 1 cup chocolate soy milk, 3x2" piece omelet, and 2 slices all-natural bread, 1 tablespoon molasses & 1 tablespoons margarine
LUNCH – banana, fat free yogurt & 10 organic 7-grain crackers

SNACK – granola bar & 8 almonds
SUPPER – chicken fajita salad
SNACK – 5 chocolate covered pretzels, shared medium
popcorn with Andrew no butter & ½ cup chocolate soy milk

DAY 134 – Thursday April 27, 2006
Morning 133.5lbs Night 135lbs

Why the f*ck can I not get under 135lbs? I was under 120lbs in
the hospital and now look at me. I was fat when I was
admitted I'm a complete f*cking cow now! SO
DISGUSTING!!!

FOOD JOURNAL for today
BREAKFAST – 1/3 cup oatmeal, 10 almonds, 1 banana & 1 cup
soy milk
LUNCH – ¾ cup black bean & corn salad, low carb flour
tortilla, fat free yogurt, banana, 8 almonds & 2 tablespoons
dried cranberries
SUPPER – Mike's hard lemonade, ¾ filet mignon, 1 cup tossed
salad & 1 tablespoon French dressing
SNACK – Smirnoff ice cooler

DAY 135 – Friday April 28, 2006
Morning 133.5lbs

Great, the weekend has come which means more food, more
fat, more drinks and more 'poor me's. Thank goodness for
purging, the one thing that exhilarates my body and puts me
into a euphoric state.

FOOD JOURNAL for today
BREAKFAST – 1/3 cup oatmeal, 1 cup soy milk, 8 almonds, 1/3 cup blueberries & 2 tablespoons natural bran
SNACK – 10 organic 12-grain crackers & 1 banana
LUNCH – ¾ cup black bean & corn salad, low carb tortilla, 3 almonds & apple
SUPPER – 6 pieces sushi, sea breeze salad & 2 glasses red wine
SNACK – nachos with hamburger, light sour cream & salsa

DAY 136 – Saturday April 29, 2006
Morning 133.5lbs

Volleyball tournament today which means I'll burn a shit ton of calories but since I won't eat much all day, I will have the biggest f*cking binge of food and alcohol tonight. God I can't wait!

FOOD JOURNAL for today
BREAKFAST – 1/3 cup oatmeal, 1 cup soy milk, 8 almonds & 1/3 cup blueberries
SNACK – at Hilltop Restaurant 2 eggs, 3 slices bacon, ¼ cup home fries, 1 slice w/w toast, 1 tablespoon jam & 2 vodka with OJ
LUNCH – apple, banana, blueberry muffin & 1 slice pineapple
SUPPER – hot dog with bun, 3 crackers with dip & 4 carrots with dip
SNACK – 1 ½ pints vodka with OJ & upsized McDonalds Big Extra Combo

---

DAY 137 – Sunday April 30, 2006
Morning 134lbs

Well holy shit, I dropped below 135lbs! Probably due to the fact that I'm completely hungover and I think I purged every last piece of anything out of me last night. I got away with it though and pretended that I was sick from the alcohol. Oh how easy it is being a bulimic whereas if I were anorexic like I was in the hospital, I got watched 24/7. People are so easily fooled.

FOOD JOURNAL for today
LUNCH – 1 cup Kraft dinner
SUPPER – 1 sausage on bun with ½ cup sauerkraut, 1 tsp mustard, 6 potato slices with cheese, ½ cup tossed salad, 1 tsp French dressing, 1 biscuit with strawberries & light cool whip

DAY 138 – Monday May 1, 2006
Morning 135lbs

Made homemade baked beans today for the first time, planted seeds for the garden and wrote 2 articles for the day therapy newsletter. It's the beginning of a new week, fingers crossed it goes well.

FOOD JOURNAL for today
BREAKFAST – 1/3 omelet, 1 cup chocolate soy milk & 2 slices all natural bread with light jam
LUNCH – 1/3 omelet & yogurt
SNACK – apple, 2 all natural crackers, 4 almonds & 1 square dark chocolate

SUPPER – ½ cup baked beans, 1 hot dog, 2 slices raisin brown bread, 1 cup tossed salad with 1 tablespoon light French dressing, ½ cup homemade fruit cobbler & yogurt ice-cream
SNACK – banana

DAY 139 – Tuesday May 2, 2006
Morning 134.5lbs

Woke up this morning felling a little irritated, not exactly sure why. My mood lately seems to be so sporadic, up one day and down the next. I don't 'feel' myself lately and I can't seem to use my coping skills that I've learnt.

Not feeling my best today but I went into the hospital and typed up the 2 articles for the newsletter and spoke with Dr. Shahid and nurse Marion. I get to relationship group and most of the seats are taken so I'm somewhat freaking out because the seat that I normally sit in is gone and I hate change. Once again I'm having a hard time concentrating, nothing seems to be sinking in. Everyone is speaking around me and I just can't seem to grasp it, how frustrating. I thought leaving my anxiety group would help me refocus and not feel so overwhelmed, so much for that.

Came home to have lunch with Andrew and I lost my shit! There was really no specific reason but I lost it and had enough! I immediately get up from the dining room table where Andrew and I are having lunch, spit out my beans into the garbage, dump the bread, grab my purse and day therapy bag and leave wanting to kill myself. I can't deal with the lack of trust. I'm tired of not knowing what's right or wrong. I'm tired of being f*cked up! Running away is the only escape I feel I have right now. I get into the car and speed off up Adams Street with the intent to kill myself. I thought I'll go to Shoppers Drug Mart on the North side because I had already bought sleeping pills there once before, therefore I know where they are, and nobody will see me and I won't have to search for parking.

Well by the time I got to Queen and King Street I knew I couldn't wait that long to drive to the North side. I was going to go to Shoppers Drug Mart in Kings Place but I knew there would be too many people and I may run into someone I know, so I took the Queen Street exit thinking I will go to Atlantic Superstore on Smythe Street. Luckily I remember as I'm driving, that Ross Drugs is just up the street and there just so happened to be a parking space in front…..this is obviously meant to be, there is never parking downtown! I walk in and I know they must know what I'm thinking and doing but I don't care. It's not against the law to buy sleeping pills, they can't stop me and if they do there are a dozen more places in Fredericton I can go, so f*ck them! I pick up the biggest bottle I can find of extra-strength sleeping pills and a bottle of water, pay for them as fast as I can and get into my car to drive off before anyone tries to stop me!

At this point I don't have a plan where I was going to do it, so I drive back down King Street thinking that if I see someone I know I may not go through with it, but I didn't. I then went back down the Lincoln Road towards home and took the long way to Oromocto. Once I got to Oromocto I had come up with a plan. I then drive back to Fredericton, back through the Lincoln Road and up through Kimble Drive onto the Highway. I pull into the McDonalds on Prospect Street and run inside to pee. I knew that I wanted McDonalds to be my last supper and final meal. I then got back into my car and head into the drive- through where I swear I see Andrew sitting at Tim Horton's next to McDonalds, f*ck he had better not ruin my plan after all of this! I get to the drive through microphone and I order a double cheeseburger combo with orange pop. Mmmmmm! I can't wait to dig into those fries. I dig a little but I then quickly fold up the bag to save the rest. Now where? Where can I go that nobody will notice I'm sitting in my car, popping pills, eating McDonalds and leave me alone?

I drive to the Sears parking lot in the back of the Regent Mall and find myself a parking spot far enough away that not too many people would see me but not so far away that I will look suspicious. There are always cars in and out of there so I know I won't look suspicious in the middle of the day. I put the car in park, turn off the ignition, recline my seat slightly, get out my journal and get my pills ready. Everything is lined up perfectly and ready to go, my little place is cozy. After all, this was going to be my last supper so I wanted to make it as special as I possibly could.

I'm not fearful but happy of what's about to happen as it will all be over soon.

I'm sure the hospital is looking for me right now as I should be at my appointment with Jane and Andrew. I check my phone to see if anyone has called as I had turned it off, but nothing. I then turn it back off, get out the pen for my journal, crank up the tunes and begin to eat my fries with ketchup. Man oh man they are yummy!

Surprisingly there are a lot of cars that are parked near me, they must have needed the exercise. I figure once I get done my fries, I will begin to take the pills, after all I want to savor some of my meal. So I finish off the fries check my phone again and nothing which angers and depresses me even more! It's 2:02pm and I open up the bottle of extra-strength sleeping pills and quickly pop 10 into my mouth while chugging them back with some orange pop. I want all this information written in my journal as I know that when people find me literally dead asleep in my car and my journal by my side, my journal will have all the information they need. The rush that those 10 pills gave me is incredible! My heart begins to race and it feels almost like when I did my first line of cocaine just 3 years ago. What an incredible rush, I can't wait to do it again! I open up my burger and take a bite, aaaah heaven! Just the right amount of pickles and ketchup with yummy cheese in between two 'make believe' hamburger patties.

The pills seem to be taking too long for any effect, it must be time to take more. My heart is really pounding now, yet my body is so relaxed. I decide to have 8 more pills, but they don't seem to be working for me. I hate that my heart is uncontrollably racing! I'm very frustrated right now, almost the extremes of anxiety. I have to pee really bad, however I know that I can't walk at this point and I definitely cannot wait any longer. I feel a little guilty for Andrew as he will be waiting for me with Jane at the hospital. My 139 days have come far compared to the first day I was admitted. I'm getting very frustrated as I just want to sleep. Wow, I have to pee! I feel like opening the car door and doing it right here in the parking lot, but I don't know if I can get up. I feel like these sleeping pills are acting like a muscle relaxer as I can't really feel my legs, they feel like Jell-O. Guess that means it's time to pop another 8. OCD kicks in during these times where I strategically know the exact time and amount I will be taking. Ending up with an odd number at the bottom of the bottle would not be a good thing!

My body becomes heavy, things feel weird to touch and my heart is pounding furiously.

Gosh if I really had to fall asleep I would be frustrated, as they say to only take one and at this point I've taken 20. Or is it 30? F*ck I don't know. I'm desperately craving a cigarette right now. Probably because when I was high on cocaine I had this euphoric sense to me and that is how I'm feeling now, well minus the 'can't move' feeling. On my cocaine binges I would stay awake anywhere from 24-48 hours straight doing lines, driving around, smoking cigarettes and playing crib with no food the entire time, just a simple bottle of apple juice that wouldn't even get finished. I feel like I go to the extremes with my emotions, I can't turn them off and have no escape. I'm very paranoid right now just like I was when I was high. I don't feel guilty for what I am doing. I will on the other hand, feel terrible for my family and friends.

2:27pm 8 more pills. My French fries are so yummy! I should have gotten an extra-large…..funny it's the only time I don't

---

feel guilty and don't feel like purging. My double cheeseburger is super yummy too! At this point I decide no more cheeseburger, not sure if it's because I feel so f*cked up or I think maybe the pills would not have the best effect if I have a full stomach, so I put it aside. First time in my life that I have ever put a cheeseburger from a McDonald's combo and NOT purging afterwards!

Maybe time to take a few more, as I am still not asleep. 8 more pills, 3:18pm. The feeling is so odd, I'm sure it's mainly the anxiety.

I begin to hear voices, like a baby crying, people laughing and pumping music like I'm at a bar. I have no idea where it was coming from and I know there are no people to be seen. I begin to get very paranoid, I feel like the cars that are driving by know what I am doing and like people are staring at me. I lock all my doors to make sure no one could creep up on me. Then I get this awful urge to have to pee. I begin to freak out because I know I can't go anywhere so I open up the car door and pee in the parking lot. Thank goodness for McDonald's napkins to wipe! I quickly jump back in the car and lock all the doors. There are more pills to be taken, 8 more down and I don't remember orange pop ever tasting this amazing! I decide to write in my journal whom I want some of my insurance money to go to and notes to people who mean a lot to me. I figure it is the least I can do. I know they will find it, my journals have everything that I have been feeling or doing in them for the past 139 days.

So I guess this is it, I'm tired of feeling this way and I'm so sorry for all the frustration and hurt I may have caused my family and friends. I can't seem to get out of my thoughts. As many steps forward that I may take, I take way to many back to try and get ahead and start over. Today, was a productive day in completing the newsletter however.

Dr. David for you, you've given me self-esteem in being able to write today. I wrote two stories for the cover of May's newsletter and inserted information from our wellness group. Maybe that was my calling in life.

Surprisingly I feel so calm right now. As I popped each sleeping pill I feel relief…..finally! My heart is racing right now not sure if that's me or the pills. I figure I will keep writing until I drift off to sleep. Journaling and writing have always been my favorite things to do, my therapy. I may as well end with it.

Cosmo my cat I'm going to miss you buddy! Mommy loves you very much. I know Daddy will take great care of you. Just remember to remind Daddy that there is $2000 to go to the SPCA from the Cosmetology Association of New Brunswick. I can't forget about where you came from and how much love you've given me during my most depressing times.

Monika what a best friend you have been. I wish both you and Jamie all the best. Remember to pursue YOUR dreams and nobody else's. Go to Calgary or travel the world while you can. Take care of my "man" Kobe (dog) for me. Sorry I didn't get any scarves done for him.

Mémère et Pépère, je vous aimes beaucoup! Votre amoure et

callin depuis j'étais née est incroyable. Mémère je n'oublierai jamais vos biscuits à la melasse et Pépère moi je bois de l'eau par-ce que moi je suis beau, toi tu bois du lait par-ce que toi tes lait! Beaucoup de bisoux!

Oncle et tante, je vous aimes beaucoup! Thérèse et Florine merci d'être là pour moi toujours, vous comprenez tous!

Nanny, what a strong, compassionate women you are! The adjectives that I would use to describe you could go on and on forever! I just want you to know that I always thought Bill was my grandfather. He was such a great caring man. I know you loved him very much and it broke my heart to see him go.

He did surprisingly get the 29 hand in crib before me though. Don't ever stop smiling and remember that your laughter is contagious. I love you!

Andrew's parents where do I even begin. You took me in like no other. I know how hard it must have been for you given the circumstances initially, however you never once made me feel out of place.

Tracey thank you for all the motivational talks. I appreciate your honesty and of course your open door anytime I would come knocking with a tea in hand. Our talk got me through my first attempt.

Sandra you are beautiful as much on the outside as on the inside. You can make anyone smile and deserve that from others too especially in your job. You are such a caring, strong willed and a little stubborn......to find that last penny and balance the books, but everyone loves you! You would give your heart to anyone even though you only have one.

Sheri my sister what can I say but tough ass. I love you! We have had our rough times, but I'm glad as I think it has made us come to understand each other a little better. You are such a great friend, the most loyal I have ever known. Thank goodness for you, you keep us on our toes to stay in touch and I need that! The biggest and kindest heart ever.

Murielle it is great to share some amazing Acadian traditions with you. Your zest for life and caring demeanor truly shine through. Remember to keep ol' Lloydy in line.

I wish I would have known my biological father more, albeit I do have to admit that I have found someone that took me in like his own daughter, Bobby. Bobby thank you! I don't know how many times I can say that. You have made both Ma and I so happy. You're devoted, caring, intelligent and funny. And let's be honest, we all love it when you're 'Bobby' even if Ma likes 'Bob' better.

Ma the strongest women I know. When I think back to the life we had it was definitely not one that I would wish upon anyone, however it did make me who I am today, some positive, some negative. You are so beautiful both on the inside and out. I just wish you could realize that more like I wish I would have as well. Take care of yourself. Don't think this had anything to do with you, if anything you were my will to live this whole time. You are incredibly talented in so many different things, however there is one talent that I feel you are not fulfilling to its full potential, your calligraphy and art. You are incredible at both and I really think you should pursue that more. I love you very much and with the money from the government insurance I only ask that you donate a portion (what you feel is needed for each one) to the soup kitchen, drug rehab program, SPCA and 2SE Psych Ward at DECH to help instill better programs for both adults and teens with mental illness and mental health difficulties as there was nothing when Jess needed it so desperately.

Jessica my beautiful Jessica. I looked back at pictures exactly 2 years ago yesterday when Andrew and I had gone to Mexico and you looked like such a young little girl with your Tingley's ice-cream shirt on. You have overcome so many things these past couple of years, you should be very proud of yourself. I know that you will get better so keep going to the counsellor, it is very much worth it. Just when you think you're getting better or making progress, things can change very quickly. I want you to have my hope chest at my Ma's. Jimmy will fix it for you. As well, there is a pile of kitchen stuff in the garage and spare room. I want you to have for your first apartment. As well with any insurance money that is left, please follow your heart and become whatever feels right for you. I know you will make the best decisions possible.

Andrew I'm sure I have skipped over a few people for the time being as I'm beginning to get sleepy and I do not want to leave you out. I am so lucky to have you and I'm sure you feel the same, I just couldn't let you go on any longer with the pain

I was suffering and putting you through. You were so understanding it was unbelievable. I may have said something in the heat of the moment before leaving, however without you I don't know if I could have done all the things I have accomplished in the past 5 months. My travels with you have been incredible. You are so well educated in travel and its history, it made me interested too. Hard to believe I'm sure you're thinking. When you do get to Paris, remember me and blow me a kiss to the heavens. The only thing I ask from you is to stay motivated with work. You have such great potential it's frustrating to me to see you rarely ever using it.

I don't dare see if there are any messages on my phone as it has been going off non-stop, so I shut it off as it's not like I'm going to answer it anyways! I check one last time and there are no messages. I'm thinking I may just go home. I know Andrew is not home right now and I would rather lay to rest in my bed than in a parking lot. Maybe I should have bought 2 bottles. I'm almost positive I can't drive. My hands feel numb on the steering wheel….wait they are not on the steering wheel.

Oh my goodness I want a cigarette so bad! 10 more pills and the bottle is gone 3:25pm 60 pills complete in 60 minutes! I feel like I have finally accomplished something, something that will make a difference yet I feel so sad because they are all gone. My body feels so numb. My head is heavy. My writing is beginning to get very slow and sloppy.

I love you so much Andrew and I want you to move on once you feel up to it. You do have to find a women who can cook,

clean, give you rubbies, pick pimples, make awesome omelettes, beans, bruschetta etc. etc. etc. I'm sure you know the list goes on and on….good luck, mwah!
I'm slowly starting to fade away.

You are my best friend, and always will be my 'bud'. Thank you for loving me and saying I'm beautiful even though I didn't believe you most of the time. My jealousy and trust issues have definitely gotten in the way and have made our relationship rocky at times.

My heart is racing, hands are shaking.

Promise me as well before you are 40 years old you will purchase a cottage, trailer or chalet somewhere to relax. I know you won't have any problems with that because that is something I have always wanted and I want you to experience the joy of that too!

Slowly going to be drifting off soon, eyes are heavy.

Baby I love you so much, you deserve so much better. You tried so hard to console me however I just could not trust you for some reason. My mood swings are frequent but yet you kept your cool most of the time. I'm writing so much I'm going to be out of room in my journal soon. One last thing, I forgive you as I know that is the reason I could not move on from a lot of things.

Getting dizzy.

What to do next…I'm getting very antsy. Maybe if I try and relax instead of writing it will help.

How much longer until I fall asleep? I am feeling so paranoid, it's driving me crazy! My paranoia begins to increase and I just can't stay in this parking lot any longer. I am freaking out I have to go, but where? I missed my appointment with Jane and Andrew at 3:00pm and I figure that since it is approximately 4:30pm Andrew will still be with Jenn his ex-co-worker and therefore won't be home. I have decided that I am going to go home and die in my own bed with Cosmo. He will just purr and not say anything until I pass on. I clean up the car, put away my books and empty pill bottle into my day therapy bag and turn on the car. Not sure if driving is a good idea or not, but I'm too anxious and frustrated to stay here. I'm beginning to hallucinate. Have I left the parking lot? Are my hands on the wheel, which one is gas and which one is brake? Seriously, is that my right foot on the brake or my left foot on the gas. I can do this or can I?

I begin to accelerate but it feels so weird, where are the brakes? I instantly hit the brake, I am so f*cked up its even scaring me a little. At the top of my lunge I yell "Oh my God, there is no way I can f*cking drive!" But I am so paranoid at this point that I have to get the hell out of here. I get on the highway and take the Kimble Drive exit. Don't ask me how I stayed on the road. I then drive down Kimble Drive to the Lincoln Road. The drugs have really kicked in at this point because my eyes are closing and I feel really f*cked up. All I know is as I pass the potato experimental farm and go down the steep hill I am way beyond my lane and driving in the lane with oncoming cars. As cars are coming I'm swerving and thinking 'they can't f*cking drive'.

I pull into the driveway (crooked so I was told later) and try my hardest to walk. Wow, I am really f*cked up. My pupils are dilated just like I'm on cocaine. I can hardly make it up the stairs, as my body feels so heavy, and my legs won't lift or bend, so I crawl up the stairs on my hands and knees instead. I stand up, grab the door handle to get myself up and finally get the door open to walk in and find Andrew standing at the top of the stairs. What the hell, he isn't supposed to be home! He says "Where have you been?" As soon as he comes down the stairs and looks at me a bit closer he knows something is up. He grabs a hold of me and says "What did you do!" I say "Please don't be mad at me." He says "Tell me!" I say "I took some pills." He says "What kind of pills?" I say "Sleeping pills, but they are not making me go to sleep." He says "Oh my God, where are they?" I pull out the bottle out of my bag and hand it to him. He says "They are empty, where are the rest?" I say "I took them all." He says "Oh my f*ck, how many?" I say "60" He says "Oh my God why would you do this?" He is freaking, but I am calm and say "I gotta go pee." Well easier said than done, I can hardly get up the first stair. He calls his sister Tracy and Tele-Care. He is yelling for me to go to the bathroom and puke them up, like I'm in a state to do that. I just wanna go pee, and not in a parking lot. He then says "Get in the car! I'm taking you to the hospital!" He runs downstairs to the basement to ask his friend Mike who is a police officer what he should do. I barely make it down the stairs after using the washroom, as I trip and grab a hold of the railing landing on my ass instead of my face. Andrew comes back up and says "Get in the car, don't forget your purse!" I pick up my purse and he goes ahead of me. However once he sees me trying to go down the stairs, on my ass, he realizes it is impossible at this point. He has to help me, my legs are just not functioning. We get into the car and he speeds off like a mad man as Mike yells at him 'Get her there as quickly as you can and don't worry about the police!" I have no idea what Mike said to me outside before I got in the car and I don't remember any of the drive.

He pulls up to the ER doors, quickly parks the car on the side of the curb and says "Let's Go!" I thought I was walking quickly, yet obviously I wasn't because he continues to say "Come on let's go! Hurry up!" We walk in the doors and Andrew immediately goes over to the nurse's station and tells them what is going on. I couldn't hear exactly what he said but the next thing I know I am sitting on the floor and they pick me up to put me in a wheelchair. At this point I can't stand, so they bring me over to the registration desk inside the ER. They ask me a few questions, but I'm just slurring my words, even though to me I sound fantastic. By the looks on their faces I'm going to assume I make no f*cking sense.

They take my blood pressure and now I'm being rushed off to a bed inside the ER. Next thing I know they rip off my shirt, and one of the nurses says "Don't worry about her pants." They shove all these sticky things on my stomach, chest, breasts, and legs to monitor my heart. My pulse is over 160 and I don't think that is bad, but as I watch the monitor it keeps going up, and up and up to almost 200 and my blood pressure is no better! 2 more nurses come in and they begin to poke at me. Blood out of my left arm, blood out of my right arm and an intravenous line in my right as well. The intravenous in my right arm f*cking hurts! I don't yell but my face says it all. The next thing I know Tracy is by my side while Andrew is talking to the Doctor. Tracy seems worried and I'm not sure why. Everyone is freaking out for some reason. Tracy asks if it's ok to call my Ma and Bobby. I'm like sure, but why? The nurses give me some drink, this large glass of blueberry milkshake, why the hell am I drinking a milkshake? Guess I was wrong as it was far from a blueberry milkshake! It is f*cking charcoal with water to try and inhibit the rest of the drugs from getting into my bloodstream. I had no idea that would work but I guess it works on alcohol so maybe it's the same for sleeping pills. As I'm trying to drink my 'blueberry milkshake I keep forgetting where I am and what I'm supposed to do.

Andrew keeps saying "Drink up" and I keep saying "What, why and where am I?" My lips and my teeth are all black. After drinking that big ass glass I have to pee, what a chore that is! I can't sit up on my own or lift my legs at this point and all I can think of is how the hell am I not passed out? Tracy helps me and brings me to the washroom. Soon after, Ma and Bobby arrive. I honestly don't remember anything about them being there, other than when they left and Ma saying "Thank-You" to Andrew. I assume for being home so I didn't die.

Before leaving, Ma takes me back to the washroom and I now have black diarrhea, what the hell is wrong with me?!? Ma asked if that was normal and the nurses assure her that this is a good thing. At this point Andrew says that I was talking pretty odd. I got talking about seeing Dr. Grass (not sure who that is) in the Co-op and then my story stopped and all I said was "Yeah, maple brie." I guess I was a little comic relief for them as I do remember laughing at myself quite loudly at times. I'm sure the other patients in the ER had a good chuckle.

Dr. Shahid comes in to see me and says "Didn't I just see you this morning?" I say "Yeah." He says "What happened?" I say "Not sure." And then I remember saying something about a dog. I believe he walks away soon after that, must have made him a little frustrated with my random answers which I think were funny at the time. I'm not sure what time Andrew left, he was going to stay with me but I told him to go home to get some sleep and I would see him in the morning. What a terrible time I had trying to sleep. I still have my jeans on and all the wires and lines hooked up to me. This was not how things were supposed to turnout. I even failed at suicide???

FOOD JOURNAL for today
BREAKFAST – 1/3 cup oatmeal, 1 cup soy milk, 8 almonds & banana
SNACK – orange, 10 baked organic chips & yogurt
LUNCH – ½ cup baked beans, 1 cup tossed salad, 1 tablespoon French dressing, ½ piece raisin brown bread & ½ cup chocolate soy milk
MY LAST SUPPER – McDonalds large fry, ½ double cheeseburger, ¼ medium orange pop & 60 extra-strength sleeping pills

DAY 140 – Wednesday May 3, 2006
Morning 133.3

As I awake, Andrew was right beside me looking tired and mentally drained, yet he still looked so handsome. Always done up to perfection with jeans and a short sleeved T-shirt that shows off his strong muscular body. His hair is so perfectly done. He reaches over, gives me a kiss on the forehead and he smells like my Andrew, so yummy. At this point I feel like such a failure, I can't even kill myself and I hope Andrew doesn't feel like he caused any of this. I'm still drugged the f*ck up, but man I'm hungry.

As I come back to reality of where I am, I realize that the heart monitor is still hooked up to me, my heart rate has now come down to the low 60's quite a jump from last night and my intravenous is still pumping into me. I remember them changing the bag a couple times last night. I feel so bloated in my right hand. I can hardly close my fingers as they are so swollen as well as my lips are swollen too. I assume it must be all the fluid they've put into me. They drop off my breakfast tray, definitely less then appetizing, that was not going anywhere near my mouth. Andrew the wonderful man he is, goes to the cafeteria and got me a slice of w/w toast, yogurt and a banana. Mmmmm food tasted so good especially the toast with orange marmalade.

The psychiatric nurse then came in and asked "What can we do for you?" I just look at her with great confusion as she asks again "What can I do for you?" and I reply "I don't' understand what you are asking." She says "I will have the

Psychologist come in and talk to you." She unhooks my heart rate monitor and soon after another nurse comes in and unhooks my IV. They then brought Andrew and myself into the quiet room to wait for the Psychiatrist. He finally arrives around 10am and begins asking me many questions as to why, how, where etc. And then questions me if I was really at the hospital every day for day therapy sessions. I get really irritated with him and say "You obviously don't believe me, so go check my charts." He then says "Oh no, it's just that none of my patients are at the hospital every day for day therapy." I then say "Well I'm not your damn patient!" It really irritates me that he doesn't believe me. He then asks "What do you want to do, go back to 2SE Psych ward or go home?" I tell him "I'm not in the right mind frame to make that kind of decision." I mean seriously how could you ask someone who has just overdosed on sleeping pills and tried to commit suicide less than 12 hours ago whether or not they want to stay at the hospital or go home? I guess the point he was trying to make was they offer a short term stay inside the unit at CNC – Critical Nursing Care aka the locked up padded rooms. I say to him once again "I can't make that decision." He says "I have to ask because admittance is on a voluntary basis and you will have to sign a release form." He then brings Andrew in and explains things to him and Andrew decides it may be best for me to be in CNC on 2SE. I sign the release form and no sooner after, I'm hugging Andrew and crying on his shoulder as I wouldn't get to see him until visiting hours between 4:00pm-8:00pm.

They whisk me away and I take the back elevator up with my ER Psych nurse and walk back through the doors of 2SE. I haven't been through them since I left on January 13th, 2006.

We head to the nurses station and the ER Psych nurse asks what room, they say 1CNC and through the guarded door I went. I am so frightened as it is a locked compound, there is no roaming other than in your room. I walked into my room which consisted of a bed, blankets, chair, roll-away table tray to eat and 2 pillows. Nothing else but a johnny shirt to wear during my stay.

You are not allowed to wear any of your own clothes inside the CNC unit other than your underwear. My CNC nurse came in and told me to strip down and put my johnny shirt on. Once my johnny shirt was on she had thoroughly examined my jeans, socks, t-shirt and sweatshirt I was told to shake out my underwear. What the f*ck!??! I quickly learnt that this means pulling down your underwear to your ankles and shaking them out. I applaud the person who would hide anything in a little itty bitty pair of G-string panties that barely cover me. You do what you got to do I guess. She asked if I wanted some toast as I would not be receiving a dinner tray. I requested 2 slices of w/w toast with jam and water. I was exhausted by the time I got done. My nurse came back in to get my vitals and brought me in a warm blanket. I crashed hard until I was awoken by Dr. David.

I remained lying in bed, as I felt like I had been run over by a Mac truck. I never once looked Dr. David in the eye during our whole discussion. He asked what happened, what went wrong and I told him that I was tired of feeling the pain. I didn't know what was right or wrong anymore. I was just so confused and I wanted it all to just go away. He asked how this happened and I told him that I got into one of those extreme moods of depression and there was no way out. I didn't know of any other way to cope. He asked how we could prevent this again. I said well I guess I would need coping mechanisms. After a lengthy and emotional chat, Dr. David made another appointment for us tomorrow at 1:00pm.

My nurse Michelle came in and talked about what the short stay unit was about and gave me homework to do. Surprise, surprise, more homework! It was to determine why this occurred and to find the underlying event that caused it. I also had a checklist to fill out on how I was feeling, needless to say it was pretty low. On a scale of 1-10 as they love to use that scale in here, I felt a 2 at best. The nurse left and I didn't want to talk to anyone else…..no such luck!

Jane my social worker came in to see me. We talked about what happened and how I was going to leave relationship group as I didn't feel I had gotten it, however I would like to join again once it comes back. She left and no sooner did Marion my day therapy nurse stop by. We talked about what happened to set me off, as she had just seen me in the morning before my attempt and wondered how this could have happened in such a short period of time.

After she left I laid down to catch some more Zzzz's, but prior to I called the nurse to go use the washroom. I looked in the mirror and I looked awful! Dark circles under my eyes, eyes were puffy, skin was pale and I didn't look good at all! It reminded me of the way I looked after a long 24-48 hours cocaine snorting binge. As soon as the nurse brought me back to my room, I fell asleep.

Andrew came by to visit, not sure what time it is since there is no clock and he brought me 2 bags full of clothes and toiletries. I had to tell him that no clothes were allowed, they didn't tell us that prior to coming up to CNC from the ER that all my toiletries had to be locked up behind the nurse's station. The only thing I was allowed in my room was my journal, puzzle book and one pen. This was definitely going to be a time to reflect on what I did. NO fresh air or looking outside into reality for 72 hours. No windows, nothing! I was the only one on Day 1 in the CNC unit, thank goodness. I didn't want to see anyone walking by my window or even worse someone that I know.

They brought in my supper and I nearly puked. Turkey on a piece of white bread, loaded with gravy, carrots and potatoes, f*cking disgusting, yuck! Soggy white bread, how disgusting! There was no way I was eating that! Andrew went to the cafeteria and got me sushi instead, unfortunately no chopsticks allowed in the unit. It just wasn't the same eating with a plastic fork. Andrew stayed until 8:00pm and I laid on his shoulder while we did Sudoku together. He said that he had only told his Dad about what had happened as he needed someone to talk to while I was being worked on in the ER. He said I gave him quite a scare and he didn't know what to do. The nurses told him as well that the worse wasn't over once they got the charcoal drink into me as I was at high risk for a seizure during the night. I didn't realize this until he told me. He then said "I want to be with you the rest of my life, grow old with you, have children etc. I hope you want that too." I said "I do but that seems so far away and impossible right now. I'm sorry." He said "Don't say sorry, just say you'll never do it again." I began to cry and said "I just want the pain to go away! I'm tired of feeling this way. I've been through enough in my life. I feel I have been punished enough. This was the only way I knew it would stop!" He held me close and said "We are going to get through it." He kissed me goodnight and I began to cry again. He said "You don' like it when I leave?" I said "No, I don't."

My night nurse came in and asked if I was ok and talked to me. She was funny. She kept calling me honey, dear, darlin'. She said she remembered me from when I was in the unit. We talked about how I have to learn to lean on other people such as my friends as that is what they are there for. I just feel I don't want to bother them with my problems as I'm sure they have enough to deal with. She said "No honey. Wouldn't you want your friend to call?" I said "Yes." She said "Why don't you go have a shower, you'll feel better." I said "Ok." So I got up thinking a shower will make me feel better but little did I know that you are you not allowed to have a shower alone. Nope, the door stays open and the nurse stands in front of the door so she can see you to make sure you are not going to do anything to harm yourself. It did make me feel better after I was done, well minus the audience. She then gave me my meds and a warm blanket and almost instantly I crashed hard. It's been a long 24 hours and my body needed to rest. I did wake up a couple of times in the night to the flashlight shining through my door window making sure I was ok. Every hour on the hour usually.

DAY 141 – Thursday May 4, 2006

Woke up to the sound of the breakfast tray hitting the table. I wonder what delicious sludge they have brought me today. Porridge, tea, toast with butter and an egg. So I eat the porridge, egg white and tea. Thank goodness Andrew has brought me some fruit to snack on. Little do I know that my day is to be filled by psychological assessments and a lot of talking back and forth with the psych doctors and nurses.

My day nurse came in to check on me to see how I was doing and I decided to have another 'watch me wash my ass shower' since it made me feel better last night, well minus the eyes on me the whole time. There are no luxuries here, no hairdryers, straighteners, soft plush towels or 'me time' to be found. After my shower, I get working on my homework from Dr. David and my day nurse – coping mechanisms for stressful situations. Surprisingly I gather my thoughts and the writing flows easily. I am pleasantly surprised with the ideas I have come up with.

Halfway through the morning I get a knock on the door and it's Dr. Vianney's intern. I was in in for a treat......as cute as he was, he's an intern from Dalhousie University and it was the longest interrogation I have ever been through. I failed to mention, I have already discussed all my past info with many doctors. Very frustrating and repetitive, all the same I tried to remain calm as I knew he was just doing his job. Finally after 2 hours, yes 2 f*cking hours he was done or should I say I was saved by the lunch tray coming into my room.

Never did I think I would be so happy for shitty hospital food. Here I thought breakfast was bad, lunch was tuna or should I say miracle whip with a side of brown tuna. I did however eat the chicken noodle soup with 2 crackers and an apple.

Ma and Bobby are supposed to come visit me tonight along with my hubby. Andrew has been so supportive, caring and loving. I really don't know how I would have done it without him these past 6 months. He is my angel, my rock and of course my knight in shining armor.

Got a roommate this morning. Well not a roommate, but someone else in a CNC room down the hall. An older lady, schizophrenic I believe. She's cute. This afternoon another women in her mid-30's or so came in. Very obese and was asking to wear her own t-shirt and shorts as the johnny shirts here are not large enough. They insisted she must wear the hospital clothes and that all personal belongings and street clothes were not allowed. She puts on the johnny shirt, comes out of her room and the poor women looked so uncomfortable. The johnny shirt did not go past her waist, and was so tight I don't know how she moved around, my heart broke for her. What a terrible way to feel and be treated. I know they were only doing their job, however if they could not supply the appropriate clothing for her there should have been another alternative. They didn't even allow her to wear her own shorts therefore she just had undies one which you could see since her shirt was so small. Later on during the day once they had inspected her clothes, they gave her the t-shirt and shorts she had brought in to wear.

Yet another appointment this afternoon at 1:00pm with Dr. David. He came in to talk and went over my coping skills homework and was very impressed by them. He also gave me general coping skills as well. He asked "How are you feeling about leaving tomorrow?" I said "I'm a little nervous, but more positive since I have something to look at during stressful situations instead of trying to figure it all out when I'm in a volatile state." Once Dr. David left Jane came in and gave me some info on trust and boundaries, things they would be covering in the relationship group. I told her that I felt it may be best if I left the group for now. I would however like to take it again when it comes up. She thought that whatever decision I made would be fine with her, as she understood my situation. Jane left and Dr. Vianney came in and spoke with me. He told me that he felt I should be put on a stronger dose of Zoloft from 100mg to 150mg. We talked about what led to my suicide attempt and how it was not a pre-meditated event. My mood influenced and directed my decision. This was not something I was thinking of doing on Monday May 1, however on Tuesday May 2, I was triggered to end my life which is worse as erratic moods or behaviors could easily cause this again. My confusion, self-doubt and not knowing what was right or wrong anymore drove me to stop all the rage, depression, doubt, tears and hurt that were going on inside of me. I had a plan and I was going to go through with it. Dr. Vianney talked to me about my mood swings and asked "Has this been a problem in the past?" I said "Yes. I can go from 0-100 in no time at all!" Finally he was gone and soon after Bobby and Andrew showed up.

Supper tonight makes me want to vomit! Roast beef, mashed

potatoes, peas and gravy. NO THANK-YOU! So I give it to Bobby, who was more than happy to eat it since he has to leave soon to go golfing and Andrew being a sweetie goes to the cafeteria and gets me a sandwich. Bobby stays for about 45 minutes and as he begins to leave, he asks Andrew to leave the room so he can have a minute with his daughter. I was shocked and scared. I didn't know what he was going to say. He kneels down by my bed and says "I love you so much. You really don't know how much you mean to me. I love you like my other 2 daughters. And if there is anything that I can do for you, I will. I want you to know that your mother is sometimes hard to understand, however she loves you very much and is very protective of you. I also want you to know you can come to me anytime you need to talk." Of course tears begin to well up in my eyes. I have never had any father/father figure say this to me in my life or be able to look into my eyes while they were sober and truly mean what they were saying. Bobby is definitely the best Dad I have ever had in the past 10 years. He is so open, caring, honest, truthful, loyal and hardworking.

Andrew leaves around 8:00pm as he is going to play tennis with Dave. I of course begin to cry. I miss not having him by my side when I'm here. That is definitely one of the hardest things to deal with while staying at the hospital. I just wrap my arms around him and don't want to let go. I love him so much. I probably would be 6 feet under if it weren't for him. I just want him to stay all night, hold me and tell me that things are going to get better. I am going to get better. I will love myself someday. He unwillingly leaves and says "Bonne nuit mia bella principessa" (Italian for good-night my beautiful princess). I give him a grin, he knows what to say to make me smile even when I am down. The door shuts and I am once again left in the dungeon alone. My night nurse comes in and ask if I plan on going to bed soon as she will bring in my meds. I quickly say "YES!"

Today has been a long exhausting day. I just want to go to sleep and wake up in the morning to go home. The nurse brings in my meds and as I am about to take them I notice something new, a different color pill than I'm used to. I refrain from taking them and ask "What is that?" as I point to the orange horse pill accompanied by 5 others. She says "It's Epival." I say "What is that?" She says "Didn't Dr. Vianney explain that to you?" I say "No, I didn't know I was going to be put on more meds, just an increase in Zoloft from 100mg to 150mg and my usual Ativan." The nurse explains to me that Epival is a mood stabilizer that is often used for Bi-Polar Disorders or Epileptic as it helps to stabilize erratic brain waves. She then says "It will also make you drowsy and he is starting you on 250mg with an increase to 500mg in a week." I accept, I mean anything to help me at this point. Unfortunately I have a hard time getting to sleep once again, so I journal for 20 pages and then do Sudoku as I figure the journaling is stimulating and therefore preventing me from relaxing to get to sleep.

I wake in the night, around 4am to the older lady roaming the halls. Ummm how did she get out of her room? I was never allowed out. Anyhow......she is roaming and yelling she is hungry. The night nurse escorts her back to her room and tells her she will have to wait for breakfast. 1 hour later she comes out again but breakfast has already been served and therefore the staff have taken breakfast tray away. Oh for the love of God, she's going to freak. Note to self, keep my door closed! I felt bad, as when she finally does wake up and says she's hungry, they will tell her she missed breakfast and give her a slice of toast until lunch. Get me out of here before that shit goes down!

For my breakfast I get 1 egg, buttered toast and 2 prunes. I refuse to eat the buttered toast and ask the staff to bring me in unbuttered w/w toast NOT white. I tell them if they want me to eat it has to be whole wheat toast and unbuttered. I know I have to eat in order to get out, and I know it's not very nice of me, but I refuse to eat white buttered toast that probably isn't butter but some chemical shit storm that looks like butter. They finally come back after an hour and bring me white toast to which I say "I'm sorry I can't eat that." So they go out looking for w/w and 1 hour later they say sorry there is none. I am very hungry, irritated, anxious and agitated. I'm more than ready to leave this place…..hopefully for good!

Dr. David comes in to check on me and see how I'm doing and also makes an appointment for Monday. Dr. Vianney comes in and asks how I'm doing and also what other options I have as far as help if I need it and what to do if my mood elevates.

I now try to await discharge patiently but it seems to take forever. Finally Dr. Vianney has signed off and the nurse does the rest. I am free to go and Andrew is here to pick me up. I am so hungry, we decide to go to Zellers restaurant for lunch.

When we get home I am happily greeted by Cosmo. He is so happy to see me. He begins to purr instantly as I pet him. I'm sure he has missed me a lot. I know I sure missed him.

DAY 142-144 Friday May 5 – Sunday May 7, 2006

If I thought I was lost before……..I'm feeling completely hopeless now. I feel like I'm starting all over again and yet I don't even feel like I've started.

DAY 145 – Monday May 8, 2006

Had an appointment with Dr. David today and it was good, but more homework. I don't know if my brain can handle this, I'm overwhelmed as it is. Dr. David discussed his concerns with my erratic emotional behavior and decided that he would like for me to come up with stressful scenarios that may come up in the future and to create coping mechanisms for each one so that way when I get into a state of 'crazy' I can use my cue cards to help me get from A to B instead of A to Z.

DAY 146 – Tuesday May 9, 2006

So I have come up with some coping mechanisms that Dr.

David suggested. Seems quite extreme for every situation but I guess I'm up for anything, especially if it offers help and hope.

COPING SKILLS FOR STRESSFUL SITUATIONS

GENERALLY
- Acceptance of having a bad day.
- Trying too hard which leads to frustration; need a time-out.
- Important to take time-outs before I get to that point.
- Being aware of my emotions or bad days; can become more easily upset, angry etc.
- Be aware that during stressful times (tired, not sleeping well, hungry, etc.) I am more vulnerable to self-abusive behavior.

WITH MY HUSBAND
Automatic time-out for 15 minutes and I must do one of the following things during my time-out:
- Write in journal – thoughts, emotions, resolutions etc.
- Deep breathing techniques.
- Write a thought record.
  - Must stay on the property.
  - Not allowed to drive anywhere.
  - Not allowed to run off on my own unless for a run, but I must return within 15 minutes.
- After 15 minute time-out, I will re-evaluate the situation to see if more time is needed.
- Discuss openly, honestly and rationally the situation and take more time-outs if needed.
- Think back to a time when I was upset and now looking back on it, it was ok.
- Try to gain perspective on the situation; will I feel this way tomorrow with the same intensity.
- Look at the situation in an hour, 6 hours, 1day, 2 days, a week, a month, 6 months a year etc.
- Try and step back outside of what's happening and observe my emotions such as feeling stupid.

- Accept that you're emotional and this is how I'm feeling; not to be judgmental. Find a way to distract myself if the above does not work such as:
  - Cook, find a new recipe, make a baked good for someone, etc.
  - Brush the cat.
  - Do laundry, clean, etc.
  - Take a bath.
  - Do exercises, go for a run etc.
  - Watch TV.
  - Listen to music.

SOCIAL SITUATIONS

Mall or Grocery Store
- Have a list and focus prior to walking in on what you are there to get.
- Try to keep focusing on the items you are picking up or the list and not those around you.

Movies
- Focus prior to going in that everyone is coming for the same reason , the movies.
- Prior to going to the movies decide whether buying items at the concession stand is an option:
  - If **YES**, these options are ok with me:
    - Small popcorn no butter
    - Juice or water
    - Chocolate covered raisins or almonds
    - Licorice
  - If **NO**, bring these options from home so not to deprive myself. (No would be an option on days that I am feeling depressed, agitated, fat, not worked out or done any physical activity)
    - Baked Lays chips
    - Baked tortilla chips and salsa

- Water or juice
- Homemade healthy cookies
- Homemade popcorn
- Cut up veggies and dip
- Cut up fruit and yogurt
- Cheese and crackers

- If **MAYBE**, I may be craving the concession food before I get there however I am not feeling so good about myself that day even after working out. I will however allow myself ONE item from the concession and bring anything else that I want from home.
  - Remind myself that while I am eating my food everyone is either concentrating on the movie or their food and therefore they are not worried about what I am doing or eating.
  - Focus on the seat you are going to be sitting in and not everyone else around you as you feel them staring at you.
  - Never arrive at the movies too early as this will only increase my anxiety.

Restaurant
- Try to sit or request a table on the outside of a restaurant not a table in the middle of everyone.
- Focus on the conversation or the person I am with.
- Remind myself that everyone is here to eat.
- Don't look around to see what others are eating – then judge them based on what they are consuming.
- If anxiety gets high or begins to increase excuse yourself and go to the washroom and do one of the following:
  - Deep breathing.
  - Count back from 100 by 7's.
  - Try to figure out how they prepared a certain dish to re-create at home.
  - Freshen up my face, lipstick etc.

o   Focus on something in the washroom and all its
    possible uses.

Family Gathering or Supper
- Discuss prior to going the length of time you will be gone.
- Have a signal with my husband which means I need to go
  now, I am ok or let's stay a little longer.
- Realize that your friends and family love and support you.
- Discuss only the things you are comfortable with and say
  "I'm not really comfortable talking about that.".
- If at a family gathering allow yourself dessert only if:
    o   You have worked out or done physical activity.
    o   Have not binged or overstuffed yourself at supper.
    o   Are feeling honestly ok with your body.
    o   You are too stuffed and box it up to savor later on.

Playing Volleyball
- Focus on the sport and not on what you look like playing it.
- If a mistake is made, acknowledge it and move on.
- Realize that those playing sports professionally or in the
  Olympics make mistakes too.
- Accept positive feedback.
- Give yourself positive mental feedback when you make a
  great play.

Party with Friends not at our Home
- Never go empty handed.
- Walking in with my husband.
- Look for someone I know.
- If there is nobody I know, stick with Andrew in the
  beginning and make him aware of this.
- Try and meet someone you don't know. Limit conversation
  so you don't feel you have to stay longer than you feel
  comfortable with and use the following to get out:
    o   Well, I should go see where Andrew is…

- I'm going to go and mix another drink...
- I should go talk to hostess...
- I'm going to see (name) and see if he/she will give me the recipe for his/her dish she brought...
- Going to run to the bathroom now...
- Going out for some fresh air...
- Remind myself when meeting someone new that they are probably nervous too.
- Ask questions, people love talking about themselves and what they do.
- Find a common interest.
- Ask different questions, not the standard ones – find out more about them on a deeper level than just 'What do you do for a living?".
- If feeling anxious, find Andrew or go to the washroom and do one of the following:
  - Deep breathing.
  - Count back from 100 by 7's.
  - Freshen up my face, lipstick etc.
  - Focus on something in the washroom and all its possible uses.
  - Call a friend for reassurance on my cell.

DAY 147-186 Wednesday May 10 – Sunday June 18, 2006

The past 5 weeks have been exhausting and frustrating wrapped up with a big f*cking blue bow. I was told to take a slight break from journaling, mainly because with my homework I can sometimes feel pressure to do it all, since I have perfectionistic tendencies and I never want to disappoint anyone in the process.

THIRD QUARTER
OF THE NAKED TRUTH

warr;or

MUST HAVES

Mint Chocolate Chip Ice-Cream.
Lots Of Coffee.
Hugs.

DAY 187 – Monday June 19, 2006
Morning 133.5lbs

Woke up feeling very tired this morning. I did take time to get ready and I felt good about myself. My hair seemed to go just right, I felt tall but still self-conscious. Maybe the heels were not my best choice as I feel they made me look even taller which brings more attention to myself, which is not good!

Assertiveness class went well, time seemed to fly by. My anxiety was ok but I'm still having somewhat of a problem concentrating making me have to read over sentences and paragraphs over and over again.

Went to visit Tracy and the kids, had a great conversation with Tracy as usual. Talked to her about my options for the future and going back to school. We decided that I would come over on Wednesday night to have supper together, as Chris and Andrew will be away for work.

I then went to the gym and went on the treadmill for 20 minutes and went 2km just as my warmup as today was supposed to be my rest day. I then went and did 3 circuits in the weight room and also an ab routine. I felt very strong, motivated, energized and empowered afterwards.

I finished all my homework/research for tomorrow I am so proud of myself. The homework from Jane took so long. I began to cry as it was a reflection of my past, which unfortunately is not pretty.

FOOD JOURNAL for today

BREAKFAST – ½ cup oatmeal, 1 banana, 8 almonds, ¾ soy milk & ½ tsp honey

SNACK – yogurt

LUNCH – w/w pita, 2 tablespoons soy nut butter, 2 celery stalks, 5 baby carrots, 1 yogurt & 1 apple

SNACK – banana & 1oz cheese

SUPPER – haddock kebab with red & green peppers, 5 sweet potato slices, ½ cup broccoli & 1 glass red wine

SNACK – 15 chocolate macaroons & 4 Willow Crisp chocolates, 3 cups air popped popcorn with butter & 20 baked blue organic tortillas with light cheddar cheese, fat free sour cream & salsa

DAY 188 – Tuesday June 20, 2006
Morning 134lbs

Woke up surprisingly with excess energy and anxiety. I have an appointment with Dr. David at 10:00am, Nancy at 11:00am and Jane at 1:00pm.

My meeting with Dr. David went well, however my energy and anxiety level were very high, it was truly unbelievable! I was rocking back and forth in the chair, Dr. David made a comment at one point that I was going to start spinning or have lift off! We figured out that it was probably due to my decision on schooling, Andrew going away for work and a multitude of things I'm sure. My homework was to keep writing in my journal, try to get to bed before 11:00pm, wake-up before 9:00am and discuss my plans with Andrew regarding schooling and how this will affect our family plans. With so much energy built up I knew I would have to go for a run at lunch after my appointment with Nancy and Suzanne. Suzanne will be taking over for Nancy when she goes on maternity leave. She is really nice and I got to meet her for the first time during assertiveness class as she sits in with Jane and Marion.

My meeting with the OT's (Occupational Therapists) Nancy and Suzanne was emotional. I guess I have been pondering my life choices for a while and have been feeling inadequate for even longer for not accomplishing some things in my life. I told them that I planned to go back to university. Saint Thomas University probably in January to take my Arts degree with a major in Psychology, then go on to do my Education degree. I told them that I didn't feel I was ready for opening my own business as the risk factor was just too high to take at this point in my life. We talked about all my options as far as funding. I still felt overwhelmed, anxious and full of excess energy.

Since I got done my meeting early I decided to go to University of New Brunswick for my run outside. I saw Chris on the train bridge with his running club. It was really hot out so by the time I was done I was super red in the face and drenched, but it felt so good to get my fat ass out there on the trails.

FOOD JOURNAL for today
BREAKFAST – ½ cup oatmeal, 2 tablespoons cranberries, 8 almonds & ½ cup soy milk

SNACK – banana

LUNCH – 10 cherries, yogurt, 5 sweet potato wedges & 1 haddock skewer

SUPPER – baked beans & 1 slice brown bread

DAY 189 – Wednesday June 21, 2006
Morning 133lbs

Woke up feeling a little down, absolutely no energy, very tired and super depressed. Andrew is getting ready to leave for Miramichi today. I woke up at 9:30am had breakfast and when Andrew left I went back to bed at 11:00am. The past weekend I ran out of my prescription for Epical and hadn't taken it for 3 days and now that I'm back taking it I'm absolutely exhausted. I only woke back up at 2:15pm. So much for going to TAG today.

I don't feel like going to Tracy's for supper, making supper or going to the gym. I feel so blah, so exhausted. I just want to keep to myself and cry. It is disappointing to be feeling this way, as I thought I was doing so well. I am now questioning as to whether or not I was doing good or just hiding it, keeping it to myself, being busy all the time which I know I have been guilty of doing especially in the past. I just want to call Tracy and cancel, but I feel so guilty to do so as I'm sure she would appreciate the help at suppertime and I may feel better when I see the kids.

So I decide to order out for pizza and make my traditional Greek salad to bring over. Well, ordering a pizza from

Superstore was not a good idea for today! I pull out my coping mechanisms key chain that I made and look over what to do when walking into a grocery store, mall etc. 'Focus on what you are here to get not others around you.' Ok, I need to get the pizza, olives and strawberries. So I go in, get the olives and strawberries for *Stewart* and walk over to the pizza counter. Unfortunately the pizza is not ready and it's going to be 10 minutes. Well I SHOULD have said "No problem" and waited out in the car. I'm stating a 'should' statement here because I didn't think of this option at the time but instead I stayed where I was trying to focus on all the foods or items in the seafood section. I did not want to walk around for fear I would run into someone I know and have to talk to them.

I began to get disgusted as there were so many obese people waiting in line at the 'Foods to Go' or should I say 'Fat to Go' food counter. I just don't understand how people can keep doing that to their bodies. Coleslaw, potato salad, fried chicken, macaroni salad, taters – all full of hydrogenated fats! Now I'm obviously assuming that these people were:

1. Going to eat these foods themselves
2. Eat this food quite often
3. Don't care about their body image or health

I catch myself doing this quite often now, looking in people's shopping carts and judging them based on what is in there. I know this is not right and I don't feel good doing it, however it has become an obsession since I myself am so obsessed with food and of course my own food choices and of course my own dysmorphic body issues......so Dr. David says.

I was somewhat glad I went to Tracy's as it was some comic relief for me to watch the kids interact, play and have a bath. I got to snuggle and read to the kids. When I left Tracy's I felt like driving around, not sure why, but I just felt so down. Thoughts of suicide rolled around in my head, however since my last attempts, I feel the bond between Andrew and I has become so much better and I now feel it would be so selfish of me to do so. Sometimes I guess that's a good thing but other times it's frustrating when you just don't want to be around anymore or deal with all the struggles and stigmas around you.

Andrew called for the second time tonight and I had been in bed crying and began to cry even more once I heard his voice. When I hung up the phone with him I began to let it all out, but I couldn't figure out why, there just didn't seem to be a specific reason why. Depression has a funny way of creeping up I guess. As I was crying Cosmo came up from the bottom of the bed and laid on my chest, as soon as I began to pet him, he began to purr. It was an instant relief to know that he was by my side and there to remain for comfort the rest of the night.

FOOD JOURNAL for today
BREAKFAST – ½ cup oatmeal, 2 tablespoons cranberries, 8 almonds & ½ cup soy milk
LUNCH – 1 cup baked beans & 1 slice brown bread
SUPPER – 1 slice pizza & homemade traditional Greek salad homemade dressing
SNACK – slice of pizza & slice brown bread with cheese

DAY 190 – Thursday June 22, 2006

My journal writing seems to not be working the way I had planned out. On the other hand, if I think of it in a more positive light, I am here today journaling and so what if I have missed a few days in between.

Got up at 7:30am and went for a run since we are leaving to go camping in Mactaquac Park today. During our drive I began to relive a lot of bad memories. We took the North side way to Mactaquac and that was the last road that *Mitch* and I took on our final 48 hour cocaine binge. I wonder when those flashbacks will ever go away. Those memories do not bring back happiness, only shame, stupidity and being stoned are the three words that definitely come to mind. I know I have to forget the past, however it's hard when there isn't a day that goes by that something doesn't trigger a memory to the stupid shit we pulled. Driving at night in the pouring rain on the back roads while hitting many raccoons and porcupines along the way. Driving to Marysville, Miramichi, Moncton and Bathurst. Now that I think of it, we drove anywhere and everywhere in New Brunswick!

I was looking through the pamphlets they gave us when we arrived at the park and I found out they have hiking trails. I should have assumed, since it is a park. They range from 0.3km – 2.4km. I'll have to inquire at the front gate desk if that is one way or return. I brought my running stuff and I'm going to try my hardest to run every day. My stomach just keeps getting fatter and fatter along with my hips and butt. I'm having a love hate relationship with Epival. I love the effects that it keeps my mood under control, however hate the fact that it has made me put on about 10lbs. I know it was the Epival because I was working out like crazy and within about 7 days I had gained the weight. I feel so disgusting! Every time I look down at my belly I pull at the fat and loose skin in a great big bunch and think 'why can't I just cut all this shit off', liposuction would be so awesome right now! I do so many sit ups and run a lot so I know there is muscle somewhere, but that great big layer of fat on top prevents me from seeing anything good.

FOOD JOURNAL for today
BREAKFAST – honey w/w bagel with light strawberry cream cheese & green tea
LUNCH - sundried tomato pesto salad with veggies & cheese & 10 cherries

DAY 191 Friday June 23, 2006 - 207 Sunday July 9, 2006

The crazy in my head won't go away and the crazier the thoughts get the numbness increases too. I have begun to cut with my razor blade because it's the only thing that allows me to feel but that too feels incomplete.

I'm using my Venus razor to cut my wrists back and forth and yet as many marks as I have and as many times that I go over and over the feeling remains the same, no pain. How can that possibly be? I do get a euphoric high just like I did when I purged every time I see blood pouring out from my veins though. I'm not sure what will be the next thing to try when cutting no longer works.

DAY 208 – Monday July 10, 2006

Is it my day to go? Woke up this morning feeling upset, depressed and lonely. Dropped my husband off at the airport for work at 9:00am and had thoughts of ending my life. I don't remember the last time I woke up thinking suicide. Oh wait, that was just 8 weeks ago! Was this going to be the start of a good or bad day?

I begin tidying up the house wondering if this can possibly distract my mind, nope it doesn't. I then question whether I should distract or dig deep into my emotions and try to figure out where all this is coming from. I did neither, as my mind and body were both exhausted. At 12:00pm I cancelled my appointment with Dr. David and began to cry. My suicidal thoughts had come on stronger and I didn't even want to have a shower let alone leave the house. I told Dr. David's receptionist that I would see Dr. David on Friday and reschedule as I did not want him calling. So much for that, he obviously sensed something was up, I began to cry and told him that I should not be home alone.

Although I did not want to come into the hospital it was probably my best option for me right now. As soon as I sat down in the rocking chair in Dr. David's office, I began to cry. Prior to coming in, I had tried on so many pairs of pants, shorts, capris etc., you name it and I tried it on. Nothing fits the way it used to, which makes me cry even more. I'm so fat. I've gained so much weight, damn Epival! I'm sure I have not been eating that good, small enough portions or exercising to the intensity I could be doing, but why me?

Dr. David and I try to come up with solutions as I will be on my own after this appointment. I tell him all I want to do is binge on McDonalds and just keep driving in my car far far away. I want to be alone on an island with nobody around me but the animals, that way there will be no judgments, no diets, no self-harm, no criticism. Just me and the nature that surrounds me. I have this in my head and I know at this point nobody is going to stop me. Dr. David on the other hand suggests that I will feel worse afterwards if I do so. At this point I am ready to take those chances. As far as suicide, what am I to try this time? Obviously a stronger pill as the bottle of sleeping pills did not work the last time. What could possibly be stronger than extra-strength sleeping pills that I can get my hands on?

Dr. David asks me "Do you feel ok? Do you feel safe to leave and be by yourself?" I quickly answer "Yes!" as I just want to get the hell out of there! I leave and walk out to my car, red eyed from crying and have my initial plan in place. I drive to McDonalds and get 2 cheeseburgers, 1 large fry, 1 apple pie and a bottle of water. I eat one cheeseburger before I even hit the first set of lights on Prospect Street. I then drive to the Mactaquac dam and park in the parking area overlooking the dam.

As I sit in my car I start eating my fries. Suddenly I ask the question, "If my family and friends were like my fries would I savor, enjoy and not take any one of them for granted?" The analogy I know is odd yet it cause me to think. There are a lot of fries in a box. Do I have that many friends and family that I truly care about? Each one is different, small, big, tall, short, soft, and hard – just like their emotions. Some more greasy and worse for you than others. Is ketchup the disguise that surrounds the fry like the makeup we put on our faces, the walls we build around us, the fad diets we succumb ourselves to, the exercising we don't necessarily enjoy doing? What are we or those that surround us really like in our natural state? Are we all truly boring and abnormal in comparison to the freshly picked potato from the garden prior to it being peeled like the naked untouched body? Potatoes being cut up into smaller pieces like the fad diets and exercise regimes we put ourselves through to get smaller.

Who instilled into us what we should and shouldn't be? Who makes our minds think like the devil when we have negative thoughts about ourselves? Is it us? Society? Our friends? Past relationships? Family? Peer pressure? Media? The rich and famous? Unfortunately I believe it is all of these things and that is why those negative thoughts and views we have about ourselves are so hard to release. Some of these people you may personally get an apology from for things that were said or done. With others, there is no possible way to receive the apologies you deserve for some of the horrors you see; trash magazines, TV infomercials ads you hear on the radio etc. When society begins to base their judgment upon us by how tall, skinny and beautiful we are, we automatically fail. When did our physical attributes become better than our mental or emotional ones? What is sexy anymore? Is there any one person who can answer these questions? Well I thought I used to know but now I don't know what to believe!

The distortional views I have on my body as well as the

societal critics don't allow me to accept myself at 5'10" tall and 140lbs. That is so f*cking 'fat' to me! I have a spare tire around my hips, cellulite on my ass and thighs, stretch marks on my breasts, thighs and hips and I can make myself jiggle in places I had no idea could jiggle when I stand up. I hardly think that is 'beautiful' yet my husband calls me beautiful all the time and honestly who do I believe at this point?

I eat my fries, cheeseburger and then ½ of my apple pie. The other ½ I share with a seagull as I felt bad for the little bugger. I downed the entire bottle of water and then purged in the parking area, Aaaaaah relief and the biggest f*cking high ever, that never gets old! The feeling when the food is all done is always complete sadness. If McDonalds were closer I would go get the same thing and do it all over again but its 30 minutes away.

Journaling has really help distract my mind from my suicidal thoughts. As I was eating I was writing at the same time. Journaling over the past 208 days has helped me get my emotions on paper and also distract my mind from crazy f*cking thoughts. I have to admit it does work, even though sometimes I hate starting that first word on paper, I feel so lost. Right now I don't feel any better about myself other than feeling super fat after eating McDonalds even though I purged. Andrew will be calling soon so I need to get home so he doesn't wonder what's going on and figure out something happened. I don't want him asking questions or being disappointed in me, that's not what I need right now. One more purge before I hit the road as I won't have a chance when I get home.

What a day this has been I guess it wasn't my time to go. If I had not gone to my appointment with Dr. David, who knows what would have happened. The more extreme mood swings I have the more I begin to wonder if I am bi-polar?!?

DAY 209 - 262 – Tuesday July 11, 2006 – Saturday September 2, 2006

I'm taking another break from journaling. I wish I didn't go to the extreme with everything. I go all in and then exhaust myself. During these times I don't need sleep, I don't eat, and I fixate on very specific things which usually are not good; drugs, binging, purging, spending money etc. I just wish I would have broken my leg, as that seems like it would have been a much easier rehab to overcome.

DAY 263 – Sunday September 3, 2006

I need food and I need it now! How am I possibly going to get away on my own to do just that! I just feel like driving around in my car all day long and stuffing my face full of crap and stopping on the side of the road to puke and start all over again! Come on Sam you are somewhat smart, you can come up with a plan to do just that! Ok, I'm off to get groceries, then go to my Ma's and then stop by Monika's? But wait, what if Andrew calls them and figures me out? F*ck, why does this have to be so difficult! Think Sam, think!

Ok, going to the grocery store and then shopping. He may catch on as I hate shopping for clothes but we'll go with that.

He buys it and I get in the car, feeling a sense of relief because I know that this craving will soon be filled. My first stop, the Irving on Lincoln Road for Joe Louis' and Vachon cakes to get in my belly! I have to make sure that I put my binge in order, always start and end with something sweet and remember to drink lots of water and juice along the way too. There is nothing worse than choking on your puke because it is too thick to make it back up into your mouth and ends up hovering in the back of your throat.

After the Irving, next stop is Burger King for a whopper, fries and onion rings. Mmmmmm I love those little onion rings especially with ketchup. I'm on the most euphoric high and it's only going to get better! I drive to Morell Park, stop and park the car to the side and puke out my door. There's only a few cars here and to be honest it only gets my heart racing even faster when others are around, which makes me want to do it even more!

Hearing someone else binge is the ultimate! When I went to esthetic school in 1997 one of my roommates was bulimic and I would tiptoe outside the bathroom door to listen to her. The best f*cking high ever that didn't cost a cent!

The one thing I do hate about binging is the stopping for food. I swear the people who ring me through the cash know what I'm doing. I get so paranoid that they are going to call someone and tell on me. Next stop Dairy Queen for a huge ass blizzard just when I thought it couldn't get any better. The sweetness of ice cream, Oreos and peanut butter make my mouth drool and help to cool down my burning throat from all the acid. Oh the possibilities of where to go to next.

I decide to take a drive out to Mactaquac but of course I need snacks for the road so I stop into the Tim Hortons drive through for a bagel with double cream cheese, a half dozen donuts and the gas station next door for a large bag of chips, onion dip and a gallon of water. This is simply the best day ever!!!

DAY 264 – Monday September 4, 2006

Went to Victory and decided to make a stew on this rainy day, seems like such a comforting choice for today. Got home, got it started and it feels great to cook again. What a relaxing feeling to cook. I was going to bake some cookies but I think I'll wait until Wednesday when I go into the SPCA to volunteer and bring some to the staff and other volunteers.

I have to get back to exercising and honestly I think running and the Power90 tapes are the only thing that is going to work. Now I am on new birth control which has made me gain more weight. F*ck this is so frustrating, first Epival and now birth control!

DAY 265 – Tuesday September 5, 2006

Dr. David feels that it is important for me to start looking into my past traumas that really shaped me into who I am today which oftentimes makes me think and react the way I do. This is really tough for me. In my heart I know that I have not dealt with most of what happened and it's scary to have to bring up the past especially because it was not a happy time for me. I have suppressed for so many years every thought that came into my mind when it had to do with these situations because they are painful and they do bring me to my knees in tears.

So, I have decided to call these flashbacks '**THE NAKED PAST**' and write about them truthfully whenever they come into my head. My heart is racing, my palms are sweaty and I feel like I'm going to be sick at just the thought about being open about my feelings and how these situations made me feel. I am also worried about hurting anyone that is involved in these situations. That is something I never want to do, but then I have to remember they have hurt me, even it wasn't intentional. I have to remember that feelings are not right or wrong, they are just that, feelings.

THE NAKED PAST – Alcoholic Step-Father

Ok, I can do this. It is not easy to talk about the situations that arose when I was young. That is not to say that I didn't have any positive memories with my step-Dad but it was far from rainbows and unicorns.

My Step-Father *Don* was an alcoholic and a terrible one at that. Gosh, this is so tough! I think when I was young and naïve I just thought 'this is the norm' of most families and it's me who has the issue of being pissed off. But as I got older, I felt like I gained more sympathy in the sense that I realized there was more going on in his head than just alcoholism, such as depression, anxiety etc. Alcoholism is usually a bi-product of many other things. But nonetheless, it's my past and I've told Dr. David I will do my best because it's really important to be honest with myself.

I didn't know much about what 'payday' meant exactly, but I knew it was every 2 weeks when I was only 6 years old because it meant that *Don* was going to be gone for 2-3 days on a bender. His hangout was the Chris Rock in Moncton. Where he went the hours when it was closed, I have no idea. One thing I do know is that he was not home. He never came home at a 'normal' time after his bender either, it was always in the wee hours of the morning when I had to wake up and go to school. He would come in stumbling and shouting and I remember being so fearful of what he would do next. I always slept with my Ma on those nights that he was gone because I was scared to sleep by myself even with my dog Heidi by my side. My heart would begin to race and my stomach felt so sick when I heard him coming up the stairs to the bedroom. I knew he was going to try and climb in bed like nothing was wrong and he'd have the most putrid breathe I'd ever smelt. Then the yelling would begin. My Ma was upset because he would begin pushing me to get out of bed and she would scream for him to get the hell out of the bedroom while he would yell back that he just wants to go to sleep. This would go back and forth until it escalated to me leaving the bedroom yelling too. There were so many nights were I would lie awake as he vomited in the bathroom and then found him on the floor the next morning. I wanted him to change so bad! The times he was a normal step-Dad he was amazing, but I was just a kid and I knew no matter how hard I tried he was not going to stop.

It saddened me so much because not only was he completely drunk when he arrived but it also meant that the bank account was empty too. My Ma was left to figure it out almost every 2 weeks and I knew she was beyond frustrated with it all. Her way of venting was to slam cupboard doors to which *Don* would say "What's wrong?" which would only piss her off even more. I remember so many nights that I was home alone with him and he had been drinking but I was so young, around 6 when it started that he would run out of beer and would put me in the Sherriff's car and we would head out to town speeding to get more. Why I thought that was ok I'm not sure, but I do know that when my Ma found out, it was the beginning of WWIII and yet he continued to do it many more times.

There were many nights where Ma and I would leave him at the house to either drink with his buddies or on his own. We would escape the house and take the car and sleep at motels to get away. One time I can remember we were at my grandfather's house and he began to drink and my Ma did not have her driver's license at that time so we hitchhiked in the middle of nowhere, about 45 minutes from home. We always felt stranded, never knowing when the bottle would rule over everything else in his life.

There was this one night that I believe was the final straw for my Ma and I. He had come home in his usual state after 3 days and I had had enough. I was a bit older, around 13 at the time and it was a Friday night. I remember this because I had a volleyball tournament the next day. He came home and I was so mad that he would wake us up once again cursing swearing, so I stormed out of the bedroom and say "Stop saying f*ck!" He ran after me and said "What the fuck did you just say to me?" My Ma quickly hurried behind him because this was escalating too quickly, faster than usual. I said to him "You keep swearing and I don't like it. Just go to bed, I have to get up early in the morning!" He left the kitchen and went to the coat closet and grabbed his rifle. I remember feeling so scared and helpless. I ran out the door to the shed which was a heated dog house for our 2 Rottweilers and I was going to lock myself in and sleep the night with them. Instead he ran after me and said "I'm going to kill your f*cking dog and give you a reason to be upset!" I opened the shed door and grabbed Geisla and hugged her. I knew he would not shoot her if I was on top of her. He looked at me and said "Don't even think about going to that volleyball tournament tomorrow!"

After a few more incidents my Ma divorced my step-Dad and I continued to visit a while after he had gotten help. He had a new place and it was good to see him being the loving man that I knew.

My last conversation with him happened when I came home for the weekend to be with him and there was a new family living with him. 2 new kids living in my room. They had taken over my room, my things were gone. He said "You are always welcome but I had to make room." That was it, I was done. I was done trying and I was certainly done loving a man that had put other people and the bottle before his own daughter.

I feel that a lot of my trust issues truly began with him. He had been unfaithful to my Mother many times and I'm glad she told me about that. It just solidified the jerk he truly was at the time. I know that people do stupid things when they are drunk and although at the time I did not understand or appreciate his illness it will never excuse the way he threw me out like trash from my bedroom and the way he continually treated my Ma.

DAY 266 – Wednesday September 8, 2006
THE NAKED PAST – Being Touched

Dr. David and I have talked about this one a few times and I just can't seem to relive it completely. We are not sure if it is so traumatizing that I have completely blocked it out or if that is where the story ends. I truly feel however that I have blocked it out because I have never spoken to anyone about this, EVER! I was a child, about 5 or 6 years years old. I didn't realize it was 'wrong' per say. I knew it felt wrong, but I had never really been talked about it specifically when I was a child about people touching me when they shouldn't or without my permission. I now realize this is so important when I have kids.

From the age of 4 I used to go and visit with my Aunt *Katrina* and Uncle *Bob* quite a bit on the weekends as my Ma worked shift work at a jail as a prison guard. I can remember my Uncle having me in the bedroom alone and for some reason my cousins were not in there and the door was shut. He used to call it 'play time' and I can remember him wrestling with me on the bed with my clothes on and touching my vagina through my clothes. I felt so bad because it felt comforting in one way yet wrong in another. So instead of telling anyone, I became embarrassed that I would feel this way. This specific memory is the one that I remember over and over again. One day I can remember him asking me to open the top drawer of the dresser where I found my Aunts panties and bras. I remember feeling awkward and I was not sure why he asked me to do this. He said pick out something and at that moment as I held a pair of panties in my hand my Aunt opened the door. The 'play time' stopped and it never happened again when I went to visit.

I don't remember feeling sad about it stopping and nobody talked to me about what happened, but looking back I do know it was wrong. It was so f*cking wrong and I can't believe that until today I have never talked about it other than a couple times to Dr. David. I can't believe that I as a child had to live with this all my life alone. I was made to believe that it was all a lie and that it never happened. To this day I can't even look at a picture of my Uncle or hear others talk about how he is doing or just how great he is because my racing heart and upset stomach tell me the truth every damn time.

DAY 267 – Thursday September 7, 2006

Went for a run this morning for 35 minutes, pretty proud of myself even if I was sucking wind the entire time.

Anxiety and stress group today went well, however by the time stress group came, I had honestly had enough. I really don't want to be taking 2 classes at once but I may not get a chance to take then again. After all, it will only be for another couple weeks with both.

So, tomorrow is 'D' day. I can't believe the time has passed by so quickly. It seems like yesterday was April and I was doing vocational work with Nancy, my OT.

Tomorrow will be September 8th, the first day of my university classes and also my future. I have so many feelings I'm not sure where to begin. I'm scared for a new challenge, scared what others will think of me, intimidated by pretty girls, intimidated by the work that will be asked of me, excited for a new challenge, excited to use my creativity, fearful that I will not succeed, curious to meet new people and afraid that this course will be too hard for me and I will fail.

So many overwhelming feelings and emotion. My heart has been racing all day. I've had hot flashes and felt heavy chested most of the day and they haven't stopped until now as I am in bed crying. My emotions are depressed and sad that Andrew's not here and that we will not be having children until later. I want to believe in the following: I am determined. I am beautiful. I am strong. I am smart. I am organized. I am a leader. I am a student. I will excel. I will persevere. I will make new friends. I will work hard. I will not procrastinate. I will not be let down. I will not let myself down. I will not give up. I will ask for help. I will ask questions in class. I will be proud of me. I will apply school like a 9-5 job. I will take time for me every day.

FOOD JOURNAL for today
BREAKFAST – ½ cup oatmeal, ½ cup blueberries, 8 almonds
& skim milk
LUNCH – wrap with tomatoes, roast beef, lettuce skim milk
mozzarella & mustard, 8 cucumber slices & yogurt
SNACK – apple
SUPPER – homemade taco salad with homemade veggie chili,
baked blue corn tortillas & skim milk mozzarella cheese
SNACK – 2 chocolate chip almond cookies & yogurt with
granola

DAY 268 – Friday September 8, 2006

My 1st day of my future at Saint Thomas University! The
alarm goes off and before I can open my eyes, panic and
excitement run through my body like a 1000 volts of
electricity. I can't believe that this day is here, the summer has
gone by so quickly. I hit snooze a couple of times hoping that
this day will go away and quickly fast forward to 2 months
from now when I'm into the full swing of things. As my
hospital session indicated yesterday, some stress is good and
this is a good stress, so nothing to be worried about……right?

I get up and quickly head out for a walk to ease my anxiety.
Listening to music, deep breathing, positive affirmations and
focusing my energy on each and every footstep to help do just
that. I drop off cookies to Erin that I made last night. Still no
signs of a new little baby, maybe these will help.

After my walk I jump in the shower and try not to count
down the hours, the minutes, and the seconds before I must

leave. I'm not sure how food will settle today so I decide to make a protein shake. As I begin to get ready and put my makeup on, I wonder what others will look like. What will they be wearing? How old will they be? How many people will be in my class? Will I be able to find my classroom?

What in the hell have I gotten myself into?!? Andrew called me this morning to tell me how proud he was of me which felt really good, and I didn't cry. Sheri and Tracy also called me to wish me good luck. Andrew's family is so sweet and caring, they don't miss anyone's anything. I am very lucky to have found Andrew and to have his family in my life. I decided to wear jeans, my new green top, black belt and my pointy toed shoes with my beige biker jacket. Ma and I are having lunch after my first class.

Well, I'm off! Honestly I don't think I should be driving, my mind is in the clouds and all I can think of are the 'what if's'. I drive on campus and now today has become a reality! The next dilemma, where to park? I decide instead of parking behind the Woo center I will park where Andrew and I had gotten married, a lot closer near the STU Chapel. I open the backseat door, gather my things and take a deep breathe. Wow, this is really happening!

I begin to walk to the Edmund Casey building and fear sets in, so many young kids, so many pretty girls, uh! As I approach the building, a sigh of relief exhales from my breath. Ok, you have made it this far, you have found the building no problem. I decide to sit outside on the ledge and begin to write in my journal as I know this will be the only thing that will take me to another place where my worries will be minimized and my thoughts will be on me and not what others are thinking or doing. I ask the guy sitting next to me "What time is it?" He says "11:20am" so I figure I had better go find my classroom.

I walk in the building and am panicked by where to go, North or South wing. I pick south as I have to use the ladies room and that is to the South. No luck, I didn't find the washroom. I do however notice that the numbers on the classrooms are in O11's, O12, 014 etc. So I must have to go up a few floors. I go up 3 floors and begin walking down the hall, hallelujah I have found it, Room O320 in the Edmund Casey building. Not so bad after all. I place my bag on a chair the one closest to the door and go find a washroom.

When I return the class has almost filled up. A VERY small classroom with 3 large tables all put together with chairs around, boardroom style, very cozy yet very uncomfortable, however it does remind me of the day therapy room which is comforting. As we sit there I am writing in my journal as I can't stand the silence or the fear on everyone's faces, and journaling calms me. I decide that I am going to have to say something, as the room is freaking me out! But just as I'm about to say "Ok I don't know about everyone else, however this room is way too quiet, what is everyone's name and where are you from? Let's start with the one and only lucky guy in the class!"

The professor walks in. He is pretty good looking, however I honestly don't know of too many black men that aren't attractive other than one that I dated, he was an asshole. He gives us our syllabus and it is VERY VERY detailed and organized, my type of guy! We go around the room saying our name and what year you are in. Most of us are in our first year and a couple in their 2nd and 3rd year as some are transfer students from UNB. I am quickly startled as the sounds of French that comes out of the students mouths is definitely the pronunciation and articulation of core French level. I begin to wonder if I am too advanced for this class, however I quickly realize this might be an easy 'A' and for my first class I'll take that and be proud. The professor seems pretty strict with respect to attendance and participation in class which is great! There are 15 students in my class including me. 1 male and 14 females and I am the oldest.

The classroom is very small and definitely too cramped for all of us. It's funny, at Dalhousie University where I went in 1995-1997, my smallest class was German with about 75 people at the beginning and then of course dwindled down to about 40 in the end. I thought that class was super small, this is awesome, and I love it! We are required to purchase our book which is $118 at the bookstore, absolutely ridiculous as well as a French English dictionary and Bescherelle. The professor asks how many years we have been studying French it ranged from 2-10 therefore I have been studying the longest.

Dr. Mbarga decides to end his class at noon and says that he will see us on Monday. I am excited for Monday's class, but less enthused to walk through the campus. I hope that anxiety will subside soon, I'm sure it will. I am really looking forward to learning French once again. As I look through the syllabus, I notice a lot of information that will be instructed that I already know but probably have forgotten over the years so this will be a great refresher for me.

I am happy that the anticipation for today is over. I am happy to be going back to university. I am happy that I have worked so hard these past few months to make myself better and to able to have this option. I am happy most of all for my husband and family who support me and will love me unconditionally no matter what the outcome may be.

DAY 269 – Saturday September 9, 2006
THE NAKED PAST – Last Name F*ck-Ups

You know when this came to mind today about my past, I didn't think too much about it but then I realized that I am embarrassed by it all. I truly think I have the most amount of last names even before I got married, 5 of them to be exact! Multiply that by 3 and I think it would be the number of times I moved before I was 20!
It was so hard growing up, because it seemed like every time a new school year rolled around when I was younger my last name would change and the amount of questions you would get from your friends let alone the confusion on the teachers faces was enough to run home crying.

When I was born I was a Belliveau which is my biological father's last name. That last for about 2 years I believe until my Ma decided that she was going to have custody of me full-time and had it changed back to her maiden name of Dinan.

About 3 years later, she met *Don* and when I was 9 years old they married and her last name became Shaffer. After the marriage, *Don* came to me and asked if I wanted to legally become his step-daughter. At that time I had no clue what that meant and to be honest I didn't care. He said that if I wanted to have the same last name as my Ma he would have to adopt me legally through the courts. Still not knowing what all that meant or who it would effect, I said yes. Thinking about this now, it must have broken my biological fathers heart! I was just a kid, I had no idea that it would mean that I would no longer carry the Belliveau or Dinan name. To this day I feel guilty for saying yes, because at that time my Dad was still in my life. He called, he visited, I visited him, I was very close with my Mémère & Pépère as well as my aunts and uncles. In saying yes, my last name then became Shaffer. I would make myself feel better by telling people I was of German decent. I was nowhere near German decent, I was Acadian & Native.

After my Ma and step-Dad divorced I went back to Dinan as that was my Ma's maiden name.
Fast forward to the year 2000 and my Ma remarried again to an amazing man named Bob. Since she changed her name to Scott, I decided to go back to Shaffer because I didn't feel linked in any way. I was lost. I was confused.

In 2005 I married Andrew and became a Sutherland. I vowed that when I got married and if anything ever happened I would never allow the Shaffer name to be a part of me anymore.

I guess all this to say that I have never felt part of any family name. If I would have had a choice, I would have remained a Belliveau until the day I got married. It's amazing how getting these situations on paper is making me feel better. If I'm feeling it, I write it.

DAY 270 – Sunday September 10, 2006
THE NAKED PAST – Daddy

Daddy, the one man in my life that caused pain but I love so much. I pushed him away, he pushed me away, I pushed him away and it went back and forth from a young age. Up until the time I was about 12 or 13 we spent many weekends together. My Dad was a truck driver and I thought that was coolest. He would take me on day trips with him to Saint John when he worked for McKay's Dairy and Coca-Cola.

Being with him was amazing. I loved that he was my Dad. To me, he was handsome and funny. He even had a tattoo of my name put on his arm with a heart. I knew that even though we didn't live together all the time he loved me.

Up until I was about 2 years old I lived with him full-time with my Mémère & Pépère. Then around the age of 3 I can remember moving in with my Ma and we lived in a one bedroom apartment right beside the KFC off St. George Boulevard.

I used to see my Dad on the weekends and in the Summer and spent a lot of time with him until one weekend I came to visit and I can remember not seeing him. I was confused. I thought I had done something wrong. My grandparents re-assured me that it was not me and that my Dad just needed some time in the basement to himself. I was so sad, I just wanted to go downstairs and give my Dad a hug and kiss like I always did. Why didn't he want to be with me? Later I found out, my Dad was an alcoholic and the reason he was in the basement was because when he tried to quit, he began suffering with depression. My Dad never drank in front of me and if he did it may be one beer but that would be it. I would never see my Dad intoxicated like my step-Dad so it just never made sense to me. The whole time I just wanted to be Daddy's little girl and I could feel him pushing me away, but why? As a little girl, I was told never to ask questions and things were always so hush hush around me and the situations I was in. Because of this, I truly believe I felt guilty and was blaming myself for everything that was happening.

Years later my Dad met a women who had a son from a previous relationship and then they had a son together. I can remember feeling so jealous! He was not able to spend time with me as we drifted apart yet he was able to take care of a new baby. I wanted to be that baby again. I wanted the attention that I deserved. I wanted to be loved. I wanted to be comforted. I wanted to be Daddy's little girl.

I've never told my Dad how all that made me feel. I know he didn't push me away on purpose but I do feel like it paved the way for my future life in how I allowed men to treat me.

It broke my heart not to have my Dad walk me down the aisle

at my wedding. It was one of the toughest decisions I had to make. My wedding was nothing like I had envisioned it when I was a young girl and one should never feel awkward on their wedding day. I had my Step-Dad Bobby walk me down the aisle and honestly I would never have changed that but I would have loved for my Dad to be on my other side instead of just sitting in a pew at the back of the church. His love means the world to me and I hope one day that it will be like it was when I was a little girl.

DAY 271 – Monday September 11, 2006

Got up at 7am this morning to go for a 35 minute interval power walk.

It's day 2 of my French class and I'm finding it a little difficult to understand my French teacher. He as a different type of French dialect and I have to pay close attention to what he is saying. I was a little more at ease walking on campus today even though we switched classrooms and I hate change. Luckily this classroom is so much better. I sat with 2 others girls who seem really friendly. I'm finding it hard to keep this 'going to school' secret away from Suzanne, my OT. I know this does not help my anxiety but it is for the best. I am just going to try and not let it bother me…..easier said than done. I'm only keeping it a secret because if I fail, there will be less people to disappoint.

I had a nap today from 5:00pm-6:30pm. I was so exhausted, so Andrew made me go have a nap. I seem to only be able to go about 4-6 days before I exhaust myself and need a nap. I feel physically and mentally exhausted.

FOOD JOURNAL for today
BREAKFAST – ½ cup oatmeal, banana & 12 almonds
SNACK – w/w flour tortilla, can tuna & 2 tablespoons light mayo
LUNCH – yogurt, ½ cup pasta salad & shrimp
SNACK – apple
SUPPER – salmon with stir fried veggies & 1 cup milk
SNACK – 1 serving fat free chocolate pudding, ½ banana & ½ cup milk

FOURTH QUARTER
OF THE NAKED TRUTH

Warr;or

MUST HAVES

Popcorn With Real Butter.
Flip-Flops.
One Million Hair Elastics.

DAY 272-285 – Tuesday September 12 – Monday September 25, 2006
THE NAKED PAST – My Ma

This one is so tough, because how does one talk negatively about the strongest and most thoughtful human on the planet? It's f*cking hard, but it is all part of the healing process and perhaps why I hid things for so long and kept the secret tucked away to take to my grave.

My Ma was a model when I was growing up and I can remember just looking at her thinking 'Wow, this I my Ma, I'm the coolest kid ever!" She would take me to fashion shows, Miss NB Pageants, Miss Moncton Pageants where she would teach the girls how to walk and talk. She wore her makeup just so and always looked amazing. My Ma and I were always busy together doing lots of activities from swimming in the river, cross-country skiing on the trails at Centennial Park, playing dress up with all her work clothes or just baking up a storm in the kitchen. That is the Ma that I know and love to pieces. But there is another side of her that really shaped me to who I am today and that I am trying to slowly fix. This is not easy.

It is easy to talk about someone who is an as*hole and who deliberately tries to hurt you, but it is another thing when you realize that the women who gave birth to you was emotionally withdrawn. As difficult as this is to say, I don't remember my Ma ever saying "I love you" when I was a child, never tucking me into bed and being affectionate when I needed it the most. I remember being told to be quiet about how I was feeling for fear it may embarrass the family. I was asked "What are you crying for?" but never in an empathetic way. I was told not to cry because that is weak. I cried a lot as a child and as a teen. I can remember being very emotional and angry with the world. I thought about suicide a lot and would retreat to a secluded place so nobody could find me. I wanted to be alone and then felt like such a failure when I couldn't do it. I had so much pain and hurt inside of me and I had no one to listen to any of it. It makes more sense now that at the age of 13 I turned to ED. My Ma had no idea that I had started binging and purging at the age of 13 because at that time I did not live with either of my parents. I'm not exactly sure why, but I was sent to live with my step Dad *Don's* sister and 4 kids. I lived there for almost a year and rarely saw my parents. I didn't understand it at all, but I was not allowed to ask either. I can remember on Thanksgiving just having had enough and when I purged the very first time I felt free for the first time in my life. Something that I had control over.

My Ma worked so hard to support the two of us. She worked 2-3 jobs and never gave up. And I know now that she didn't necessarily allow me in because she herself was just trying to survive and doing the best she knew.

During my first year at Dalhousie University I came home at Christmas break. I was so sick. My skin was beyond pale. I was purging almost every time I ate. I had moved in with my best friend Erin to a dorm so I could try and get better but that only made me eat more because I binged in the cafeteria and then purged in the shower where nobody would hear me. I was out of control. When I came home, my Ma didn't say anything which at the time I was relieved. But a few nights later, I had a couple of my friends over for a party and when my Ma came home my best friend Erin told her. At first I was upset with Erin, but then I didn't care because I was going to do what I wanted to do and nobody was going to f*cking stop me! I remember sitting down on the bed with my Ma and Erin. Erin was distraught and my Ma just sat there like she was ordering a cheeseburger from McDonalds. Erin to this day still recalls that night vividly.

After that night, I had to quit University for my second semester. I was so unwell, I needed desperate help. Ma made me go see an eating disorder counsellor which I thought was complete bullshit. It was a waste of my time, her time and her money. I went to a couple sessions and I can vividly remember the counsellor making me point to a stick figure where I felt worse about myself. I just looked at her with eyes of death and that was my last session. I used to pretend to go to my sessions but walk out the back door until Ma found out. I guess after that point, she thought I was healed as she never made me go see anyone else ever again. I knew I wasn't healed, but I didn't want to be. I had too much rage pent up inside and ED made me feel way too good to ever let him go.

DAY 286 – Tuesday September 26, 2006

Today is going to be the biggest day of my life. I'm headed to 'Mind Over Mood` class and it`s like no other! Normally this would not be a big day but today we are throwing out a piece of our past that no longer serves us! You'll never guess what mine is, my F*CKING SCALE! That's right, today I'm saying "F*CK THE SCALE!"

I never thought this day would come, but I have to start making changes even if I can't quit binging just yet.

I have been working with Dr. David on body image and although I think that is the hardest part of all the day therapy classes I'm starting to like parts of my body which is a huge step from not liking ANY of it for most of my life and always seeing fault in each part.

I arrive to class with my scale in tow and the looks I receive from others, is a bit overwhelming but I know they get it whether they are man or women. The class begins and the teacher makes us go around and talk about why we are throwing out that specific piece of our life and how it has affected us negatively. As my turn approaches I'm nervous as this is a huge deal for me. I have relied on those f*cking numbers for over 16 years now and they have determined my self-worth 100%. Whether I was going to have a good or bad day. If I was going to wear something specific. If I was going to feel sexy. If I was going hide behind yet another pair of sweats with a baggy shirt.

The garbage can is beside me and in one foul swoop I pick up the scale and toss it in with a furry. I knew that if I didn't do it quickly, it was never going to happen. WOW, instead of feeling anxious I feel a sense of relief! This is truly a huge day for me and one that I never thought would happen......EVER!

DAY 287-293 – Wednesday September 27 – Wednesday October 3, 2006
THE NAKED PAST – Car Accident

Anytime the subject comes up today, I somehow manage to brush it off as a joke like it was no big deal that I got hit by a car while walking across the street. Funny enough as I write this, my accident actually occurred at the end of September, the day that this memory came up and I felt I should write about this trauma. Funny how memories come up and if we ignore them we feel like they are no big deal but our subconscious is really trying to tell us the opposite.

Rewind back to 2003 in my Grade 11 year at Harrison Trimble High school that had just started. It was a cool and crisp Fall day and I put on a pair of Guess Jeans, flip-flops, Sweatshirt and my LL Bean backpack and headed out the door to catch the bus. Ma wasn't home because she was in Fredericton for meetings since the day before. I got to St. George Boulevard beside the old CKCW radio station and waited for the 4 lanes of traffic to slow down and stop so I could cross. Across the street in front of the Wesleyan Church there were 2 other women waiting to do the same. I couldn't wait to get to school because I had just found out that I had made the Soccer team and my first practice was that night. The lane closest to me had stopped as well as the 2 lanes closest to the women so we all proceeded to cross until I hit the second lane near me and the SUV didn't stop. I was thrown about 30 feet away landing on my right knee and my left knee turned inwards.

But guess what? My Guess jeans did not rip and my head was

---

saved from my big ass L.L. Bean bookbag on both shoulders. There's a lesson for all you cool kids, wear Guess jeans and your bookbag on both shoulders.

I don't remember being hit, I just remember waking up and wondering if I was in Heaven. Within minutes an ambulance arrived and brought me to the hospital and the next thing I knew my Ma was on her way back from Fredericton. The accident itself I don't believe caused any emotional trauma even though it sure did cause quite a few physically for many years to come. What I do remember causing emotional trauma however was not being able to play soccer that year with my team. Being frustrated playing volleyball because I had to wear a knee brace. Feeling like a failure when I couldn't try out for the University volleyball team in 1995 and 1996 because I had yet another surgery to go to. Missing weeks of esthetic school in 1997 because I had yet another surgery and it came with complications. The surgery that I had in 2005 just before I got married is the one that really set me back. They decided to remove my staples from my knee that had been there for almost 10 years and it was excruciating the pain I had after surgery. My healing took many weeks and I was off work during that time as well. I had way too much time to think, stress, eat and binge. I wasn't sleeping. I began hearing things. I was crying every day and yet I hid it all from my fiancé at the time. I just wanted it all to go away, had I not been through enough. Why was life not on my side and why did I have to suffer so much, I was such a good person.

DAY 294 – Thursday October 4, 2006

My binging and purging is starting to become better, however when I get these urges to puke or need a euphoric high they come on so strong it is nearly impossible to control. For some that may not make sense but it really is no different than a drug or alcohol addict trying to rehab and now needing a fix. The only downside, mine is legal and is less frowned upon in society. I'm now realizing that this type of behavior is NOT normal and is NOT healthy for my body. My throat has scars. The enamel on my teeth has broken down. And to think that is all that I can see……on the outside. I can only imagine what my insides must look like.

I need a binge but I promise myself it won't be so much. I head to the Irving to get 'gas', so I tell Andrew and walk out of the Irving with no gas but 2 Vachon cakes and 2 caramel cakes. From the time I leave the Irving on Lincoln Road to the time I get to Adams Street about 5 minutes away, they are gone and my taste buds are salivating for more. I pull over on Lonewater Street and purge until there is nothing more to come up. I've become such a pro that after 3 shoves of my 2 fingers down my throat there is nothing left and away I head home on a euphoric high…….but this time instead of feeling a sense of accomplishment I feel guilty??? This is new……

DAY 295 - 317 – Friday October 5 – Friday October 27, 2006
THE NAKED PAST – Past Relationship Bullshit

Once a cheater always a cheater? I hate to sound cliché, but I swear this quote was written for me. I had my first serious relationship when I was in 1993 while I was in grade 10, the first love of my life and his name was *Marcelle*. We had an amazing time together, playing sports, watching movies, hanging out with friends, going to parties and just being young kids in love. I can remember him going away one Summer for Leadership camp and me being so jealous and nervous at the same time. I thought for sure he was cheating on me and if I couldn't figure it out for sure, I was going to do the same on him. It made sense but in no way did it make me feel good.

The next relationship was in 1997 while I was at Dalhousie University to *Carl* and we had known each other in high school and had even worked together in the Summers as camp counsellors. He used to go away in the Summer to his relatives to work in Illinois and I just knew he was cheating on me based on his behavior. So, when he came back the second Summer I once again I did the same on him for revenge.

The next one, a real ladies man. I had no f*cking clue what the heck I was doing. I had such terrible self-esteem that I knew that once a man cheated on me and I returned the 'favor' that was not working so I vowed never to do it again. But somehow, the guy in my relationships just never got the memo. I probably could go on and on about stories regarding this guy, the one that sticks in my head goes a little something like this.

We had been dating for some time and he lived in a fancy apartment building downtown on Queen Street. He never used his key, but the code that allowed him into the building. I knew that code of course because I used it too when I would come over to visit. Long story short, he was sick one day and didn't make it to work so when I got done work I thought it would be so nice of me to drop off some homemade soup and muffins. I made my way up to the apartment and knocked on his door. I heard people but nobody answered. That was odd…..or was it?

The next day when he called he didn't even mention the soup and in my head I thought shit, he must be really sick he hasn't left the apartment. Why the f*ck I was so naïve to believe that is beyond me. Fast forward a few days and we were heading into his place and he said you can't use that code anymore, the fire marshal has been here and they know that people are using that code and who is using it and it's only for them during emergencies. I was like, jeez ok. Once again, dumb and naïve.

That night when I am getting ready for bed, I can't find my toothbrush in the drawer and my shampoo, conditioner and soap is not in the shower. I holler out to him to ask to which his reply is "The cleaning lady must have moved it." Once again, dumb and naïve.

I know, I know at this point I'm the moron. Seriously this went on for a couple more months until I realized it wasn't the f*cking cleaning lady, he was hiding my things because there was another women.

Moral of the story, if you don't have access to your boyfriends apartment, if your shower stuff is put away AND if he isn't grateful for you, DUMP HIS ASS ASAP because you are just too damn good for that bullshit.

The next guy, was my now husband Andrew. I always felt like he was being unfaithful and I did catch him a few times but had to somehow convince not only myself but him that I was right. I've always hated the fact that you would have to 'justify' the feelings you were feeling. I knew I had very little self-esteem and that Andrew was a dream guy. He was handsome, educated, had a great job and we played volleyball together. I was lucky to have him. He had made mistakes but he would never do that when we were married. He just needed to feel settled to feel secure didn't he? Why do I continue to check his email account? Why do I question where he is? Why do I hate when he goes out without me? There is something wrong with me. I'm just the jealous type and I need to get over this or I am going to lose him.

DAY 318 – Saturday October 28, 2006

Dave and Laura are having a party tonight and I'm sure there will be a house full. I went for a run today to try and feel as good about myself as I can for tonight. Although 'ED' and I are still acquaintances and the cutting still occurs during stressful times, somehow it allows me to feel alive and know that I have some kind of feeling inside of me. It has become a bit of a substitute for food and drugs.

We arrive at Dave's late which frustrates me because by that

---

time there are a lot of people which make me feel so self-conscious walking in. I quickly head over to the corner of the kitchen to mix a drink and find a familiar face. My heart is racing and I just want to hide, but I have to do something to not make myself even more noticeable. So after making my drink, I get food prepared, the one thing that brings me a little relief, feeding people's bellies. After a few drinks I'm feeling a bit better and got to talk to a few people, however no sooner I'm easily irritated because I don't feel that Andrew is paying any attention to me and it frustrates me. I know I may be overreacting but he knows how much I dislike being alone.

I become so upset that I run to the bathroom, slam the door, break down and begin bawling my eyes out sitting on the toilet. I don't know what to feel anymore. I second guess every one of my decisions and I don't know any more what is right or wrong. Am I overreacting? Am I asking too much? Am I drunk? Am I me? Am I helpless at this point? As I look at myself in the mirror, I ask myself the same question over and over "Why? Why can't I stop this! I'm so confused!" As Andrew bangs on the door and I look in the mirror with mascara running down my face and snot running down my face. A thought quickly comes to mind, a razor!

There has got to be a razor here somewhere, I know Laura uses this shower, so I know she has one! I tear open the shower curtain and there it is staring directly at me, my relief. I quickly grab the razor, run to the mirror and begin to cut both wrists. I watch my expression on my face as it fades from sadness to happiness and my pupils begin to dilate. Although it hardly even stings, it makes me feel alive and takes away the emotional craziness that I am feeling right now. Alive enough to know that it feels exhilarating and that there is no confusion into what I am doing to myself. It almost feels like that first snort of cocaine. That 'feel good f*cking feeling' that one never forgets and leaves you wanting more. As the blood streams down my hands and onto the floor it's like I awaken a new person.

I clean up the blood on my wrists and the makeup streaming down my face and try to put myself together as best as I can. Crap, I didn't wear a long sleeve shirt. Ok, so hold your arms by your side, and tell Andrew you want to go home. Or he can stay and you'll get a cab home as it's the only way to get out of here without a million questions. He decides to come home and I as soon as I arrive I get ready for bed, I'll figure out a way to hide it in the morning from Andrew and as for volleyball I'll figure it out. It's not that bad......is it?

DAY 319 – Sunday October 29, 2006

I stare at my wrists they have deep red lines from the razor blade digging into them over and over again. They are painful today, something that was void while as I was doing the cutting. The cutting itself is almost numbing yet euphoric at the same time. I'm going to play volleyball this afternoon and because Andrew caught a glimpse of my wrists he was very unhappy. He made me tape them up.

As we head to volleyball he asks "How are you planning to hide that from everyone?" I say "I'm keeping my long sleeve on, nobody will even notice." As we begin to play, it hurts intensely every time I bump the ball. I begin hoping that every serve or hard hit ball is not coming to me but no such luck. I'm bleeding through my tape around both wrists and we still have 11 points left to go in this game before I can get to a washroom and wipe it off. Part of me wants to hide the tape under my sleeves, however the other part of me wants everyone to see them. I want you to worry about me. I want you to be impressed. I want you to be a little afraid. I don't get any of those feelings from my scars, so let me live vicariously through you.

DAY 320 - 338 – Monday October 30 – Friday November 17, 2006
THE NAKED PAST – Back in the Summer of 96'

I felt like I could never be good enough for anyone because I didn't think I was good enough for myself. I didn't know who I was. Who I was supposed to become. Where my life was headed. And most importantly, if things would get better. It sure felt like 'rock bottom', but I would later find out it was far from it. I guess that's the thing with rock bottom or anything in life, there is always a worse scenario no matter what situation you may be facing right now.

I was forced to leave University because I was so sick, both mentally and physically. But in leaving, I was left with time on my hands. You see time and me DO NOT get along. We butt heads and dream up all the bad that could happen and that is happening and that happened in the past.

I had gone to 2 counselling sessions in January of 1996 and decided that was more than enough for me. I just needed to stay busy and the thoughts of suicide and showing my fingers down my throat would go away. I showed up at Burger King in Dieppe with a resume in my hand ready to work. I got the job on the spot and became the best damn employee BK had ever seen. I was only 18 years old and they asked if I would be interested in becoming a manager down the road. Although I was flattered BK was not going to be for me. It was a filler and a way to make money to feed my habit of shopping at Club Monaco and drinking my face off every chance I got which helped to ease the f*cking pain and memories.

BK is where I met *Peter* and he was the 'bad boy' in some respects but the sweetest, even to this day. He was into drugs, nothing too heavy, just marijuana. We partied like it was the Summer of 69' every night that we weren't working. We played pool at the Broken Q non-stop, ordered drinks at the bar (with fake ID's of course) and had many sleepless nights. I was living it up, or so I thought. I had left school. I was binging and purging every day. I was spending all my money on addictions. I was pushing everyone away from me. I didn't give a shit either. I was once again feeling so lost. I truly didn't care if my life ended until this one night that I scared even myself.

It was a hot Summer June night in 1996 and *Peter* and I had been invited to a going away party for one of his friends. We went over and within just a couple hours I had shot an entire pint of tequila, played Frisbee in the streets, smoked a few joints and not eaten a damn thing. Since I was the most 'sober' out of about 15 people, 3 of us headed out in my Ma's little red Honda hatchback Civic to the liquor store for more. I did a pretty good job of driving and to be honest was more nervous that the cashier was not going to sell me another pint of tequila because I was already feeling good. Back to the house and I shot another pint with lemon and salt. At around 2am the party was winding down and I had to get home to work the next morning. My only way home, to drive since I had my Ma's car. This is where the specific details are a bit blurry. I do however remember feeling scared shitless. As I drove down Mountain Road, I remember crossing into the other lane many times and dozing off. When I arrived home, I was grateful that I had made it. I was so worried about getting into an accident and something happening to my Ma's car. To this day, I have only had tequila once. I tried a shot and it came right back up. Needless to say it's off limits now. I think that night really put a fear into me and I swore I would never drink and drive again, it was beyond selfish.

That Summer I quit my job at BK and got my previous Summer job as an Outdoor Adventure camp counsellor at Camp Centennial. This truly helped me see that I was a somebody. Those kids needed me probably just as much as I needed them. It gave me the confidence to stop drinking all the time, quit drugs (for the time being) and register for Dalhousie University in the Fall. I thought the past would go away.......

DAY 339 – Saturday November 18, 2006

Tonight is the annual Wine Expo and we are headed to Moncton with Monika and Jamie. I'm excited to drink wine all night long with my bestie and stay in a hotel downtown.

School has been really intense and although I'm not doing as good as I had hoped I am studying the best that I can. I'm finding it difficult to concentrate and remember things but overall I'm passing which is further than I ever got when I went to Dalhousie University back in 1995-1997. I keep questioning whether University is for me because I feel like it's the 'thing to do' but I do know that if I can make it to being a teacher in some capacity it will be pretty amazing!

We arrive in Moncton and get ready to head to the Coliseum. The Wine Expo is an annual event held in Moncton, NB and we go on the 'Grand Tasting' featuring hundreds of wine to taste. Yeah I know, doesn't get much better than that! I'm feeling pretty for the first time in a long time and I'm looking forward to letting my hair down and getting wined out!

As we head to the expo I feel a sense of panic, as there are a lot of people and I always feel like others are staring at me. Now by staring I don't mean in a good way. I either assume that they are staring because they think I'm disgusting or staring because I'm pretty and they hate me. There is no happy medium to this thinking in my head. I hold Andrew's hand and we walk in together and he never leaves my side. After countless sips of wine we are all ready to head back to the hotel and get some food!

When we get back I get this crazy feeling to have sex and within seconds the next thing I know Andrew and I are on the bathroom floor while Monika and Jamie are just outside the door in the room. You see, most of my life I've gotten used to having 'XYZ NOW!' to fill the void and by 'XYZ I mean something immediate which was binging, purging, drugs, cutting etc. and this was just one of those moments. I figured sex was a better alternative to self-harm. After we walk out, I can sense a change in the mood of the room and they are not happy. But to be honest I understand why deep down inside but immediately react by justifying and saying "It's not like you could hear us or see us!" This sets off my mood to immediate frustration and embarrassment and my only escape is to run to the bathroom and lock the door.

As I stand there and look in the mirror I realize that this is the first time I shouldn't cut but I don't know what else to do. I need something to dull the craziness inside my head and I reach over for my razor and the cutting begins once again. As tears stream down my face the blood drips into the tub. I've never felt guilty for cutting before, but I know I've worked hard over the past 3 weeks to not cut or purge. I have short sleeves on so when I come out of the bathroom I do my best to hide my wrists because this is one time that I don't want any attention for my actions. I just want the pain of hurting my friend to go away and cutting was the only way I knew how.

DAY 340-364 – Sunday November 19 – Wednesday December 13, 2006
THE NAKED PAST – Cocaine Dreams

You know when Dr. David suggested that I journal anytime my past came up I thought "Sure, no big deal. I've dealt with it all." I was simply bullshitting myself into believing that f*cking lie. I'm coming to the realization that I have not dealt with any of it. I simply thought I was strong enough to set it aside and if I didn't continue to 'worry' about it I was over it. I realized that on a daily basis I've had severe anxiety when I come to this specific past trauma, which made me STOP dead in my tracks and come to the realization I had not dealt with any of the shit that happened during my cocaine dreams.

At the end of the day I'm a fixer. I want to help others more than I want to help myself. I'm caring and compassionate but the downside is that I get sucked into other people's bullshit really fast because I believe that I can help them. By trying to 'fix them' it's a way for me ignore all the shit that goes on in my own head and life.

The first time I laid eyes on him, I melted. He had eyes like nobody I had ever seen, so blue, so innocent, so captivating and so f*cking sexy. I had met him at the Rockin' Rodeo a bar I worked at for almost 5 years while working 2 other jobs. He had a girlfriend at the time and she was beyond beautiful, so I immediately knew he was way out of my league.

Months past, and I saw him at Dolan's pub downtown and we got talking. He had broken up with his girlfriend quite a while ago and I was single. We chit chatted but I still felt like there was no way he could possibly be into me. A few weekends later, I saw him at the same pub and he asked for my number. The next morning, he called asked me out on a breakfast date and arrived with flowers in his hands. Needless to say he had me at "Hello".

We spent the next couple months having so much fun together! We went on so many weekend getaways and just enjoyed each other's company. It all felt like such a dream come true until incident after incident the pieces came together like a nightmare.

FIRST INCIDENT
"The first step towards getting somewhere is to decide that you are not going to stay where you are."
~Unknown

One night, when I went to visit him at work he asked for money and not just your typical $20, but $1000. I quickly replied "What do you need that for?" He assured me that he would pay me back and he needed to pick up a trailer but the boss hadn't left him the money to pick it up and it had to be picked up that night. I told him "If I had it I would give it to you." He told me "No problem, I will make arrangements and I'll give you a call when I'm on my way back from getting it." I waited for his call all night, but he never called and he never picked up his phone when I called him either. The next morning, same thing, I began to get worried, where the f*ck could he be? I quickly called his best friend *Jared* to ask him if he had heard from him. He said "No" but didn't seem too worried, which shocked me. He then asked "What exactly did he say to you last night?" I told him and the next thing I knew he said I'm coming to get you with *Katherine* and we'll head out driving around to see if we can find him. We drove all day long from one end of Fredericton to another in hopes of finding him. We stopped and asked people if they had seen him from one of the photos I had. No such luck. *Jared and Katherine* dropped me off and said "He will show up, try not to worry." Later that evening I got a phone call from him and he said that he had lost cell service, gotten the trailer stuck and had been up all night. I felt awful that he had to go through all that and wished I could have helped him.

SECOND INCIDENT
"It's not the drugs that make a drug addict, it's the need to escape reality."
~Unknown

A few weeks later I was in Dieppe visiting my Mémère and Pépère and *Mitch* was going to come down the following day. Before I left we stopped at Scott's Nursery to pick up some flowers. He said that since he couldn't come down with me now, he wanted to give something to them. I thought that was simply the sweetest thing ever. He called the next morning to let me know that the night before he had gotten oil in his eye while working on a truck out towards Marysville. I asked questions about how but his answers were vague. I asked him if he wanted me to come home and he said "No. I just got home from the hospital, I'm going to go to bed. My eye hurts and it's all red." I felt terrible, he had been at the ER getting his eye flushed and I wasn't there to help him. When I arrived home the next day, his eye seemed fine. He looked a bit tired, but otherwise nothing a little Visine couldn't fix. It all sounded so strange, but who was I to question. But then I got thinking, did he buy the flowers because he knew he was never going to show up?

THIRD INCIDENT
"Addiction is a family disease. One person may use, but the whole family suffers."
~Anonymous

Things started to feel weird. I was living on Biggs Street in Fredericton and that night I was home alone watching TV and went to bed early. When I woke up the next morning, I found a man sleeping on my couch! I didn't know whether to scream or call the cops but he rolled over and it was *Mitch*. I was in shock! My first words were "How did you get in here?" He said "The patio door was open." I said "Why didn't you call and where have you been?" He said "I was out drinking with the boys and I didn't want to wake you and the door just happened to be open. I'm sorry." Me being me, I forgave him but things just didn't add up.

FOURTH INCIDENT
"Once the enabling stops, the recovery is given the opportunity to start."
~Unknown

After the last time when I found him on my couch I knew something was going on, but I had no idea. I talked to *Jared* and he told me that *Mitch* had a drug problem in the past and that he believed he was up to his old ways once again. He knew the day that we went driving around looking for him, but didn't have the heart to tell me. He wanted to be sure that he was right before telling me. He knew his suspicions were right when *Mitch* came to him asking for money, he was doing cocaine once again. He told me never to lend him money because I would never see it again. He told me he needed help and I just knew that I could be that person.

I began leaving the patio door open for him on nights that I couldn't get in touch with him or where I thought he was not being truthful about where he was. I would wake up half of the mornings happy that he was safe on my couch and the other half worried sick that he was in a ditch somewhere dead. We argued continuously for him to stop and I told him repeatedly that I was going to leave him if he didn't get help. He told me he had gone to see Additions Services and I do believe he had gone once perhaps twice, but never truly made the effort to stop. I loved him so much and I was losing him.

FIFTH INCIDENT
"Recovery is not for people who need it, it's for people who want it." ~Anonymous

The back and forth went on for weeks until I realized that if I can't beat him, join him. He had asked me a few times to just do one line with him, but I quickly said "No, absolutely not!" I was scared of becoming addicted like him. He said "You don't get addicted after just one try. Seriously I've done it in the past and quit and can do the same thing again when I want." I remember that night like it was yesterday, it was a

Friday after a very busy week and I didn't have to work at the Rockin' Rodeo like most Friday nights. He asked me again if I wanted to go out with him to the crack shack in Penniac and if I wanted to do it with him I could and if not that was ok too. I told him I was not going to do it, but that I would take the drive with him.

We drove to Penniac and my heart was furiously beating. As he put on his blinker to turn I remember asking him "Where are we going?" He said "The 'house' is just up this hill." We drive up a steep hill and pull up to the 'house'. You know when they say 'crack shack' that is exactly what this was. It was no bigger than a large baby barn, shades over all the windows, siding falling off, an old beat up car outside with the windows busted out and nobody to be seen. This felt so wrong. Mike said "Wait here, I'll just be a minute. You can't come in, you're safer here." I said "I'm what?" I'm sure the look on my face said it all as he slammed the door. Within him slamming the door I locked all the doors, and slumped down in my seat. Mike came back about 10 minutes later which seemed like an hour and I said "What took you so long?" He said "Well I had to sample it to make sure it was good before I bought any." I remember feeling so scared, like I was being watched and I just wanted to get the f*ck out of there.

We drove to the store picked-up a couple bottles of juice and a handful of straws (I thought this was odd), headed to his work, turned on some music and sat at his desk. He pulled out the homemade paper envelope of cocaine and I couldn't get over how small it was. I didn't bother asking then how much it was or how much it cost. He pulled out a piece of glass from his drawer and carefully dumped out the contents on the glass. He then pulled out a plastic card, almost like a debit card, but reassured me you never use a debit card because the products gets stuck in the numbers and that's a waste of time and money. This card was flat as he began to crush the coke and form it into the most perfect white line I have ever seen. It was exactly like you see in the movies and it was the craziest shit I had ever been a part of. None of my friends had ever done cocaine, I had never seen or been around it and this felt so wrong. I was so nervous we were going to get caught but yet I was intrigued to watch him do it. He took one of the straws and within a millisecond the line was gone. When I had seen people do it in movies, they had always just used their nose or a special type of pen. I asked him why the straw and he said "Because a straw you can cut open after a few times and get the residue to put on your gums." On my gums I thought? Wow, I was completely confused now.

After each line he asked if I wanted to try and I said "No, not yet." After his 5th line, I was ready. I had watched him do it and I didn't think I could screw it up. He created the line in front of me because I was not going to be responsible for f*cking that up, took my straw in hand, had my apple juice ready in case it tasted like shit, plugged one of my nostrils, bowed my head down to the white God's and snorted it up like a kid on a cold winter day. Fuck it burnt a little and tasted so bitter! I quickly reached for my bottle of apple juice and was told only to take a little sip so I wouldn't dilute what was running down the back of my nose and into my throat.

The exhilaration was immediate! I felt on fire! I felt energized! I wanted more!

The night continued with more cocaine being smashed and snorted. We took another trip out to Penniac because the drugs were gone and we both wanted more. The next thing I knew the sun was coming up, having the time of our lives and high on life and coke!

SIXTH INCIDENT
"It is not the cocaine that makes one an addict, it is the need to escape from a harsh reality."
~Anonymous

For the next 48 hours I couldn't stop thinking about that night. I felt guilty, but yet proud. I felt, I felt like I wanted f*cking more! It was so odd, I mean I had only done it one, is that possible to want more so quickly? I mean when I've had alcohol in the past I NEVER wake up the next morning or two mornings later wanting more, at least lately I haven't. I was embarrassed to tell *Mitch* how I was feeling so when he asked me if I would do it again, I simply brushed it off like it was no big deal. But inside, I was wanting f*cking more! I was hoping he would want to go and get some and I would just 'tag along' for the ride. By Tuesday night, just 4 days later we were headed back to the crack shack. I had money. I was excited. I had butterflies in my tummy. I had no idea how I was going to go to work the next day. I simply didn't think things through and nor did I care.

Weeks went on and we would only go about 2-3 days before

---

we were heading back to the shack. Every time I would bring most of the money, anywhere from $300 - $1000. When I knew how much money was being spent I was always so amazed at how little we got. I never questioned it in the beginning however because I knew that cocaine was a 'rich man's' drug. I can vividly remember heading up to the shack, and handing over $800. *Mitch* came back to the car and gave me the envelope and it was about 2 ½ very small pieces of unbroken cocaine with a little bit of dust. Immediately I said "Is that all we get for $800? Where the f*ck is the rest of it?" *Mitch* replied "That is what he gave me." I said "Did you do some of ours while you were in there?" He said "No, I just sampled what he gave me." I said "Well you had better f*cking go back in there and tell him that he ripped us f*cking off, or I will!" *Mitch* quickly got out of the car and back to the shack doors. He had a very quick conversation with *Teddy* and the next thing I knew *Teddy* had a baseball bat and started beating on the windshield of a car that was in the driveway. I was freaking out! *Mitch* ran to our car and said "It's ok, he's just frustrated because he's tired of people questioning whether or not they got their value." Listen, I was in no way going to question him at that point, this guy was f*cking nuts and if I wanted to get another fix anytime soon, I just wanted the hell out of there and didn't want him mad at me.

We bolted out of the driveway and as soon as we got about 20 seconds away, we pulled over on the side of the road, snorted a couple lines and immediately felt relief and exhilaration. Every damn time we do that first line, I have to use the bathroom. *Mitch* says it's just because I'm nervous being on the side of the road but that we are safe. I trust him but I would much rather just wait until we got home or out of sight. I hate trying to crush and create lines in a moving vehicle.

Later I would find out that *Mitch* was going to the shack without me and without money. He was using the money that I was giving him when we went together to pay for some of his previous debts and therefore WE weren't being shortchanged, I was in the end. That is why *Teddy* reacted the way he did that day because he couldn't believe that *Mitch* would call him out on something like that considering he was giving product without payment every now and then.

SEVENTH INCIDENT
"Don't hate the addict, hate the disease. Don't hate the person, hate the behavior. If it's that hard to watch it, imagine how hard it must be to live it."
~Anonymous

If I could count the hours that we spent driving I think we would have driven across Canada and back. There were times were we would just go to my apartment to play crib, smoke multiple packages of cigarettes, listen to old country tunes like Keith Whitley and Randy Travis and do lines all damn night with big smiles on our face until it was gone. Then most nights, we would drive around New Brunswick like it was no big deal. We drove every back road possible and oftentimes got lost. This is where my paranoia would take over. I was so scared of getting caught by the cops that I was constantly looking over my shoulder which only made *Mitch* more frustrated. I remember driving at around 3am and not knowing where we were and suddenly we drove by an RCMP vehicle who was parked on the side of the road. My heart stopped! We had a little bit of coke left but the fact that we were both higher than a kite was what freaked me out. *Mitch* told me to pretend that I was sleeping but that was never going to happen. His eyes were the size of saucers and so were mine. I was shaking and worried that we had been caught. The RCMP car swung around and started following us. Shit just got real and I was freaking out even more! I just wanted to gun it and get away as fast as we could, but *Mitch* just stayed as calm as he could and the next thing I knew the RCMP turned another direction. There were so many times that we dodged deer, moose and hit so many raccoons and skunks along the way. I think that is why to this day I have such anxiety driving at night not to mention almost being caught by the cops.

We always took the same route to the crack shack. Across the Princess Margaret bridge, Marysville exit, down Bridge Street, past my work at the old Cotton Mill, turned right onto River Street, stopping at the little corner store just before Penniac to pick up my bottle of apple juice. To this day, driving to Marysville and my work gives me flashbacks every damn time. There is not one day that has passed since 2003 when driving to work it doesn't remind me of the shit we did. How we managed to never get caught is beyond me and my reasoning.

EIGHTH INCIDENT
"Drugs may be the road to nowhere, but at least they're the scenic route"
~Anonymous

I was not sleeping much. I was losing weight. I looked like shit. I was broke unless it was for drugs. And oddly enough, I still couldn't figure out why. I mean, I was in f*cking denial to believe it could possibly be the cocaine. Did I have an addiction? I had only been using for 4 months at this point and I looked like hell! I called into my Government job so many times 'sick'. I wasn't even home to call in 'sick' most times, I would call from a pay phone in the middle of God knows where to let them know I wasn't feeling well. A.K.A. had been on a bender for 24 hours and was ready go to at it for another 24. People at work started questioning me. I was falling asleep at my desk because I hadn't slept in days and my boss was worried when I showed up at really important meetings that I was to be the lead at with my eyes like giant saucers, my nose running constantly and I couldn't answer simple questions. That man had the patience of a Saint for what I put him through. This was not me and he knew it, but he also didn't know how to help. I think this is when he went to see Mica and asked what he should do. Mica was there all the mornings I would come in high after not having slept for at least 24 hours and I just tried to pretend that everything was 'A' ok. Mica asked if I would go and talk with someone and I agreed. I truly appreciated her care and concern but I think she knew that it would be the only session I would go to.

I'm not sure how much weight I had lost up to that point, but I do know that I was only about 140lbs when I started and by the end I was under 120lbs. My clothes would fall off me without a belt. When I would go to work at the Rockin' Rodeo I would have to adjust my money belt every time to stay up. I was on a steady intake of Rooster caffeine pills and coffee to try and get me through the day and night when I wasn't high.

I had no money to buy groceries and when I did I would buy potatoes because they were cheap and I knew they would fill me up the most. At times, my Ma and *Mitch's* Mom would drop off groceries because we complained that we were poor and just trying to get by. Little did they know we had money most times, but it was gone with one swift snort. I can remember there was going to be a bake sale at work and I was part of the committee to help raise money. I always helped out every time there was a bake sale. This time however I had no money to buy anything but there was no way I was going to back out because people already had a reason to think something was up. So, I had potatoes, one can of corn and a bag of apples. I stole ground beef from my roommate and I made individual potato pot pies and applesauce. People raved about how delicious it was and I felt so guilty.

NINTH INCIDENT
"Be careful fighting someone else's demons, it may awaken your own."
~Anonymous

The one thing with addiction is that you will find any way to get it! They say winners figure it out....we'll I felt far from being a f*cking winner but I sure did figure it out when I wanted my next fix. I had 3 jobs and made really good money for only being 26 years young but yet I had nothing to show for it other than debt owed to many. I had racked up my credit cards. I had gotten more loans than I can account for with Easy Financial telling them a new lie every time. I was quite proud of myself when they would ask too, coming up with something cool every time. I had gotten multiple pay advances with Payday loans. Had borrowed money from my parents and lied every damn time to their face. I had borrowed money from *Mitch's* Dad because he told me to tell him that I needed it for rent now that he was living with me. And last but certainly not least, I had committed fraud multiple times until I got caught. You see in my head I truly thought it was no big deal. We wanted our second fix on our second day and we had no cash in hand but I did know that in a couple days I would be working at the club so I would get tip money or I would have a paycheck coming in from Moosehead or my Government job so I figured that 'depositing' cash and taking it out especially on a weekend when the banks were not open would be no biggie. So, in the wee hours of the morning I would go into an ATM, deposit a check from myself and made out to myself from one of my other banks and withdrawal the money immediately in one transaction so it wouldn't put a hold on my account. I had done this so many times it seemed like a flawless plan.....until one night I f*cked up! I deposited the check like normal but instead of it being under $1000 like it always was in the past it would not allow me to withdrawal any funds! F*ck! So back to the car I went and wrote out another check for less than $1000 and used *Mitch's* bank card to withdrawal the money. Phewf, that was a close one....so I thought.

That Monday I received a call from the bank asking me to come in to speak with the Manager. I had no idea what was going on. I figured no biggie, just explain that I deposited money and that I couldn't get it out because there was a hold and weasel my way out like usual. This time it was different, he was mad. He told me he should call the police because what I was doing was fraud and that there were multiple times that I had made deposits when there was absolutely no money in my account. He asked me why I should have a chance. I explained to him that I was trying my best to get by. That I had always been a great client. I had a car. I had a job. He then froze my account, would not allow me to make any deposits or withdrawals at an ATM for at least 3 months and that I would have to come in every time to see a teller and that if I messed up one time, there would be repercussions to my actions. I nearly shit my pants! What was I doing? This had to stop, but how?

In the end I had hit rock bottom financially. I had lost my job with the Rockin' Rodeo because I knew I was going to get fired due to lack of sales and showing up stoned. I had lost my apartment because I couldn't financially make it on my own anymore and had to move back in with my Ma and Bobby. And, I had racked up over $10, 000 in debt from my drug addiction in the short span of 6 months.

TENTH INCIDENT
"You don't get over an addiction by stopping using. You recover by creating a new life where it is easier to not use. If you don't create a new life, then all the factors that brought you to your addiction will catch up with you again."
~Anonymous

Over the past 6 months *Mitch* and I didn't go out or meet up with friends much. I had distanced myself from everyone because I knew they would figure out exactly what was going on or get the idea. When I began to realize that I was losing everything and everyone I knew I had to make a change, but how? We had talked about stopping, but in the end one of us would convince the other that it was ok. I knew I had to cut off my ties and break up with *Mitch* but I loved him and I knew that if I wasn't with him, he would continue to do it and I was fearful of what would happen.

One night I decided to go out with my girlfriends and I can remember them being so happy to go out with me. We headed to Dolan's which was ironic since that is where *Mitch* and I had exchanged numbers. I had a lot of friends that were police officers, since I had dated on in the past and one of the girls that I was with that night, her boyfriend was a cop. We had a few drinks and suddenly he walked over. I was happy to see him and gave him a hug. It felt odd however this time. He looked me straight in the eyes and said "Sam, I know what you've been doing, you've gotta get out before you get caught." I froze, I had no idea what to say and I'm sure the look on my face said it all. How did he know? He then said "We see you go up to the shack, we watch you on surveillance, you are on tape and there are eyes on you and others." My heart stopped. I finally opened my mouth and said "What the f*ck do you mean you have seen me? There is nobody there when we go." He said "Sam, we are in the bushes, doing undercover, I see you in the car waiting for *Mitch* to come out of the shack." In that instant, I wanted to run, but I didn't. I let things sink in and said "I will stop." He then replied "Sam you have to, or you are going to get caught too. I'm being serious, this is real."

Something felt different inside of me. This whole time I thought it was no big deal. I wasn't dealing the drugs, I was just using them a lot. I was failing at everything in my life, but why would that matter to the police. I then realized that the place we were getting our fix at was larger than I had thought. Up from the shack was a beautiful house, with a beautiful garage, big fancy cars and a drug Lord that ruled it all. This was big time, and I was part of it even though I was only buying from the sidelines. I knew I had to get out and I knew it wasn't going to be easy, but the only way was to cut off ties completely and become a complete bitch to the man that I thought I loved.

The next day, I called *Mitch* and ended it with him. I knew it was not the right thing to do over the phone but I also knew that if I did it in person I could not face him and the way always justified the behaviors. Two weeks went by and I never spoke to him until that one time I picked up my phone because I truly cared and wanted to be sure he was ok. He said "I just want to talk. Can I come and get you and we can go for a little drive?" I hesitated but said "Sure." He showed up just 10 minutes later and as soon as I got in the car, there it was in the usual spot it always was, in front of the cup holder. That little piece of origami folded paper that I knew would only contain one thing, misery in the end. I told him that I didn't want to do any, he said not to worry, he wouldn't ask.

We drove and barely talked and the longer we drove the more I wanted it. He would stop and do lines, but the sound, the smell and even the taste was all there like it was just the other day. I couldn't stand it any longer, I had to have some. I said "Give me some." He said "No, I don't want you doing it because you stopped." I said "I will make that decision." And in matter of seconds we had stopped, done a couple lines and were back on the road to find a gas station so I could have my usual apple juice. You see apple juice is the only thing that I ate or drank the entire time we were on a bender. I would buy a 355ml bottle of apple juice and in 48 hours it might be ¾ of the way gone. Writing this now, I realize why I lost so much weight. That little drive turned into a 48 hour episode whereby I once again called into work sick. My Ma and Bobby were out looking for me only after calling a hundred times. I felt like a failure for giving in but at the end of the 48 hours I was done.

I woke up the next morning to having had a couple hours sleep and having to play in a volleyball tournament all day. I couldn't eat. I was lethargic. My eyes were bugged out of my head. I looked like death and tried to pretend it was just a hangover from the night before. That was it, I had hit my rock bottom. I had enough and I was done with *Mitch* once and for all. I had to tell myself that whatever happened thereafter was not my fault. Helping was only enabling him and I was not becoming the person that I wanted to be. Looking back, I realize that there was a reason he wanted me to try it, because I had money and money is what he needed. I was his 'good girl' sidekick that made people think he couldn't possibly be addicted once again. Thankfully my addiction only lasted 6 months….but it felt like an eternity and I carry the wounds from it all to this day.

I'M TIRED OF F*CKING INCIDENTS

"I don't care who you are or what you've done, anyone who chooses recovery over a life of addiction is a warrior in my book."
~Sam

'Those people', you hear it all the time when it comes to drug addicts. The ones that people seem to look down upon, until they are put into a similar situation and then want sympathy. I thought those people were losers. I thought those people came from poor and uneducated families. I thought those people had no goals in life. I thought those people had no job. I thought those people had terrible friends. I thought those people weren't part of society. I thought those people were just weak. I thought wrong! 'Those people' became me and I quickly realized that 'those people' can easily become any one of us.

I will never be able to recall each and every crazy f*cking thing we did, but looking back I realize just how dumb we were. I am far from proud of the shit we did, however it gives me an appreciation for those who continue to have drug addictions and can't seem to get out of the madness of it all. My only wish was that you *Mitch* got the help that you so desperately needed. The day I got the phone call that you had been in an accident was a day that I will never forget. You had a heart of gold but you got lost somewhere along the way. Writing this has been the most difficult part of all my journal writings, but I needed to do it to heal. *Mitch* I just hope you know how much you meant to me and everyone around you.

DAY 365 – Thursday December 14, 2006

The healing begins to 'click'. I begin feeling more confident. I have not purged in a few weeks and although I have my good and bad days, 'ED' was now only an acquaintance and not a partner in crime which I thought he had been for so long. I thank 'ED' for all that he has taught me about myself and thankfully only have a few of his scars remain.

I've also not cut in a few weeks either. The scars remind me every day of the self-mutilation that I have done to my body and I really need to find another way to release. What that is, I'm still seeking out but I'm willing to listen to suggestions. I know I have a ways to go, but I feel slightly better in the sense that I am willing to try a little harder.
I enjoy communicating now, I truly do! It releases something within me which is a great feeling as well as a great sense of accomplishment. From where I was just 365 days ago, to where I am now, I truly am a new woman. I am not the girl that was 'taught' to be strong and hold in all that emotion all the time. Looking a certain way does not determine your self-worth, nor does the f*cking number on the scale. I am becoming a strong women that believes in herself just a little bit more every day.

Even though I have done all the work myself, I thank Andrew each and every day for his kind words, encouragement, shoulder and helping hand through my journey. I know I don't thank him enough. Not because I don't want to, but because it was a very difficult time for me and it's still hard for me to relive moments from the past.

I know that my mental illness will be in remission but I'm hoping with my hard work and dedication it will never come back.

"Always remember
you are braver than you believe,
stronger than you seem,
smarter than you think and
twice as beautiful as you'd ever imagined."

THE END?
New Beginning, shouting F*CK THE SCALE!

May 2, 2018

"Binge on life. Purge negativity. Starve guilty feelings. Restrict unhappy thoughts. Count blessings not calories. The only weight you ever need to lose is the weight of the world on your shoulders."
~Unknown

Today marks my 12 year attempted suicide anniversary. Why do I celebrate you ask? My life, by the graces of God continued with a ';' (semi-colon) instead of a '.' (period) By far the biggest obstacle we all face in taking action is our fears. Conscious and unconscious fears hold us back from so many of life's accomplishments. It is important to be very clear in what our fears are in order to move ahead and succeed.

I believe that you always have a choice! No matter what situation you are in you have a choice. No matter how bad things are you have a choice. No matter what you think you can or cannot do you have a choice. Now with saying that, it may not be an easy choice by any means, but YOU have the power to make a choice for YOU! It may be a very difficult choice and the road you decide to take may be a tough one. It may push you way out of your comfort zone. It may mean that in the initial stages your life may get even harder than it already is. But it is a choice nonetheless.

Oftentimes we get stuck in the mindset to believe that when life gets hard there must not be a choice. I'm here to tell you an amazing life is out there but it's YOUR choice whether YOU want to find it and fight for it. I'm not saying it is going to be easy, but I promise you it will be worth it.

I want to read you once again the passage that was repeated to me over and over again during my stay at the DECH by an amazing nurse. The nurse herself had succeeded in breaking free from 'ED' and I repeated this verse every night and most of those nights with her by my side. At the time I know I may have repeated it for the sake of making her happy but little did she realize that many years later I still repeat this verse before I go to bed to acknowledge that I am grateful for my day.

"God, grant me the serenity to accept the things I cannot change, Courage to change the things I can, and wisdom to know the difference."

I am grateful for the days I have ahead. Most of all I am proud of who I was, to make me the women I am today. In closing, we must always remember the past and some of the mistakes or challenges that have occurred in our life because those my friends, create the spark. That spark will ignite the fire within each and every one of you to pursue, succeed and most importantly be mindful of you, your value, your time and your needs for today and every day.

I always believed that one day I would be lucky enough to share my story in a book. I hope I have given you some hope to realize that with time you will believe in yourself, have the power and the courage to take that first step in the journey ahead called a *warr;ors* life!

Sending you Much Love & Courage,
Sam xo

NEXT BOOK
Calling all my BRAVE *warr;ors*

I have already started writing my next book! What can I say, I have the gift of gab. If you or someone you know would like to be a part of my next book and share your #nakedtruth story (anonymously or name attached) with respect to any type of mental illness, please reach out as it would be my privilege to help you heal and share your #nakedtruth story for others to realize they too are not alone.

If you would like to have me attend a private or public function, please contact me directly as I would be honored to spread the *warr;or* love.

 thenakedtruthwarrior.com

 Sam@thenakedtruthwarrior.com

 Sam_the_Naked_Truth_Warrior

 Sam The Naked Truth Warr;or

♥My body. My vessel. My mountain.
My body is my tool. A gift given to me which I experience
and appreciate myself and the world in which I live. A world
that, thanks to my body can smell, taste, hear and see; to be
one with it. I love my body.

♥I love every inch, muscle, nerve, hair.
Not because I am a size 7, because I am not. I am comfortable,
beautiful and dynamic size 14. I love my body because when I
break it, it heals me, it helps me soar with legs as my wings
and it gives my spirit and mind and together creates me;
unique, individual and beautiful me.

**♥My measurements are two feet that carry me over
mountains, two legs that give me strength to run, a body that
keeps me alive, arms to embrace and a mind to help guide
me along the path.**
And inside this is a spirit that won't accept limitations. All
these measurements are mine. I own them, only I empower
my body, no one can take that freedom from me. And so…I
celebrate!

♥My relationship with my body is a healthy one.
One I had developed by ignoring the status 'ideal' of society
and changing my attitude. I told myself that I will not cheat
my body out of its destined experiences because of imagined
limitations. I will wear sexy clothing and look good, not being
a size 6. And if I want to dress comfortably for myself I will. I
am, in my own skin, comfortable and have discovered new
and different ways to move through life, physically and
mentally. I will love my body before I expect anyone else to
love it.

♥I would not change my body for anyone else's even a model.

Every scar and wrinkle on my body represents moments of life. I celebrate myself feeling alive. Running through fields of daisies after the rain, jumping in a lake and feeling the water rush over my naked skin. Climbing so hard that it hurts every muscle in my body and I keep pushing until it cries out for more. The sweet taste of someone's lips upon my own. I know for the rest of my days, I will celebrate life. I know I will not let female stereotypes harness my freedom. And when I die, I will thank my body for giving me the strength and the chance to experience life.

♥I will accept me, and in doing so love me. And I do.

5 RANDOM & PECULIAR THINGS ABOUT ME

Things you didn't know, you didn't' know.

ONE

There's no need to take my potty mouth as a lack of education or upbringing. There is just something about the word F*CK that takes things to a whole other level. My mother will however disagree, especially when it came to the title of this book. I may or may not be grounded for life after she reads this book.

TWO

I am a science geek at heart. In 1991 I traveled to Iqaluit, Baffin Island as part of a Grade 8 science team to do research on beluga whales and narwhales. To this day I still have a huge passion for all things "whale" and go crazy at the sight of one. What can I say, I'm a sap for anything animals.

THREE

In Grade 11 (circa 1993) I was hit by a car while walking across the street. Since that time I have had plastic surgery (liposuction on my hip – don't get all jealous ladies it was for medical reasons and very painful), six arthroscopic surgeries on my knees, ACL surgery on my knee, staples removed from my knee and countless hours of physio. Although my road rash was extreme, my Guess Jeans were still intact. (Insert plug for Guess Jeans here and please send all free swag to me at ….) I've got the knees of a 100 year old but the spirit of a 20 year old. Lesson learned, always use a crosswalk!

FOUR

I'm stinkin' terrified of balloons and snakes, I know, it makes no sense whatsoever. As for balloons, it's the lack of control when one is about to burst! Crazy? Yup, you're on the right track! As for snakes, when I was a kid I lifted a rock from a pile and found a small snake and these little white things. To my surprise when I smashed the white things with a rock baby snakes began to crawl all over the place….what the!!!! To a nine-year-old discovering this by herself, that's gottta be a sure recipe for PTSD and a fear of all things snake like!

FIVE

I have the most amazing and supportive spouse on the planet. Back away ladies and gentlemen Mike's all mine! His guidance, patience and huge heart have helped push me through times when I thought writing a book was the craziest thing ever. I also have the most incredible daughters – my 10 year old daughter Madyson and my 15 year old step-daughter Kaleigh mean the world to me. They each shine in their own way and I truly believe they have the biggest hearts on the planet. They've taught me patience and love on a whole new level.

LOVE & APPRECIATION

While becoming a *warrior*

I would like to thank the following wonderful people who are in my life today and those that were very much a part of my life during a time that seemed impossible to escape:

Julia Bannister, (Counsellor at Family Enrichment and Counselling Service) had it not of been for you and your intuition on December 15th, 2005 and knowing I desperately needed medical intervention, I truly believe that my life would be very different today. I've never had the chance to thank-you in person or see you since that day. I'm unsure as to where you are as I write this, but I truly hope you are able to know just how much you mean to me and how much your support during that time was life changing.

Andrew, although you are now my ex-husband, I thank God every day that you were in my life during a time that seemed impossible to take on. You had such patience, insight and comfort when the world around me seemed to spin uncontrollably. Had it not been for you, I would not be here today helping to inspire other women that they are enough, just as they are. So thank- you from the bottom of my heart. I will never forget all that you did.

Ma and Bobby, I can't even imagine what it must have been like for you to see your own daughter struggle the way I did. I know you supported me each day, even if I tried to push everyone around me away. You showed me that no matter how many times I lashed out during fits of rage and uncontrollable emotions, your love for me never diminished. I love you from the bottom of my heart.

Monika, where do I even begin? You were the one that sat with me on the first night I was brought into the hospital. You never complained, even when you had to sleep overnight in the most uncomfortable chair that didn't even recline. I always felt like you calmed me and I could just be 'me' around you. I never worried that you judged me, you simply just wanted the best for me and offered me support every step of the way. If it hadn't been for you, the Doctor that was on call would have thought I was faking all those bodily twitches and pacing back and forth. It was because of you and your determination for me to get help, that I am here today writing this book.

Tracy and Sheri, gosh you both have the best listening ears one could ever ask for. You sat, you cried, you offered me guidance, you never once judged me and it didn't matter what time of day or night that I showed up on your doorstep, you welcomed me with open arms. Although I don't have blood sisters to call my own, I feel just as connected to you as if you were.

To all the Doctors and Nurses from the Dr. Everett Chalmers Regional Hospital thank-you for all the care that you gave me over 2005-2007. You made sure that I was always given the best care available. Your compassionate attention and professional care saved my life. There are not enough words for me to be able to express my appreciation and gratitude.

♥Dr. Shahid - Psychiatrist– In-patient and Outpatient program

♥Dr. David Calquhoun - Psychologist – In-patient and Outpatient program

♥Leo Burke - Psychologist – In-patient program

♥Jane Higgins - Social Worker – In-patient and Outpatient program

♥Nurses on 2SE Psych Ward

♥Nurse Marion – In patient & day therapy outpatient program

♥Nancy and Suzanne - Occupational Therapist – In-patient and outpatient program

♥TAKE ACTION♥

If you or someone you know is
thinking of self-harm or suicide,
please reach out for support.

Emergency ♥ 911
Canada Suicice Prevention Service CSPS ♥ 1-833-456-4566
Kids Help Phone ♥ 1-800-668-6868

LEARNING MORE from MAYO CLINIC
www.mayoclinic.org

GENERALIZED ANXIETY DISORDER
Generalized anxiety disorder can be defined as excessive, ongoing anxiety and worry that interferes with day-to-day activities. It has symptoms that are similar to panic disorder, obsessive-compulsive disorder and other types of anxiety, but they're all different conditions.

SYMPTOMS IN ADULTS
- Persistent worrying or obsession about small or large concerns that's out of proportion to the impact of the event
- Inability to set aside or let go of a worry
- Inability to relax, restlessness, and feeling keyed up or on edge
- Difficulty concentrating, or the feeling that your mind "goes blank"
- Worrying about excessively worrying
- Distress about making decisions for fear of making the wrong decision
- Carrying every option in a situation all the way out to its possible negative conclusion
- Difficulty handling uncertainty or indecisiveness
- Fatigue
- Irritability
- Muscle tension or muscle aches
- Trembling, feeling twitchy
- Being easily startled

- Trouble sleeping
- Sweating
- Nausea, diarrhea or irritable bowel syndrome
- Headaches

There may be times when your worries don't completely consume you, but you still feel anxious even when there's no apparent reason. For example, you may feel intense worry about your safety or that of your loved ones, or you may have a general sense that something bad is about to happen.

Your anxiety, worry or physical symptoms cause you significant distress in social, work or other areas of your life. Worries can shift from one concern to another and may change with time and age.

SYMPTOMS IN CHILDREN and TEENAGERS

In addition to the symptoms above, children and teenagers who have generalized anxiety disorder may have excessive worries about:
- Performance at school or sporting events
- Being on time (punctuality)
- Earthquakes, nuclear war or other catastrophic events

A child or teen with generalized anxiety disorder may also:
- Feel overly anxious to fit in
- Be a perfectionist
- Redo tasks because they aren't perfect the

first time
- Spend excessive time doing homework
- Lack confidence
- Strive for approval
- Require a lot of reassurance about
  performance

WHEN TO SEE A DOCTOR

- You feel like you're worrying too much, and
  it's interfering with your work, relationships
  or other parts of your life
- You feel depressed, have trouble with
  drinking or drugs, or you have other mental
  health concerns along with anxiety
- You have suicidal thoughts or behaviors —
  seek emergency treatment immediately

Your worries are unlikely to simply go away on their own, and they may actually get worse over time. Try to seek professional help before your anxiety becomes severe — it may be easier to treat early on.

PANICK ATTACKS

A panic attack is a sudden episode of intense fear that triggers severe physical reactions when there is no real danger or apparent cause. Panic attacks can be very frightening. When panic attacks occur, you might think you're losing control, having a heart attack or even dying.

Many people have just one or two panic attacks in their lifetimes, and the problem goes away, perhaps when a stressful situation ends. But if you've had recurrent, unexpected panic attacks and spent long periods in constant fear of another attack, you may have a condition called panic disorder.

Although panic attacks themselves aren't life-threatening, they can be frightening and significantly affect your quality of life. But treatment can be very effective.

Panic attacks typically begin suddenly, without warning. They can strike at any time — when you're driving a car, at the mall, sound asleep or in the middle of a business meeting. You may have occasional panic attacks or they may occur frequently.

Panic attacks have many variations, but symptoms usually peak within minutes. You may feel fatigued and worn out after a panic attack subsides.

SYMPTOMS
- Sense of impending doom or danger
- Fear of loss of control or death
- Rapid, pounding heart rate
- Sweating
- Trembling or shaking
- Shortness of breath or tightness in your throat
- Chills

- Hot flashes
- Nausea
- Abdominal cramping
- Chest pain
- Headache
- Dizziness, lightheadedness or faintness
- Numbness or tingling sensation
- Feeling of unreality or detachment

One of the worst things about panic attacks is the intense fear that you'll have another one. You may fear having a panic attack so much that you avoid situations where they may occur.

WHEN TO SEE A DOCTOR

If you have panic attack symptoms, seek medical help as soon as possible. Panic attacks, while intensely uncomfortable, are not dangerous. But panic attacks are hard to manage on your own, and they may get worse without treatment.

Because panic attack symptoms can also resemble other serious health problems, such as a heart attack, it's important to get evaluated by your health care provider if you aren't sure what's causing your symptoms.

CAUSES
- Genetics
- Major stress
- Certain changes in the way parts of your brain function
- Temperament that is more sensitive to

stress or prone to negative emotions
- Certain changes in the way parts of your brain function

Panic attacks may start off by coming on suddenly and without warning, but over time, they're usually triggered by certain situations.

Some research suggests that your body's natural fight-or-flight response to danger is involved in panic attacks. For example, if a grizzly bear came after you, your body would react instinctively. Your heart rate and breathing would speed up as your body prepared itself for a life-threatening situation. Many of the same reactions occur in a panic attack. But it's not known why a panic attack occurs when there's no obvious danger present.

RISK FACTORS

Symptoms of panic disorder often start in the late teens or early adulthood and affect more women than men.
Factors that may increase the risk of developing panic attacks or panic disorder include:
- Family history of panic attacks or panic disorder
- Major life stress, such as the death or serious illness of a loved one
- A traumatic event, such as sexual assault or a serious accident
- Major changes in your life, such as a divorce or the addition of a baby
- Smoking or excessive caffeine intake
- History of childhood physical or sexual abuse

COMPLICATIONS

Left untreated, panic attacks and panic disorder can affect almost every area of your life. You may be so afraid of having more panic attacks that you live in a constant state of fear, ruining your quality of life.

- Development of specific phobias, such as fear of driving or leaving your home
- Frequent medical care for health concerns and other medical conditions
- Avoidance of social situations
- Problems at work or school
- Depression, anxiety disorder and other psychiatric disorders
- Increased risk of suicide or suicidal thoughts
- Alcohol or other substance misuse
- Financial problems

For some people, panic disorder may include agoraphobia — avoiding places or situations that cause you anxiety because you fear not being able to escape or get help if you have a panic attack. Or you may become reliant on others to be with you in order to leave your home.

DEPRESSION

Depression is a mood disorder that causes a persistent feeling of sadness and loss of interest. Also called major depressive disorder or clinical depression, it affects how you feel, think and behave and can lead to a variety of emotional and physical problems. You may have trouble doing normal day-to-day activities, and sometimes you may feel as if life isn't worth living.

More than just a bout of the blues, depression isn't a weakness and you can't simply "snap out" of it. Depression may require long-term treatment. But don't get discouraged. Most people with depression feel better with medication, psychotherapy or both.

Although depression may occur only once during your life, people typically have multiple episodes. During these episodes, symptoms occur most of the day, nearly every day.

SYMPTOMS
- Feelings of sadness, tearfulness, emptiness or hopelessness
- Angry outbursts, irritability or frustration, even over small matters
- Loss of interest or pleasure in most or all normal activities, such as sex, hobbies or sports
- Sleep disturbances, including insomnia or sleeping too much
- Tiredness and lack of energy, so even small tasks take extra effort
- Reduced appetite and weight loss or increased cravings for food and weight gain
- Anxiety, agitation or restlessness
- Slowed thinking, speaking or body movements
- Feelings of worthlessness or guilt, fixating on past failures or self-blame
- Trouble thinking, concentrating, making decisions and remembering things
- Frequent or recurrent thoughts of death, suicidal thoughts, suicide attempts or suicide

- Unexplained physical problems, such as back pain or headaches

For many people with depression, symptoms usually are severe enough to cause noticeable problems in day-to-day activities, such as work, school, social activities or relationships with others. Some people may feel generally miserable or unhappy without really knowing why.

SYMPTOMS in CHILDREN and TEENAGERS
- In younger children, symptoms of depression may include sadness, irritability, clinginess, worry, aches and pains, refusing to go to school, or being underweight.
- In teens, symptoms may include sadness, irritability, feeling negative and worthless, anger, poor performance or poor attendance at school, feeling misunderstood and extremely sensitive, using recreational drugs or alcohol, eating or sleeping too much, self-harm, loss of interest in normal activities, and avoidance of social interaction.

SYMPTOMS in OLDER ADULTS
- Memory difficulties or personality changes
- Physical aches or pain
- Fatigue, loss of appetite, sleep problems or loss of interest in sex — not caused by a medical condition or medication
- Often wanting to stay at home, rather than going out to socialize or doing new things
- Suicidal thinking or feelings, especially in older men

WHEN TO SEE A DOCTOR

If you feel depressed, make an appointment to see your doctor or mental health professional as soon as you can. If you're reluctant to seek treatment, talk to a friend or loved one, any health care professional, a faith leader, or someone else you trust.

CAUSES

- Biological differences. People with depression appear to have physical changes in their brains. The significance of these changes is still uncertain, but may eventually help pinpoint causes.
- Brain chemistry. Neurotransmitters are naturally occurring brain chemicals that likely play a role in depression. Recent research indicates that changes in the function and effect of these neurotransmitters and how they interact with neurocircuits involved in maintaining mood stability may play a significant role in depression and its treatment.
- Hormones. Changes in the body's balance of hormones may be involved in causing or triggering depression. Hormone changes can result with pregnancy and during the weeks or months after delivery (postpartum) and from thyroid problems, menopause or a number of other conditions.
- Inherited traits. Depression is more common in people whose blood relatives also have this condition. Researchers are trying to find genes that may be involved in causing depression.

RISK FACTORS

- Certain personality traits, such as low self-esteem and being too dependent, self-critical or pessimistic
- Traumatic or stressful events, such as physical or sexual abuse, the death or loss of a loved one, a difficult relationship, or financial problems
- Blood relatives with a history of depression, bipolar disorder, alcoholism or suicide
- Being lesbian, gay, bisexual or transgender, or having variations in the development of genital organs that aren't clearly male or female (intersex) in an unsupportive situation
- History of other mental health disorders, such as anxiety disorder, eating disorders or post-traumatic stress disorder
- Abuse of alcohol or recreational drugs
- Serious or chronic illness, including cancer, stroke, chronic pain or heart disease
- Certain medications, such as some high blood pressure medications or sleeping pills (talk to your doctor before stopping any medication)

COMPLICATIONS

Depression is a serious disorder that can take a terrible toll on you and your family. Depression often gets worse if it isn't treated, resulting in emotional, behavioral and health problems that affect every area of your life.

- Excess weight or obesity, which can lead to heart disease and diabetes
- Pain or physical illness

- Alcohol or drug misuse
- Anxiety, panic disorder or social phobia
- Family conflicts, relationship difficulties, and work or school problems
- Social isolation
- Suicidal feelings, suicide attempts or suicide
- Self-mutilation, such as cutting
- Premature death from medical conditions

TYPES OF DEPRESSION

- Anxious distress — depression with unusual restlessness or worry about possible events or loss of control
- Mixed features — simultaneous depression and mania, which includes elevated self-esteem, talking too much and increased energy
- Melancholic features — severe depression with lack of response to something that used to bring pleasure and associated with early morning awakening, worsened mood in the morning, major changes in appetite, and feelings of guilt, agitation or sluggishness
- Atypical features — depression that includes the ability to temporarily be cheered by happy events, increased appetite, excessive need for sleep, sensitivity to rejection, and a heavy feeling in the arms or legs
- Psychotic features — depression accompanied by delusions or hallucinations, which may involve personal inadequacy or other negative themes
- Catatonia — depression that includes motor activity that involves either uncontrollable and purposeless movement or fixed and inflexible posture

- Peripartum onset — depression that occurs during pregnancy or in the weeks or months after delivery (postpartum)
- Seasonal pattern — depression related to changes in seasons and reduced exposure to sunlight

DISORDERS that cause DEPRESSION SYMPTOMS
- Bipolar I and II disorders. These mood disorders include mood swings that range from highs (mania) to lows (depression). It's sometimes difficult to distinguish between bipolar disorder and depression.
- Cyclothymic disorder. Cyclothymic (sy-kloe-THIE-mik) disorder involves highs and lows that are milder than those of bipolar disorder.
- Disruptive mood dysregulation disorder. This mood disorder in children includes chronic and severe irritability and anger with frequent extreme temper outbursts. This disorder typically develops into depressive disorder or anxiety disorder during the teen years or adulthood.
- Persistent depressive disorder. Sometimes called dysthymia (dis-THIE-me-uh), this is a less severe but more chronic form of depression. While it's usually not disabling, persistent depressive disorder can prevent you from functioning normally in your daily routine and from living life to its fullest.
- Premenstrual dysphoric disorder. This involves depression symptoms associated with hormone changes that begin a week before and improve within a few days after the onset of your period, and are minimal or gone after completion of your period.

- Other depression disorders. This includes depression that's caused by the use of recreational drugs, some prescribed medications or another medical condition.

♥TAKE ACTION♥
If you or someone you know is
thinking of self-harm or suicide,
please reach out for support.

Emergency ♥ 911
Canada Suicice Prevention Service CSPS ♥ 1-833-456-4566
Kids Help Phone ♥ 1-800-668-6868

EATING DISORDERS
Eating disorders are serious conditions related to persistent eating behaviors that negatively impact your health, your emotions and your ability to function in important areas of life. The most common eating disorders are anorexia nervosa, bulimia nervosa and binge-eating disorder.

Most eating disorders involve focusing too much on your weight, body shape and food, leading to dangerous eating behaviors. These behaviors can significantly impact your body's ability to get adequate nutrition. Eating disorders can harm the heart, digestive system, bones, and teeth and mouth, and lead to other diseases.
Eating disorders often develop in the teen and young adult years, although they can develop at other ages. With treatment, you can return to healthier eating habits and sometimes reverse serious complications caused by the eating disorder.

SYMPTOMS
Symptoms vary, depending on the type of eating disorder. Anorexia nervosa, bulimia nervosa and binge-eating disorder are the most common eating disorders.

ANOREXIA NERVOSA
Anorexia (an-o-REK-see-uh) nervosa — often simply called anorexia — is a potentially life-threatening eating disorder characterized by an abnormally low body weight, intense fear of gaining weight, and a distorted perception of weight or shape. People with anorexia use extreme efforts to control their weight and shape, which often significantly interferes with their health and life activities.

When you have anorexia, you excessively limit calories or use other methods to lose weight, such as excessive exercise, using laxatives or diet aids, or vomiting after eating. Efforts to reduce your weight, even when underweight, can cause severe health problems, sometimes to the point of deadly self-starvation.

BULIMIA NERVOSA
Bulimia (boo-LEE-me-uh) nervosa — commonly called bulimia — is a serious, potentially life-threatening eating disorder. When you have bulimia, you have episodes of bingeing and purging that involve feeling a lack of control over your eating. Many people with bulimia also restrict their eating during the day, which often leads to more binge eating and purging.

During these episodes, you typically eat a large amount of food in a short time, and then try to rid yourself of the extra calories in an unhealthy way. Because of guilt, shame and an intense fear of weight gain from overeating, you may force vomiting (purging bulimia), exercise too much, or use other methods, such as laxatives, to get rid of the calories (non-purging bulimia).

If you have bulimia, you're probably preoccupied with your weight and body shape, and may judge yourself severely and harshly for your self-perceived flaws. You may be at a normal weight or even a bit overweight.

BINGE EATING DISORDER
When you have binge-eating disorder, you regularly eat too much food (binge) and feel a lack of control over your eating. You may eat quickly or eat more food than intended, even when you're not hungry, and you may continue eating even long after you're uncomfortably full.

After a binge, you may feel guilty, disgusted or ashamed by your behavior and the amount of food eaten. But you don't try to compensate for this behavior with excessive exercise or purging, as someone with bulimia or anorexia might. Embarrassment can lead to eating alone to hide your bingeing. A new round of bingeing usually occurs at least once a week. You may be normal weight, overweight or obese.

OTHER EATING DISORDERS
Pica - Pica is persistently eating nonfood items, such as soap, cloth, talcum powder or dirt, over a period of at least one month. Eating such substances is not appropriate for the person's developmental level and not part of a specific cultural or social practice.

Persistently eating these nonfood items can result in medical complications such as poisoning, intestinal problems or infections. Pica often occurs along with other disorders such as autism spectrum disorder or intellectual disability.

Rumination Disorder - Rumination disorder is repeatedly and persistently regurgitating food after eating, but it's not due to a medical condition or another eating disorder such as anorexia, bulimia or binge-eating disorder. Food is brought back up into the mouth without nausea or gagging. Sometimes regurgitated food is re-chewed and re-swallowed or spit out.

The disorder may result in malnutrition if the food is spit out or if the person eats significantly less to prevent the behavior.

The occurrence of rumination disorder may be more common in infancy or in people who have an intellectual disability.

Avoidant/restrictive food intake disorder - This disorder is characterized by failing to meet your minimum daily nutrition requirements because you don't have an interest in eating; you avoid food with certain sensory characteristics, such as color, texture, smell or taste; or you're concerned about the consequences of eating, such as fear of choking. Food is not avoided because of fear of gaining weight.

The disorder can result in significant weight loss or failure to gain weight in childhood, as well as nutritional deficiencies that can cause health problems.

Avoidant/restrictive food intake disorder is not diagnosed when symptoms are part of another eating disorder, such as anorexia, or part of a medical problem or other mental disorder.

WHEN TO SEE A DOCTOR
Because of its powerful pull, an eating disorder can be difficult to manage or overcome by yourself. Eating disorders can virtually take over your life. If you're experiencing any of these problems, or if you think you may have an eating disorder, seek medical help.

Unfortunately, many people with eating disorders may not think they need treatment. If you're worried about a loved one, urge him or her to talk to a doctor. Even if your loved one isn't ready to acknowledge having an issue with food, you can open the door by expressing concern and a desire to listen. Be alert for eating patterns and beliefs that may signal unhealthy behavior, as well as peer pressure that may trigger eating disorders.

RED FLAGS that may INDICATE AN EATING DISORDER
- Skipping meals or making excuses for not eating
- Adopting an overly restrictive vegetarian diet
- Excessive focus on healthy eating
- Making own meals rather than eating what the family eats
- Withdrawing from normal social activities
- Persistent worry or complaining about being fat and talk of losing weight

- Frequent checking in the mirror for perceived flaws
- Repeatedly eating large amounts of sweets or high-fat foods
- Use of dietary supplements, laxatives or herbal products for weight loss
- Excessive exercise
- Calluses on the knuckles from inducing vomiting
- Problems with loss of tooth enamel that may be a sign of repeated vomiting
- Leaving during meals to use the toilet
- Eating much more food in a meal or snack than is considered normal
- Expressing depression, disgust, shame or guilt about eating habits
- Eating in secret

CAUSES

- **Genetics.** Certain people may have genes that increase their risk of developing eating disorders. People with first-degree relatives — siblings or parents — with an eating disorder may be more likely to develop an eating disorder, too.
- **Psychological and emotional health.** People with eating disorders may have psychological and emotional problems that contribute to the disorder. They may have low self-esteem, perfectionism, impulsive behavior and troubled relationships.
- **Society.** Success and worth are often equated with being thin in popular culture. Peer pressure and what people see in the media may fuel this desire to be thin.

RISK FACTORS

- **Being female.** Teenage girls and young women are more likely than teenage boys and young men to have anorexia or bulimia, but males can have eating disorders, too.
- **Age.** Although eating disorders can occur across a broad age range — including childhood, the teenage years and older adulthood — they are much more common during the teens and early 20s.
- **Family history.** Eating disorders are significantly more likely to occur in people who have parents or siblings who've had an eating disorder.
- **Mental health disorders.** People with depression, anxiety disorder or obsessive-compulsive disorder are more likely to have an eating disorder.
- **Dieting.** People who lose weight are often reinforced by positive comments from others and by their changing appearance. This may cause some people to take dieting too far, leading to an eating disorder.
- **Stress.** Whether it's heading off to college, moving, landing a new job, or a family or relationship issue, change can bring stress, which may increase your risk of an eating disorder.
- **Sports, work and artistic activities.** Athletes, actors, dancers and models may be at higher risk of eating disorders. Coaches and parents may unwittingly contribute to eating disorders by encouraging young athletes to lose weight.

COMPLICATIONS

- Significant medical problems
- Depression and anxiety

- Suicidal thoughts or behavior
- Problems with growth and development
- Social and relationship problems
- Substance use disorders
- Work and school issues
- Death

DIAGNOSIS

- **Physical exam.** Your doctor will likely examine you to rule out other medical causes for your eating issues. He or she may also order lab tests.
- **Psychological evaluation.** A doctor or mental health provider will likely ask about your thoughts, feelings and eating habits. You may also be asked to complete psychological self-assessment questionnaires.
- **Other studies.** Additional tests may be done to check for any complications related to your eating disorder.

Evaluation and testing may also be done to determine your nutritional requirements.

♥TAKE ACTION♥

If you or someone you know is
thinking of self-harm or suicide,
please reach out for support.

Emergency ♥ 911
Canada Suicice Prevention Service CSPS ♥ 1-833-456-4566
Kids Help Phone ♥ 1-800-668-6868

SELF-INJURY/CUTTING

Non-suicidal self-injury, often simply called self-injury, is the act of deliberately harming the surface of your own body, such as cutting or burning yourself. It's typically not meant as a suicide attempt. Rather, this type of self-injury is an unhealthy way to cope with emotional pain, intense anger and frustration.

While self-injury may bring a momentary sense of calm and a release of tension, it's usually followed by guilt and shame and the return of painful emotions. Although life-threatening injuries are usually not intended, with self-injury comes the possibility of more serious and even fatal self-aggressive actions.

Getting appropriate treatment can help you learn healthier ways to cope.

SYMPTOMS
- Scars
- Fresh cuts, scratches, bruises or other wounds
- Excessive rubbing of an area to create a burn
- Keeping sharp objects on hand
- Wearing long sleeves or long pants, even in hot weather
- Difficulties in interpersonal relationships
- Persistent questions about personal identity, such as "Who am I?" "What am I doing here?"
- Behavioral and emotional instability, impulsivity and unpredictability
- Statements of helplessness, hopelessness or worthlessness

FORMS OF SELF-INJURY

Self-injury usually occurs in private and is done in a controlled or ritualistic manner that often leaves a pattern on the skin. Examples of self-harm include:

- Cutting (cuts or severe scratches with a sharp object)
- Scratching
- Burning (with lit matches, cigarettes or hot, sharp objects like knives)
- Carving words or symbols on the skin
- Hitting or punching
- Piercing the skin with sharp objects
- Pulling out hair
- Persistently picking at or interfering with wound healing

Most frequently, the arms, legs and front of the torso are the targets of self-injury, but any area of the body may be used for self-injury. People who self-injure may use more than one method to harm themselves.

Becoming upset can trigger an urge to self-injure. Many people self-injure only a few times and then stop. But for others, self-injury can become a long-term, repetitive behavior.

Although rare, some young people may self-injure in public or in groups to bond or to show others that they have experienced pain.

CAUSES

- Non-suicidal self-injury is usually the result of an inability to cope in healthy ways with psychological pain.

- The person has a hard time regulating, expressing or understanding emotions. The mix of emotions that triggers self-injury is complex. For instance, there may be feelings of worthlessness, loneliness, panic, anger, guilt, rejection, self-hatred or confused sexuality.

Through self-injury, the person may be trying to:
- Manage or reduce severe distress or anxiety and provide a sense of relief
- Provide a distraction from painful emotions through physical pain
- Feel a sense of control over his or her body, feelings or life situations
- Feel something — anything — even if it's physical pain, when feeling emotionally empty
- Express internal feelings in an external way
- Communicate depression or distressful feelings to the outside world
- Be punished for perceived faults

DIAGNOSIS

Although some people may ask for help, sometimes self-injury is discovered by family members or friends. Or a doctor doing a routine medical exam may notice signs, such as scars or fresh injuries.

There's no diagnostic test for self-injury. Diagnosis is based on a physical and mental evaluation. A diagnosis may require evaluation by a mental health provider with experience in treating self-injury.

A mental health provider may also evaluate you for other mental illnesses that may be linked to self-injury, such as depression or personality disorders. If that's the case, evaluation may include additional tools, such as questionnaires or psychological tests.

SUICIDE

Suicide, taking your own life, is a tragic reaction to stressful life situations — and all the more tragic because suicide can be prevented. Whether you're considering suicide or know someone who feels suicidal, learn suicide warning signs and how to reach out for immediate help and professional treatment. You may save a life — your own or someone else's. It may seem like there's no way to solve your problems and that suicide is the only way to end the pain. But you can take steps to stay safe — and start enjoying your life again.

SYMPTOMS

- Talking about suicide — for example, making statements such as "I'm going to kill myself," "I wish I were dead" or "I wish I hadn't been born"
- Getting the means to take your own life, such as buying a gun or stockpiling pills
- Withdrawing from social contact and wanting to be left alone
- Having mood swings, such as being emotionally high one day and deeply discouraged the next
- Being preoccupied with death, dying or Violence

- Feeling trapped or hopeless about a situation
- Increasing use of alcohol or drugs
- Changing normal routine, including eating or sleeping patterns
- Doing risky or self-destructive things, such as using drugs or driving recklessly
- Giving away belongings or getting affairs in order when there's no other logical explanation for doing this
- Saying goodbye to people as if they won't be seen again
- Developing personality changes or being severely anxious or agitated, particularly when experiencing some of the warning signs listed above

Warning signs aren't always obvious, and they may vary from person to person. Some people make their intentions clear, while others keep suicidal thoughts and feelings secret.

CAUSES
Suicidal thoughts have many causes. Most often, suicidal thoughts are the result of feeling like you can't cope when you're faced with what seems to be an overwhelming life situation. If you don't have hope for the future, you may mistakenly think suicide is a solution. You may experience a sort of tunnel vision, where in the middle of a crisis you believe suicide is the only way out.

There also may be a genetic link to suicide. People who complete suicide or who have suicidal thoughts or behavior are more likely to have a family history of suicide.

RISK FACTORS

- Feel hopeless, worthless, agitated, socially isolated or lonely
- Experience a stressful life event, such as the loss of a loved one, military service, a breakup, or financial or legal problems
- Have a substance abuse problem — alcohol and drug abuse can worsen thoughts of suicide and make you feel reckless or impulsive enough to act on your thoughts
- Have suicidal thoughts and have access to firearms in your home
- Have an underlying psychiatric disorder, such as major depression, post-traumatic stress disorder or bipolar disorder
- Have a family history of mental disorders, substance abuse, suicide, or violence, including physical or sexual abuse
- Have a medical condition that can be linked to depression and suicidal thinking, such as chronic disease, chronic pain or terminal illness
- Are lesbian, gay, bisexual or transgender with an unsupportive family or in a hostile environment
- Attempted suicide before

CHILDREN AND TEENAGERS

Suicide in children and teenagers often follows stressful life events. What a young person sees as serious and insurmountable may seem minor to an adult — such as problems in school or the loss of a friendship. In some cases, a child or teen may feel suicidal due to certain life circumstances that he or she may not want to talk about, such as:

- Having a psychiatric disorder, including depression
- Loss or conflict with close friends or family members
- History of physical or sexual abuse
- Problems with alcohol or drugs
- Physical or medical issues, for example, becoming pregnant or having a sexually transmitted infection
- Being the victim of bullying
- Being uncertain of sexual orientation
- Reading or hearing an account of suicide or knowing a peer who died by suicide

MURDER AND SUICIDE

In rare cases, people who are suicidal are at risk of killing others and then themselves. Known as a homicide-suicide or murder-suicide, some risk factors include:
- History of conflict with a spouse or romantic partner
- Current family legal or financial problems
- History of mental health problems,

particularly depression
- Alcohol or drug abuse
- Having access to a firearm — nearly all murder-suicides are committed using a gun

STARTING ANTIDEPRESSANTS AND INCREASED SUICIDE RISK

Most antidepressants are generally safe, but the Food and Drug Administration requires that all antidepressants carry black box warnings, the strictest warnings for prescriptions. In some cases, children, teenagers and young adults under 25 may have an increase in suicidal thoughts or behavior when taking antidepressants, especially in the first few weeks after starting or when the dose is changed.

However, keep in mind that antidepressants are more likely to reduce suicide risk in the long run by improving mood.

COMPLICATIONS

Suicidal thoughts and attempted suicide take an emotional toll. For instance, you may be so consumed by suicidal thoughts that you can't function in your daily life. And while many attempted suicides are impulsive acts during a moment of crisis, they can leave you with permanent serious or severe injuries, such as organ failure or brain damage.

For those left behind after a suicide — people known as survivors of suicide — grief, anger, depression and guilt are common.

DIAGNOSIS

- **Mental health conditions.** In most cases, suicidal thoughts are linked to an underlying mental health issue that can be treated. If this is the case, you may need to see a doctor who specializes in diagnosing and treating mental illness (psychiatrist) or other mental health provider.
- **Physical health conditions.** In some cases, suicidal thinking may be linked to an underlying physical health problem. You may need blood tests and other tests to determine whether this is the case.
- **Alcohol and drug misuse.** For many people, alcohol or drugs play a role in suicidal thinking and completed suicide. Your doctor will want to know whether you have any problems with alcohol or drug use — such as bingeing or being unable to cut back or quit using alcohol or drugs on your own. Many people who feel suicidal need treatment to help them stop using alcohol or drugs to reduce their suicidal feelings.
- **Medications.** In some people, certain prescription or over-the-counter drugs can cause suicidal feelings. Tell your doctor about any medications you take to see whether they could be linked to your suicidal thinking.

CHILDREN AND TEENAGERS

Children who are feeling suicidal usually need to see a psychiatrist or psychologist experienced in diagnosing and treating children with mental health problems. The doctor will want to get an accurate picture of what's going on from a variety of sources, such as the young person, parents or guardians, others close to the child, school reports, and previous medical or psychiatric evaluations.

COPING and SUPPORT

Don't try to manage suicidal thoughts or behavior entirely on your own. You need professional help and support to overcome the problems linked to suicidal thinking. In addition:

- **Go to your appointments.** Don't skip therapy sessions or doctor's appointments, even if you don't want to go or don't feel like you need to.
- **Take medications as directed.** Even if you're feeling well, don't skip your medications. If you stop, your suicidal feelings may come back. You could also experience withdrawal-like symptoms from abruptly stopping an antidepressant or other medication.
- **Learn about your condition.** Learning about your condition can empower and motivate you to stick to your treatment plan. If you have depression, for instance, learn about its causes and treatments.
- **Pay attention to warning signs.** Work with your doctor or therapist to learn what might trigger your suicidal feelings. Learn to spot the danger signs early, and decide what steps to take ahead of time. Contact your doctor or therapist if you notice any changes in how you feel. Consider involving family members or friends in watching for warning signs.
- **Make a plan so you know what to do if suicidal thoughts return.** You may want to make a written agreement with a mental health provider or a loved one to help you anticipate the right steps to take when you don't have the best judgment. Clearly stating your suicidal intention with your therapist makes it possible to anticipate it and address it.

- **Eliminate potential means of killing yourself.** If you think you might act on suicidal thoughts, immediately get rid of any potential means of killing yourself, such as firearms, knives or dangerous medications. If you take medications that have a potential for overdose, have a family member or friend give you your medications as prescribed.
- **Seek help from a support group.** A number of organizations are available to help you cope with suicidal thinking and recognize that there are many options in your life other than suicide.

♥TAKE ACTION♥

If you or someone you know is thinking of self-harm or suicide, please reach out for support.

CANADA

Emergency ♥ 911
Canada Suicide Prevention Service CSPS ♥ 1-833-456-4566
Kids Help Phone ♥ 1-800-668-6868
Member Assistance Program ♥ 1-800-268-7708
Veterans Crisis Line ♥ 1-800-273-8255
NB CHIMO Helpline ♥ 1-800-667-5005
First Nations and Inuit Hope for Wellness ♥ 1-855-242-3310
Trans LifeLine ♥ 1-877-330-6366
Alberta Crisis Line ♥ 403-266-4357
British Columbia Crisis Line ♥ 1-800-SUICIDE
Manitoba Crisis Line ♥ 1-877-435-7170
New Brunswick Crisis Line ♥ 1-800-667-5005
Newfoundland and Labrador Crisis Line ♥ 1-888-737-4668
NWT Crisis Line ♥ 1-800-661-0844
Nova Scotia Crisis Line ♥ 1-888-429-8167
Nunavut Crisis Line ♥ 1-800-265-3333
Ontario Crisis Line ♥ 1-866-531-2600
Quebec Crisis Line ♥ 1-866-277-3553

USA

National Prevention Suicide Hotline ♥ 1-800-273-8255

*"God, grant me the serenity
to accept the things I cannot change,
Courage to change the things I can,
and wisdom to know the difference."*

HELP END THE STIGMA

Instagram or Facebook? Post a pic of you reading the book, sharing the book, leaving a book review or #bucketfilling around your community. The more we share the #nakedtruth, the closer we will get to ending the stigma that surrounds mental illness.

#nakedtruth #empower #bethechange
#mentalillness #endthestigma #warrior

SHARE THE *Warr;or* LOVE

If you would like to have me attend a private or public function, please contact me directly as I would be honored to spread the warr;or love and empower others to do the same.

 thenakedtruthwarrior.com

 Sam@thenakedtruthwarrior.com

 Sam_the_Naked_Truth_Warrior

 Sam The Naked Truth Warr;or

Much Love and Gratitude for your support!

Sam xo

ABOUT THE AUTHOR

Samantha Sutherland has been EMPOWERING thousands of women to say "F*CK the SCALE" for over 15 years and live their BEST LIFE!

Sam has overcome multiple mental illnesses and knows firsthand just how damn hard it can be to have a positive body image.

Sam has dedicated herself to building women's self-esteem, discovering how powerful their minds can be and celebrating each and every 'flaw' shamelessly. Sam truly believes the scale doesn't measure your worth. Besides, it's usually lying anyway.

A speaker and motivator (Sam prefers the term ass-kicker) that helps other women look beyond their self-imposed limitations, throw out the f*cking scale and empowers others to share their #nakedtruth story.

"*I got naked and used my story to help EMPOWER other women to speak their* #nakedtruth."

Sam xo

Made in the USA
Columbia, SC
22 February 2023

12825800R00183